D1608869

SPARTAN BAND

Burnett's 13th Texas Cavalry
in the Civil War

Thomas Reid

Number 9 in the War and the Southwest Series

University of North Texas Press
Denton, Texas

10 9 8 7 6 5 4 3 2 1

Permissions:
University of North Texas Press
P.O. Box 311336
Denton, TX 76203-1336

The paper used in this book meets the minimum requirements of the American National
Standard for Permanence of Paper for Printed Library Materials, z39.48.1984. Binding
materials have been chosen for durability.

Library of Congress Cataloging-in-Publication Data

Reid, Thomas, 1947–
Spartan band : Burnett's 13th Texas Cavalry in the Civil War / Thomas Reid.
p. cm. -- (War and the Southwest series ; no. 9)
Includes bibliographical references and index.
ISBN 1-57441-189-6 (cloth : alk. paper)
1. Confederate States of America. Army. Texas Cavalry Regiment, 13
2. Texas--History--Civil War, 1861-1865--Regimental histories.
3. United States--History--Civil War, 1861-1865--Regimental histories.
4. United States--History--Civil War, 1861-1865--Cavalry operations.
5. Southwest, Old--History--Civil War, 1861-1865--
Cavalry operations. I. Title. II. Series.
E580.513th .R45 2005
973.3'464--dc22
2004023332

Spartan Band is Number 9 in the War and the Southwest Series

Design by Angela Schmitt

This work is dedicated to my wife Paulien
whose patience and understanding surpass all
reasonable expectations.

Contents

Tables

Maps

Photos (following page 120)

Acknowledgments

In the completion of this work I owe a debt of gratitude to Ralph A. Wooster, my thesis supervisor in the history department of Lamar University-Beaumont, and to the members of the committee, Howell H. Gwin, Jr. and John W. Storey. Their scholarly recommendations, careful analysis, and friendship were the key to a credible outcome as well as a very rewarding personal experience. Thanks are also due to other members of the history department: Adrian N. Anderson, Rebecca A. Boone, Mary L. Kelley, J. Lee Thompson, James D. Seratt, Alan Autrey, and Walter A. Sutton.

Sincere thanks are also extended to Richard Lowe of the history department of the University of North Texas for his generosity in extending me the opportunity to review a draft of his now published *Walker's Texas Division: Greyhounds of the Trans-Mississippi* during the time I was completing my final revisions. The insights provided were quite useful in improving my understanding of the personalities involved and the broader strategies operating in that theatre of the war.

I also owe a debt of gratitude to the staff of the Mary and John Gray Library at Lamar, Peggy Fox at the Research Center at Hill College, and the staff at Sam Houston Regional Library and Research Center at Liberty, Texas. Their patience, enthusiasm, and expert professional assistance were invaluable.

The greatest contribution of information I received during my research, however, came from an unexpected source: the descendants of the soldiers of the 13th Texas Cavalry Regiment. Over one hundred individuals came forward with diaries, letters, photos, and family traditions that have made this history much more complete than I could ever have hoped. My particular thanks are extended to Mrs. Margie H. Malone, Charles H. Ham, Jeremiah Stark, and Jack and Manie Whitmeyer.

Introduction

The 13th Texas Cavalry Regiment was in some ways typical of Confederate units raised in Texas during the second year of the American Civil War. Many other features were quite unusual. The men who organized the regiment were two of the youngest and among the richest members of the first Texas Senate elected following secession. As a result, Burnett's Texas Mounted Volunteers, as the unit was known prior to Confederate recognition, had no significant shortages of supplies or equipment during a time when the military authorities in the state were virtually destitute. While a few of the officers had some training as a result of the Mexican War and Texas frontier service, the timing of its organization led to an enlisted force with an unusually low level of military experience. In spite of this, the regiment, while not immune to insubordination and desertions, fared far better than many other units that served with them. Unlike most Texan Confederate units, they served in a division drawn entirely from their native state. Despite enduring three years of sacrifice, hardship, and combat, the 13th Texas Cavalry inexplicably lacked a published contemporary history.

Many have commented on the limited attention paid by authors to events that took place west of the Mississippi River during the Civil War. The Union loss at Wilson's Creek, Missouri; the epic defeat of a Federal fleet at Sabine Pass, Texas, by outnumbered Confederate forces; and the Southern failures in the New Mexico territory and at the battles of Pea Ridge and Prairie Grove, Arkansas, briefly stirred the public imagination, but were overshadowed by events in the east. For

1

many years after the war, there was also a feeling among historians that the Confederate Trans-Mississippi Department was a dumping ground for general officers who had failed to measure up during the first two years of war in the east. It was also clear after Gen. Ulysses S. Grant's Vicksburg Campaign destroyed the last serious Southern threats to navigation on the Mississippi River that the Union was unlikely to assign its best or brightest to that area of operations. These facts, combined with very limited media coverage of the war in the west, contributed to an unfortunate lack of historical research for many years. Only in the past forty years or so has a serious effort been made to reconstruct the histories of the units that defended Texas, Louisiana, and Arkansas from repeated Union invasion attempts. Following the war, Confederate veterans in Texas were generally held in high regard in their communities. Such status often improved one's chances when seeking political office or in securing favorable treatment in business and employment. But even organizations like the United Confederate Veterans had their "Trans-Mississippi Department," whose members could not evoke the familiar names of Robert E. Lee or "Stonewall" Jackson or claim service in such well-known units as Hood's Brigade or participation in battles with resonant names like Gettysburg or Shiloh. It may have been an unconscious or subtle distinction, but it probably discouraged many Texans from writing about experiences in little-known units with the certain knowledge that they would be compared with others who served in the east and had grown larger than life.

Eva Gaines, daughter of Pvt. Milton P. Gaines of Company D, 13th Texas Cavalry, wrote in her typed transcript of his diary, "I feel so bad that I never read this with my father . . . so much more I would like to know." There can be little doubt that many, both descendants of the veterans and students of Texas history, feel that same sense of loss. Although many gaps still remain, this work is an attempt to reconstruct the history those veterans never wrote. To the greatest extent possible, it is drawn from the diaries, letters, and journals of those who proudly served in Burnett's 13th Texas Cavalry.

Chapter 1

Burnett's Texas Mounted Volunteers

"Nine out of every ten men I see are going to the army."
—First Sgt. John T. Stark[1]

The year 1861 had been one of crucial decisions and actions for Texans. In January a state convention was called to consider relations with the federal government. Results of the 1860 presidential election gave the Republican opponents of slavery and compromise a victory that threatened the fundamental basis of the Southern society and economy. The convention's representatives voted on February 1 to sever their ties with Abraham Lincoln's incoming administration and the Union. On February 23, Texas voters approved the measure by a large majority. The ordinance of secession, made effective March 2, 1861, reversed the 1845 annexation of Texas as a state. Gov. Sam Houston, an ardent opponent of the measures, refused to affiliate himself with the Confederacy and was forced out of office, leading to the confirmation of Lieutenant Governor Edward Clark to the governorship. In a series of quick actions, taken before the popular votes were cast, the state organized volunteers and seized federal military installations and supply depots in San Antonio. By April, word came that Confederate forces had fired on Fort Sumter. Units of Texas volunteers responded to President Jefferson Davis' call for soldiers. By August, battle lines were clearly drawn, and regular elections for state senators and representatives included few candidates not already committed to the Confederate cause.

In early 1862, Burnett's Texas Mounted Volunteers, consisting entirely of volunteers from several East Texas counties, was mustered into Confederate service as the 13th Texas Cavalry Regiment. In many ways, it was typical of the numerous Texas regiments formed in the second year of the Civil War, but like most military units, it developed a distinctive character as time passed. The first commander of the regiment, John H. Burnett, was a very successful planter from Houston County. Elected to the Texas Senate in August 1861 to represent a district that included Anderson, Houston, and Trinity Counties, Burnett, at age thirty-two, was among the county's five wealthiest men. In 1860 he owned over 3,000 acres and had personal property valued at $40,000. A native of Summerville, Georgia, Burnett was a veteran of the Mexican War and a former colonel in the Georgia militia. He came to Texas in 1854 with his family and father-in-law, Gen. John F. Beavers. Between them, they owned sixty-six slaves.[2] A supporter of secession, Burnett used his Senate campaign to develop support for raising a regiment of Confederate cavalry.[3]

Burnett soon found willing allies in the counties neighboring his district. Robert Simonton Gould, a lawyer in Leon County, and William K. Payne, a farmer from Henderson County, were supporters from the outset. Both had voted to withdraw Texas from the Union as representatives of their counties during the Secession Convention in January.[4] Following the opening of the regular session of the Ninth Legislature on November 4, 1861, Burnett gained another, even more enthusiastic colleague, in Senator Anderson Floyd Crawford, whose district encompassed Jasper, Newton, Hardin, Tyler, Orange, and Polk Counties.[5]

Senator Burnett, as a member of the Confederate Affairs Committee, introduced several bills intended to integrate Texas fully into the war effort. Shortly after the opening session, he sponsored a bill to "protect soldiers mustered into State or Confederate service" against any legal forced sale of their property until twelve months after they were discharged from the service.[6] Burnett introduced legislation on December 5, 1861, authorizing the Confederate government to seize the property of "enemy aliens" through legal actions in the Texas courts.[7] As the session came to an end, it was Burnett who introduced the bill, later vetoed by Gov. Francis Lubbock, which would have paid $75,000 to the members of the legislature for their expenses, as authorized by the constitution. Sen. Anderson F. Crawford offered an unsuccessful amendment, which if adopted, would have eliminated the ability of legislators to collect their payments in their home counties in preference to other debts of the state, but the Senate rejected it.[8] If it had passed, the state treasurer could have paid legislators' per diem at his convenience. While the defeat of this measure did not have a significant impact on wealthy men like Burnett and Crawford, it did come as a blow to representatives of lesser means. Governor Lubbock clearly believed that the state's limited resources should be dedicated to the war effort.

While building support for his regiment, Burnett was treading familiar ground by calling for cavalry rather than infantry. Texans had a strong aversion to any suggestion of walking long distances. Governor Edward Clark, in his farewell message November 1, 1861, commented, "The predilection of Texans for cavalry service—founded as it is upon their peerless horsemanship—is so powerful that they are unwilling, in many instances, to engage in service of any other description, unless required by actual necessity."[9]

By December 21, 1861, Burnett was sufficiently confident of his prospects for success that he wrote Confederate Secretary of War Judah P. Benjamin, stating "he had nearly raised a Regiment for the Confederate Service."[10] Representative John T. Bean, of Tyler County, and a member of the Texas House Committee on Confederate relations and later one of Burnett's company commanders, was an active supporter of both the senator's efforts to raise volunteers and his legislative proposals.[11] Coming from one of the state's most successful cotton production areas, Bean had also been selected to serve on the Committee on Agriculture.

Besides needing the support of politically prominent men to promote his new unit, Burnett faced several other major challenges. Unlike Texas militia units, which could appeal to the state for virtually everything they needed, units entering Confederate service were required to be armed and equipped.[12] The Confederate War Department added to the already chaotic mobilization in Texas by directly authorizing the raising of over a dozen regiments "north and east of the Trinity River" and then placing a levy on the governor for an additional fifteen regiments of infantry.[13] The third major issue facing those who raised troops that spring was the duration of enlistments. State troops had been accustomed to terms as brief as six months, but the majority of the War Department's instructions specified twelve months. On November 16, 1861, Brig. Gen. Paul O. Hebert, commanding the Confederate District of Texas, had issued General Order No. 11 directing that "no enlistment would be for any term less than that of the duration of the war."[14] All of these conflicting orders had to be addressed during the organization of the 13th Texas Cavalry.

Recruiting began in earnest when the legislature adjourned on January 14, 1862. Burnett set February 22 as the date for the initial muster of companies in Anderson, Henderson, Houston, and Leon Counties. Anderson Crawford ordered the muster of the companies from the southern counties, Angelina, Jasper, Newton, Orange, and Tyler, on March 1.[15] Concurrently, and using Colonel Burnett's authorization from the War Department, Robert S. Gould of Leon County recruited an additional five companies, which later became the 6th Texas Cavalry Battalion.[16]

Capt. John T. Smith, another of Burnett's political allies and a member of the Ninth Legislature from Houston County, conducted the muster of his company at Camp Burnett,[17] near the village of Porter's Springs, eight miles west of Crockett. A New Yorker by birth, Smith had moved to Georgia at an early age, serving in the lower house of the legislature before departing for Texas in 1849. He was forty-seven years old, a prosperous planter, and owned extensive land in the county.

Smith was one of the county's large slaveholders, listing twenty-four slaves among his property in the summer of 1860.[18]

Capt. George English raised a second company for the regiment in Houston County, despite having been an opponent of secession. English had served as a lieutenant during the Texas War for Independence. He had been commissioned by President Sam Houston as a captain to lead a company of Indian fighters in Shelby County in 1838 and 1839, and had served with Capt. John Hall during the Mexican War. English moved to Houston County about 1843. At age fifty-five, he was the oldest of Burnett's company commanders. Although unmarried, English had taken in a number of orphaned cousins when his uncle, Archibald English, died in 1857. Five of them volunteered for his company.[19] While most companies from East Texas drew their men from one county, the Houston County companies included several recruits from Cherokee County east of the Neches River.[20]

Capt. Jerome N. "Jet" Black mustered a company at Centerville, Leon County, February 21, 1862. His command had been recruited in Leon County and in Madison, Trinity, and Polk Counties along the Trinity River bottoms to the south. Aged thirty-three, Black had settled in Leon County in the 1850s after leaving his home in northern Alabama. Described as a popular man, he had served in the Mexican War and had been elected Leon County's sheriff.[21] The wider area of Black's recruiting was made necessary by Robert Gould's earlier efforts around Centerville. There was intense competition for volunteers in the spring of 1862 as recruiting officers from Texas units serving in Virginia arrived. First Lieutenant J. J. McBride of the 5th Texas Infantry was particularly persistent.[22] Captain Black discovered that McBride was enrolling soldiers already mustered into the 13th Texas Cavalry. On March 22, he demanded that a private named James Green be returned, but McBride refused. This matter was referred to Lieutenant Colonel Crawford, who complained to General Hebert, the department commander. Hebert ordered the arrest of both Lieutenant McBride and Private Green, and Green returned to his proper company.[23] McBride eventually returned to Virginia with forty new recruits for Company C, 5th Texas Infantry.[24]

In neighboring Anderson County, Capt. James Steele Hanks mustered his company at Mound Prairie, not far from Palestine. According to the 1860 census, Hanks was the wealthiest man in the county. His land and personal property, which included at least twenty-five slaves, was valued at over $63,000. This was nearly four times that of his friend and neighbor, Confederate Postmaster General and former U.S. Congressman John H. Reagan. Hanks was fifty-three in 1862, and his oldest son was already serving in Virginia. In 1893, he assisted in writing his biography, which stated "in 1861 he was a Union man, but when he found that his neighbors differed from him, he raised the largest company that ever went from Anderson County." Other sources note that out of hundreds of votes cast in the county, only seven were against secession. Hanks' Union sympathies should be viewed in the context of his purchase of new slaves as late as August 1860.[25]

To the north in Henderson County, Capt. William K. Payne's company took the oath on February 15 at Athens. Payne was a thirty-six-year-old farmer born in Alabama. His personal wealth of $7,850 was moderate in comparison to that of his fellow company commanders.[26] Capt. S. M. Drake mustered Payne's company at Camp Shiloh on February 22.[27] With eighty-five volunteers, the Henderson County company was initially the smallest in the 13th Texas Cavalry. Drake, the former commander of Company F, 1st Texas Heavy Artillery, had been detailed as the mustering officer for Burnett's regiment as representative of the Confederacy by the Department Commander, Brigadier General Hebert. Drake's company had been disbanded in November 1861 and he had been assigned to post duty in Houston.[28]

It was Drake's responsibility, as stated in the Secretary of War's authorization letter of January 17, 1862, to "muster the Regiment into service, provided it is armed and equipped."[29] In a letter to President Jefferson Davis, recruiting officer Lt. Col. Samuel A. Roberts complained from Texas, "two-thirds of their horses . . . are totally unfit for any military service, while the expense to the Government of feeding them is enormous. I have never yet known a horse rejected by any mustering officer."[30] This certainly seems to have been the case with Captain Drake. While the average value of a horse was $150, Drake accepted animals valued as little as $87.50. The majority of the horses (and mules) were not even shod.[31] There is also little evidence that he rejected men who were equally unsuited for military service.

The soldiers of Anderson F. Crawford's senatorial district mustered on March 1, 1862, at Newton, Orange, Jasper, and Woodville. Crawford, scion of an aristocratic Georgia family, had joined an elder brother in Jasper County in 1857. He was elected to the Texas House of Representatives in 1859 and to the Senate in 1861. Crawford's appraised county property was $63,000 in 1860.[32] A photograph in the album of the Eighth Legislature, taken when Crawford was thirty, shows a thin, athletic young man. Soldiers referred to him as "Colonel" even before he was elected the regiment's second in command.[33] Crawford presided over many festivities as the local company, "Crawford's Rebels," as well as the "Dreadnaughts" of Newton, were sworn into Confederate service in Jasper. Families competed for the honor of feeding and entertaining the new troops. Local ladies organized a program of patriotic music and speeches described as "enough to nerve the arm of the most cold blooded man in Newton County." Even though another company had just been among them, John Stark of Newton wrote that citizens "took us home with them every one some 95 men and fed us on the best they had."[34] On March 11 the two companies rode to a camp overlooking the Neches River in Polk County to wait for the company from Tyler County.

Elias T. Seale of Bevilport commanded the Jasper County company. Elias had settled down somewhat after an adventurous youth. He was said to have been the only "Jasper County boy" to have returned from the California gold fields with "a small fortune."[35] Seale and his younger brother William, who also volunteered, owned a large general merchandise business in Jasper. The county's contingent also included

Charles R. Beaty, later elected major of the regiment. At thirty-three, Beaty owned a sawmill, which employed seven full-time employees in 1860 and cut 500,000 board feet of oak and pine annually, producing an income of almost $10,000.[36] Major Beaty was the brother-in-law of Capt. William Blewett, the company commander from Newton County. A native of Thomasville, Georgia, Blewett was a thirty-one-year-old merchant and gentleman farmer in Newton County, and owned eleven slaves. Blewett was also a partner in one of the county's largest cotton buyers, Blewett & Co.[37]

The "Orange Greys," a state militia company originally organized April 29, 1861, had offered their services to Governor Clark and requested the necessary arms and accouterments. The governor promptly provided commissions for Capt. Samuel A. Fairchild and his officers but little else. The Orange Greys were assigned to the Second Brigade of Texas State Troops, headquartered at Jasper. By September 1861, attrition, mainly to units already in Confederate service, had reduced the company from ninety to seventy-four men. All seventy-four had horses, but only fifty were armed. The weapons, an assortment of shotguns, muskets, and revolvers, were mostly private property. Fairchild was persistent in seeking active service for his company, and was recruited by Anderson Crawford for the 13th Texas Cavalry early in 1862.[38]

Fairchild was the only native-born Texan among the company commanders. His father, William H. Fairchild, had been a sheriff and local civic leader in Angelina County. Both William and Samuel were very active in their support of the Masonic Lodge. Samuel Fairchild was thirty-three when his company joined Burnett's Cavalry. In 1862 he was serving as the Orange County treasurer, having earlier served as the sheriff from 1854–56 and county judge in 1858. The Orange Greys began their journey to Camp Burnett, west of Crockett in Houston County, early in March after mustering in Orange on March 1. Samuel was one of six brothers, all of whom volunteered for the 13th Texas Cavalry.[39]

The heavy impact that recruiting had in the spring of 1862 on these southern counties is illustrated in letters from the State Troops brigade commander to the Texas Adjutant General's office. After serving as Jasper's delegate to the Secession Convention of 1861, Dr. William Madison Neyland was commissioned as the brigadier general in command of the 2nd Brigade of Texas State Troops. Neyland was one of Jasper County's larger cotton planters, having ginned 225 bales in 1860.[40] His brigade included men from the counties of Chambers, Hardin, Jasper, Jefferson, Liberty, Newton, Orange, Polk, and Tyler.[41] In a document dated March 20, 1862, Neyland reported that there were only 200 white males left in Jasper County between the ages of 18 and 50, including invalids. He said that from his area, "the probable number entering the Confederate service since the enrollment, about 800, four companies to Burnett's Regiment, three to Carter's Regiment,[42] one to Whitfield's Battalion[43] in Missouri and two now organized to respond to the Governor's call for 15,000 infantry, also about 150, enlisted as recruits in companies of Virginia." Neyland also stated that of 1,673 firearms reported earlier, several hundred had "been taken off by the volunteers in said regiments."[44]

East of the Neches River in Angelina County, Capt. Hiram Brown, a forty-seven-year-old merchant, organized a company at the county seat of Homer.[45] Brown faced intense competition for volunteers from both the officers recruiting for Texas units serving in Virginia and from recruiters for Col. R. B. Hubbard's 22nd Texas Infantry. On April 15, Brown's company was still camped near Homer when Lt. William R. Anderson led thirty of his men to desert. There had been deep divisions concerning secession in Angelina County, the only county in East Texas that opposed the measure, and these defections may have been symptomatic of that rift or of other local issues. There is nothing to suggest Brown filed any sort of official protest over these losses, and he may have welcomed the men's departures as ridding him of a disruptive, undisciplined influence. Brown overcame his losses, reporting to Camp Burnett with nearly one hundred volunteers.[46]

Capt. John Thomas Bean, known to his men simply as "Captain Jack," recruited his company in Tyler County after returning from Austin and the Ninth Legislature. He represented Tyler and Hardin Counties and had served as chairman of the House Agriculture Committee and as a member of the Committee on Confederate Relations.[47] Bean was born in Tennessee in 1817 and brought his family to Texas in 1838, settling in the community of Egypt near the Neches River. Bean's mother's family, the McQueens, were the richest planters and largest cotton growers in the county. Bean himself was less successful. His farm and four slaves, valued at about $9,000, probably produced a good living for his family of seven but little more.[48] Prior to the war, Bean had served Tyler County in a number of elected and appointed offices.

Bean's company left Woodville on March 11, 1862, and moved north to join Lieutenant Colonel Crawford at Camp Lookout on the Neches River in Polk County. That same night, about an hour before midnight, First Sgt. John Stark wrote his wife from that camp. "On every hand I hear the challenge of our sentries to men coming into camp. It seems to me to be one vast up heaving of the people . . . nine out of every ten men I see are going to the army."[49]

Secretary of War Judah P. Benjamin issued his levy on Texas for fifteen regiments of infantry on February 3, 1862. Governor Lubbock received it at Austin on February 25 and issued a proclamation calling for volunteers the next day.[50] On March 1 Lubbock traveled to Houston to confer with General Hebert regarding the difficulties faced by the state in complying with the order.[51] It was soon evident to the governor that recruiting was already proceeding on a massive scale by officers with commissions directly from Richmond. State accountability had not been established over many of the troops who left Texas each day. Based on the proclamation and Lubbock's discussions with General Hebert, Texas Adjutant General Jeremiah Y. Dashiell issued General Order No. 8 on March 13. In part it explained "men leaving the State singly, in squads, or in any other manner since the Governor's proclamation ... without reporting to their [local] brigadier general, deprive the State of the credit to which she is entitled, diminish its strength, and by this course will force upon the Executive the necessity for a draft, the very apprehension of which is so repugnant to a Texan."[52]

Both the proclamation and the General Order were published in every Texas newspaper for four weeks. The order made two facts clear: no more cavalry was being recruited, and enlistments were accepted only for three years or the war. As more evidence of the Confederate government's granting independent commissions to raise troops came to Governor Lubbock's attention, his correspondence with the Secretary of War became more heated. This culminated with a letter on March 17, 1862, in which Lubbock complained that Secretary Benjamin "should at once know the difficulties surrounding this department in raising infantry for the war. Every mail brings me letters and assurances of authority from your Department issued to parties to raise cavalry in this State. Only yesterday I was notified that J. H. Burnett, of Crockett, Tex., had authority from you to raise, in addition to a regiment, as many

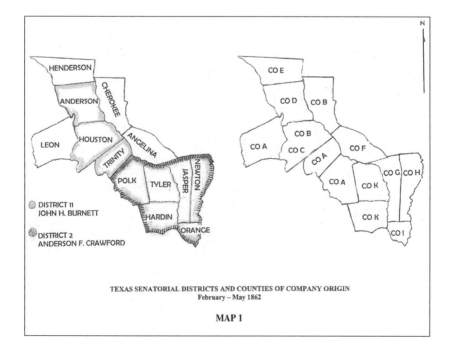

TEXAS SENATORIAL DISTRICTS AND COUNTIES OF COMPANY ORIGIN
February – May 1862

MAP 1

more men as should offer to him their services."[53] Burnett's 13th Texas Cavalry, also known at the time as the 13th Texas Mounted Volunteers, clearly had the Governor's full attention.

Lt. Col. Samuel A. Roberts, who also had authority from the War Department to raise five regiments of infantry in the area of Texas east of the Trinity River, discovered that the department had no record of him or his commission to recruit in Texas.[54] He explained to President Davis that seven cavalry regiments had been raised in the area that Secretary Benjamin had assured him was his alone in which to recruit. "As it is," he pointed out, "the fine military material of this country has gone off helter-skelter, mounted on every description of animal, and generally for a short term of service." Roberts' letter reached Richmond just after there was a major change in President Davis' cabinet: George W. Randolph had replaced Benjamin as Secretary of War.[55] The clerks at the War Department later reported that Roberts "was probably the person to whom Governor Lubbock referred in a late letter complaining of such authority." They concluded that they "were unable to find a record" of his authority or any promises from the Secretary of War. Secretary Randolph wrote an apologetic letter to Governor Lubbock stating that in the future he would refuse to grant any such authority without Lubbock's consent and that "all troops mustered into the C. S. service in Texas [would] be counted as part of the quota."[56]

The 13th Texas Cavalry Regiment slowly gathered at Camp Burnett just west of Crockett in Houston County. Discipline was not established quickly. Local soldiers continued to frequent saloons and to visit friends and relatives in Crockett. One such visit, details of which no longer exist, led to the killing of Pvt. James C. Moffatt by Privates Dempsey J. Burton and Robert Burton, all from Capt. George English's company.[57] The Burtons were listed as "surrendered to Houston County Sheriff" in the April muster. The majority of the men and officers were unfamiliar with military life and had little experience beyond that of a monthly militia drill, often more a social than a military event. Four soldiers from Captain Hanks' company, Edward Dagg, James A. Johnson, John

Petty, and James O. Goad, succumbed to the call of service in Virginia and deserted on March 30 to join Company G of the 1st Texas Infantry, Hood's Texas Brigade. The April 30 muster listed them as "deserted, (transf. w/o permission)." By mid-April, the regiment had settled into a routine of drill, horse grooming and feeding, and work details.

Behind the scenes of camp routine, the demands on Colonel Burnett's logistical staff were immense. Feeding over 1,000 men and horses was a daily challenge. The responsibility fell on the quartermaster Capt. Armstead Thompson Monroe and the commissary officer, Lt. Wilson Edwin Hail. In early March, Governor Lubbock had complained to the Secretary of War that both the department and the state "were destitute of means to provide for the organizing companies."[58] Although the citizens in many areas were already quite hesitant to extend credit to state officers, there is no evidence that this was the case in Houston County.

A. T. Monroe was ideally suited as the regiment's quartermaster. Born in Virginia, he was the son of Augustine G. Monroe, a nephew of President James Monroe. Monroe left Virginia about the age of twenty-two, traveling to New York to find a ship bound for Texas. He arrived at Galveston in 1842 or 1843 and continued inland on the Trinity River. At Alabama Crossing, a major Houston County port on that river, Monroe established a trading post, which soon became the largest cotton shipping facility on the upper river. By 1860, he was the wealthiest man in the county, with personal property assessed at $60,000.[59] While the State of Texas might have had credit problems due to a long history of poor financial management, A. T. Monroe certainly did not.

Based on the number of soldiers who were detailed as teamsters, Monroe was hauling supplies, corn, and horse fodder from a number of East Texas counties. As spring progressed and new grass grew on the prairies surrounding Camp Burnett, fodder demands diminished. Shipments of pork, beans, and milled cornmeal and flour could be diverted from the normal traffic on the Trinity and Neches Rivers. Conservative estimates indicate 1,000 working horses and mules would have consumed 10,000 pounds, or 200 modern bales, of hay, as well as 175 bushels of shelled corn daily. Due to the timing of the activation, farmers would have been quite willing to part with surplus feed and fodder. The published daily ration for a corresponding number of soldiers would have been 1,000 pounds of fresh beef or 500 pounds of bacon or pork and 1,500 pounds of cornmeal or flour. Variety was probably made available by substituting sweet potatoes for cornmeal. Beef would have been slaughtered daily, and salt pork purchased from the smokehouses of Houston County farmers. Daily distribution of rations was typically made to company supply sergeants from such central commissary sites as barns or pole sheds or directly off supply wagons.[60]

The Southern agricultural economy was based on credit, a commodity that men like Monroe, Burnett, and Hail certainly possessed. Requisitions and receipts for tons of rations for both soldiers and horses were filed along with their compiled service records in the personal papers of commanders and the 13th Cavalry's staff. There are, however, no corresponding issue documents from the Confederate Department of Texas or from the state militia Quartermaster. During the months of March and April 1862, the regiment existed on the credit of its officers.

Governor Lubbock knew that the inability of army quartermasters across Texas to meet their obligations during the 15,000-man mobilization in March 1862 could soon lead to the state's failure to provide much-needed manpower for the Confederacy. After meeting with General Hebert, Lubbock sent Horace Cone as his personal messenger to Richmond to press for funds and supplies. Cone's efforts to convey the governor's concerns to George W. Randolph, the new Secretary of War, and Christopher G. Memminger, the Secretary of the Treasury, produced results. Cone returned to Texas at the end of April with $910,000 in banknotes to fund the Army Quartermaster Department in Texas.[61]

As the state struggled with funding issues, Captain Monroe continued working to supply the regiment's training and combat readiness. On April 10, 1862, he sent a requisition to the quartermaster officer at Department Headquarters in Houston requesting that he "please forward via Navasota for the use of Col. J. H. Burnett's Regt. the amount of ammunition necessary for twelve-hundred men armed[,] say four fifths with Double Barrel Shotguns and the remainder with rifles."[62] A response was received, and on April 15 Lieutenant Colonel Crawford gave Monroe written orders to "proceed without delay to Houston, deliver the dispatches to the Commanding General, and receive such ammunition and supplies as he may furnish you for the use of this regiment."[63]

Concerning the weapons of the regiment, armed "four fifths Double Barrel Shotguns and the remainder with rifles," evidence suggests that the volunteers provided the majority of the shotguns. Shotguns, often with short barrels, were the preferred weapons for men on horseback. General Neyland of Jasper, reporting on March 20, 1862, concerning losses of military assets in his 2nd Brigade area, mentioned the departure of the four companies of Burnett's Regiment, along with "several hundred [weapons] taken off by the volunteers."[64] Of the rifles, some may have been older long rifles that were prized for hunting in East Texas, but at least 200 had probably been issued to the companies of Capt. John T. Smith and Capt. James S. Hanks. A soldier from Newton County later mentioned that the men of Smith's company were all armed with "enfield Rifles." According to a later comment by Major Robert Gould, the arsenal at Little Rock may have issued these. On January 6, 1862, the Texas Legislature had given special permission to Anderson County (in Burnett's 11th Senatorial District) to levy and collect taxes to buy 128 Morse rifles.[65] These were likely earmarked for Captain Hanks' volunteers. The only documented shortage of weapons was in Captain Fairchild's Orange Greys, who reported having twenty-four unarmed men in 1861 while still in state service.[66] Photographs of volunteers from Texas during the period indicate they were also armed with a bewildering array of derringers, pocket pistols, and revolvers.

In the absence of any nearby army depot or installation, Captain Monroe polled the companies for skilled laborers. Individual service records indicate that he soon had a respectable support organization. It was staffed with several blacksmiths, at least one wheelwright, and several carpenters, gunsmiths, and harness makers. Later, when the unit was prepared to move, a number of cowboys, or those "detailed to herd beeves," were detached to move rations still on the hoof.

While Monroe's quartermaster activities were evidently very efficient, it should not be assumed that this demonstrated any real aptitude for military logistical planning. Captain Monroe had simply replicated the type of supply and support required by any small frontier town. Operating in well-known territory, he had none of the difficulties inherent in rapid movement through unfamiliar terrain or the resupply of troops in combat. Some items, however, were in such short supply that the regimental commander became involved. Captain E. T. Seale wrote to a friend in Jasper County, "Col. Burnett is off now trying to secure tents for the regiment[.] [W]e expect him back soon."[67]

From a medical prospective, the regiment remained remarkably healthy during March and April despite crowding and primitive sanitary facilities. Dr. William F. Corley of Crockett was assigned from Captain Smith's company as Regimental Surgeon. Several other companies had physicians, but all were serving as private soldiers. It was reported, "the Boys is getting along finely. We have general good health some colds and no serious sickness." During those first two months, eight soldiers were separated on medical grounds for "disability," "inability," and "inability of mind." Pvt. Ulysses Lewtney, described by his family as "not quite right," was in the latter category. Lewtney was eager to serve, but his commander was forced to send him home on the pretext of getting his horse and treating an eye infection. He wrote Ulysses' father, "in all honesty . . . he will not do for this service."[68] One soldier, Pvt. Noah S. Alford of Newton County, died of disease, probably measles, on April 10. On May 18 the regiment lost its oldest volunteer when Pvt. Francis S. Manning of Orange died at the age of sixty-two. The greatest medical challenge was horse-related injuries, but these went unrecorded since none produced actual fatalities.

Very heavy rain curtailed activities during the latter part of March and the first week of April. The *Marshall Republican* of April 12, 1862, reported that "an immense quantity of rain has fallen within the last two or three weeks. All the streams are full, bridges have been washed away, &c." This was followed by a norther that dropped temperatures sufficiently to produce light frost, but "as it was, no serious damage was done to the fruit or the growing crops." The soldiers would have found other matters reported in East Texas newspapers that week more disturbing than the weather. Editorials discussed the Conscription Act, then being debated in the Confederate Congress. They claimed "the volunteer system has filled the army with old men and boys . . . conscription gives us an immediate and vigorous army." Such sentiments were poorly received in a camp of 1,200 volunteers. Even more galling to soldiers, idled by weather and two states removed from the action, were the reports of the Battle of Shiloh. Columns listing the dead and wounded in local units and casualty estimates in the thousands may have provoked thought in some soldiers. Those who had financial concerns at home would surely have noticed the advertisement by Capt. W. H. Smith, of Tyler, who was "prepared to pay the $50 bounty" to volunteers.[69] Burnett's Cavalry had also been promised the bounty, which remained unpaid as of the end of April.

Despite the known financial difficulties of Brigadier General Hebert's headquarters and the state treasury, the enlisted soldiers of the regiment were mustered and paid on April 30, 1862. The money, roughly $25,000, probably came from Colonels Burnett and Crawford, Major Beaty, Captain Monroe, and some of the company commanders.[70] Failing to meet the first bimonthly payroll would have had a disastrous impact on morale because many of the soldiers were subsistence farmers with families. As it was, the regiment was considerably in arrears. Besides the fifty dollar volunteer bounty, the soldiers were also due twenty-five dollars for six months "commutation of clothing" since they were not issued uniforms. Acting Secretary of War Judah P. Benjamin had discussed the clothing issue with Governor Clark in October of the previous year. "The simplest and best plan," wrote Benjamin, "is for the State of Texas to clothe her own troops, and to receive the commutation of $25 for every six months clothing furnished to each man, according to the act of Congress of 30th August last."[71] The soldiers were also due forty cents a day for the "use & risk" of their horses. This amounted to twelve dollars per month, a dollar more than privates received in wages.[72]

TABLE 1
13th Texas Cavalry, Economic Status of
Commanders and Field Officers*

NAME	RANK	UNIT	COUNTY	REAL PROP.	PERS. PROP.	SLAVES
Burnett, John H.	Col.	Staff	Houston	6,800	40,000	18
Crawford, Anderson F.	Lt.Col.	Staff	Jasper	40,000	23,000	40
Beaty, Charles R.	Maj.	Staff	Jasper	3,400	1,200	16
Monroe, Armstead T.	Capt.	Staff	Houston	10,000	60,000	1
Hail, Wilson E.	Lieut.	Staff	Houston	7,000	23,000	20
Black, Jerome N.	Capt.	Co A	Leon	1,680	1,055	0
Smith, John T.	Capt.	Co B	Houston	4,266	25,000	24
English, George	Capt.	Co C	Houston	2,000	5,200	5
Hanks, James S.	Capt.	Co D	Anderson	22,112	41,465	25
Payne, William K.	Capt.	Co E	Henderson	250	7,600	5
Brown, Hiram	Capt.	Co F	Angelina	1,500	8,000	0
Seale, Elias T.	Capt.	Co G	Jasper	0	3,400	1
Blewett, William	Capt.	Co H	Newton	8,500	17,500	11
Fairchild, Samuel A.	Capt.	Co I	Orange	800	10,000	4
Bean, John T.	Capt.	Co K	Tyler	3,200	6,125	4

* Based upon information in the manuscript returns of the Eighth United States Census, 1860.

Election of regimental officers, often a contentious matter, went quite smoothly. On March 19, 1862, Capt. Elias Seale related, "Lieut. Col. Crawford . . . is universally beloved by every body. C. R. Beaty is Elected major and hince [sic] you see the regiment is organized[.] Col Burnett nor Lieut Col Crawford had no opposition. Col Crawford could have been Elected to the first position in the Regiment but declined it."[73] Crawford, no doubt, knew that Burnett's service in the Mexican War gave him greater credibility dealing with officers in other organizations. Other appointments were made to the regimental staff. Riley J. Blair of Houston County was selected as the regiment's first sergeant major. The Rev. John B. Renfro, age forty-three, of Anderson County, assumed the duties of Chaplain and conducted his first services on Sunday, March 2. The regimental adjutant, John M. Hilliard, also over forty years old, was a physician recently arrived in Jasper County. Less than a year before he joined the regiment, he had been paid for his services in script so often he was compelled to write the author of one such note, "I am a new comer and if you cannot pay me any money I will take cows & calves."[74] The prospect of regular pay may have temporarily overcome his desire to pursue his medical career.

By the end of April 1862, the organization of the 13th Texas Cavalry was complete. Adjusted for initial losses from the original 1,125 volunteers, the strength of the regiment remained well over 1,000. Supply and equipment shortages were being quickly overcome, although not always in strict compliance with army acquisition regulations. No mission or movement orders had been received from the Department headquarters at Houston. One company commander wrote, "There is a variety of opinions as to when our regiment will leave here[.] I fear it will be three or four weeks at least."[75] It was time the unit needed for training and establishing military routines unfamiliar to most of the recruits.

The 6th Texas Cavalry Battalion[76] was raised at the same time as the 13th and mustered at Camp Burnett in May 1862. A history of the unit explained, "Capt. Gould's company was ordered to Porter's Springs, in Houston County, with a number of other companies raised under the supervision of Col. John H. Burnett. Out of these companies, after forming a regiment, it was found that there were five companies left, including Capt. Gould's. These companies were organized into a battalion with Capt. Gould as major."[77] Muster rolls from the period indicate Gould's battalion was attached from May 3–July 30, 1862.[78] This unit suffered from the same shortcomings as the other companies in the 13th Texas. First Sergeant William Wood of Company D recalled, "At the organization the men were armed with common shotguns and rifles, and a few with rough homemade substitutes for swords. With such arms and no experienced officers, the men were in no condition to meet an enemy, and as a consequence the progress made in drilling was slow."[79]

The soldiers of the 13th Texas were not sunshine patriots, encouraged by victories on distant battlefields. The spring of 1862 brought only grim reports of defeat and disappointment. Brig. Gen. Henry Sibley's campaign in the desert southwest had proven that tactical successes do not always result in strategic gains. Resupply problems forced Sibley's Brigade to retreat due to its defeat at Glorieta Pass. Two weeks after the initial muster of the 13th Texas, news arrived that Maj. Gen. Earl Van Dorn's forces had been defeated at Pea Ridge, Arkansas, and Texan Ben McCulloch had been killed. On April 6, 1862, Gen. Albert Sidney Johnston attacked Union forces near Shiloh Church in southwestern Tennessee. Johnston was wounded that afternoon and bled to death in minutes. The Confederates were compelled the next day to withdraw to Corinth, Mississippi. The combined Union and Confederate soldiers killed or wounded at Shiloh were nearly 23,000 men. Burnett's Texans do not seem to have been discouraged by these reports, perhaps because they had been raised on stories of the Alamo, Goliad, and the final victory at San Jacinto.

1. John T. Stark to Martha Stark, March 11, 1862, Hill College, Confederate Research Center.

2. "Eighth Census of the United States, Population Schedule," Houston County, TX, Microfilm M653-1297, household 191; James M. Day, ed., *Senate Journal of the Ninth Legislature of the State of Texas, Regular Session, Nov. 4, 1861–Jan. 14, 1862* (Austin: Texas State Library, 1963), 289; "Eighth Census of the United States, Slave Schedule," 1860, Houston County, TX.

3. Ron Tyler, ed., *The New Handbook of Texas* (Austin: Texas State Historical Association, 1996), 1: 835.

4. Ralph A. Wooster, "Analysis of the Membership of the Texas Secession Convention,"

Southwestern Historical Quarterly 62, no. 3 (January 1959): 322–35.

5. *Members of the Texas Legislature, 1846–1962* (Austin: Legislature of the State of Texas, 1962), 34, 38; Crawford represented the 2nd Texas Senatorial District.

6. Day, *Senate Journal, Ninth Legislature*, 40–41.

7. Ibid, 108.

8. Ibid, 209; Fredericka Ann Meiners, "The Texas Governorship, 1861–1865: Biography of an Office" (Ph. D. Dissertation, Rice University, 1975), 98.

9. Governor's Message, Nov. 1, 1861, in Stephen B. Oates, "Recruiting Confederate Cavalry in Texas," *Southwestern Historical Quarterly* 64 (April 1961): 476.

10. R. H. Chilton to General Samuel Cooper, Jan. 17, 1862, in John H. Burnett's file, Compiled Service Records of Confederate Soldiers Who Served in Organizations from The State of Texas, Microfilm 323-75, National Archives, Washington DC, personal papers. Consulted in microfilm at Lamar University, Mary and John Gray Library. (Compiled Service Records are hereafter noted as CSR. These records contain both official military records such as musters and commissions as well as personal correspondence, receipts, and other items not normally maintained in military personnel records. These are referred to as "personal papers.")

11. James M. Day, ed., *House Journal of the Ninth Legislature, Regular Session of the State of Texas, Nov. 4, 1861–Jan. 14, 1862* (Austin: Texas State Library, 1964), 19.

12. Chilton to Cooper, Jan. 17, 1862, CSR, M323-75, John H. Burnett, CSR, personal papers.

13. R. H. Chilton to Lieutenant Colonel Samuel A. Roberts, Feb. 3, 1862. In this order the War Department directed Roberts to raise five regiments of infantry "subject only to orders given by the War Department while remaining in Texas, of which fact General Hebert [Texas Department Commander] will be informed." U.S. War Department, *War of the Rebellion: A Compilation of the Official Records of the Union and Confederate Armies* (hereafter noted as O.R.), Series 4, I: 907; Col. Middleton T. Johnson to General Samuel Cooper, Adjutant General, Apr. 7, 1862, Johnson reported "under the authority of the Honorable Secretary of War, of the 18th of October last . . . I have raised five regiments of cavalry in the State of Texas and the same have been mustered into the C.S. service." O.R., Series 4, I: 982–83. Colonels William B. Ochiltree, Horace Randal, and Edward Clark also had approval to raise regiments in the spring of 1862.

14. O.R., Series 4, I: 131.

15. Janet B. Hewett, ed., *Supplement to the Official Records of the Union and Confederate Armies* (Wilmington, NC: Broadfoot Publishing Co., 1998), pt. II, 68: 3–19.

16. Gov. F. R. Lubbock to Sec. of War J. P. Benjamin, Mar. 17, 1862, O.R., Series 4, I: 1006.

17. William D. Wood, *A Partial Roster of Officers and Men Raised in Leon County, Texas* (San Marcos, Texas: by the author, 1899), 5.

18. Armistead A. Aldrich, *History of Houston County* (San Antonio, Texas: The Naylor Company, 1943), 185; "Eighth Census of the U.S., Population Schedule," 1860, Houston County, TX, M653-1297, household 689; "Eighth Census, Slave Schedule," 1860, Houston County, 33; Joseph G. C. Kennedy, *Agriculture of the United States in 1860: Compiled from the Original Returns of the Eighth Census* (Washington DC: Government Printing Office, 1864),

241. Only thirty-seven planters in Houston County owned twenty or more slaves.

19. Tyler, *New Handbook of Texas*, 2: 434; CSR, M323-76; "Eighth Census of the U.S., Population Schedule," 1860, Houston County, TX, M653-1297, household 252.

20. Muster Roll of John T. Smith's Company of Burnett's Cavalry, May 28, 1862, Texas State Archives, Austin, Texas.

21. *History of Leon County, Texas* (Dallas, TX: Curtis Media Co., 1986), 20; Wood, *Officers and Men Raised in Leon County, Texas*, 30. In "Eighth Census of the U. S., Population Schedule," Black was listed as Leon County sheriff in June 1860.

22. Janet B. Hewett, *Texas Confederate Soldiers, 1861–1865* (Wilmington, NC: Broadfoot Publishing Co., 1997), 2: 397. McBride was first lieutenant of Capt. D. M. Whaley's Company C, 5th Texas Infantry, serving in Hood's Texas Brigade. He was listed as authorized to recruit for Whaley's Company at Centerville in General Order No. 8, Adjutant General of Texas, O.R., Series 4, I: 1002.

23. Lt. Col. Anderson F. Crawford to Brig. Gen. Paul O. Hebert, Mar. 28, 1862, with undated endorsement, CSR, M323-77, James Green, personal papers.

24. Wood, *Officers and Men Raised in Leon County, Texas*, 13.

25. Michelle Ule, *Pioneer Stock* (Ukiah, CA: Published by the Author, 2000), 18–19.

26. "Eighth Census of the U.S., Slave Schedule," 1860, Henderson County, TX. Much of that appraisal consisted of five slaves. It is unlikely that Payne derived much financial benefit from their ownership. His slaves are listed as a woman, age twenty-seven, and four children under the age of twelve. A male slave, age thirty-one, was listed as employed by Payne, but he belonged to Mrs. Margaret Berton of Anderson County.

27. Hewett, *Supplement to the Official Records*, pt. II, 68: 13.

28. Hewett, *Texas Confederate Soldiers*, 1: 143; Hewett, *Supplement*, pt. II, 68: 452.

29. R. H. Chilton to Adjutant General S. Cooper, Jan. 17, 1862, in CSR, M323-75, John H. Burnett, personal papers.

30. Samuel H. Roberts to President Jefferson Davis, Apr. 2, 1862, O.R., Series 4, I: 1042–44.

31. CSR, M323-76, Ely Freeman, personal papers; Captain William Blewett to Nancy Blewett, Jul. 4, 1862, Whitmeyer family papers, Colmesneil, Texas.

32. Crawford was among the more wealthy members of the state legislature. Average wealth for House members in the 1859–60 legislature was $16,000. See Ralph A. Wooster, "Membership in Early Texas Legislatures," *Southwestern Historical Quarterly* 69 (Oct. 1965): 170.

33. "Eighth Census of the United States," 1860, Jasper County, TX; *Members of the Texas Legislature 1846-1962*, 24, 38; DeRyee and Moore, *The Texas Album of the Eighth Legislature, 1860* (Austin, TX: Miner, Lambert, & Perry, 1860), n.p.; First Sergeant John T. Stark to Martha Stark, Mar. 11, 1862, Thirteenth Texas Cavalry file, H. B. Simpson Research Center, Hill College, Hillsboro, Texas.

34. John Stark to Martha Stark, Mar. 11, 1862.

35. Nida A. Marshall, *The Jasper Journal Vol. I* (Austin, Texas: Nortex Press, 1993), 24–25.

36. "Eighth Census of the U.S., Population Schedule," 1860, Jasper County, TX, Beaty is listed as a thirty-two-year-old "machinest" who had been born in Georgia.

37. "Eighth Census of the U.S., Population Schedule," 1860, Jasper County and Newton County, Texas; Hill College, Confederate Research Center, 13th Texas Cavalry files, Letters of William Blewett and John T. Stark, transcribed and annotated by Jeremiah Stark; Marshall, *Jasper Journal*, 27.

38. Keith A. Hardison, "Orange County and the War for Southern Independence," Unpublished manuscript, Heritage House Museum, Orange, Texas, 1985.

39. Fairchild family papers; CSR, M323-76, Samuel A. Fairchild.

40. Wooster, "Analysis of the Membership of the Texas Secession Convention," 332.

41. The State Troops Brigade districts corresponded directly to the thirty-three Texas senatorial districts both in area and numerical designation.

42. Colonel George W. Carter's 21st Texas Cavalry Regiment, Hewett, *Texas Confederate Soldiers*, I: 85.

43. Colonel John T. Whitfield's 27th Texas Cavalry Regiment, Ibid, I: 570.

44. Jasper County Historical Commission files, cited in Marshall, *Jasper Journal*, 35–36; Texas State Troops Correspondence, Second Brigade, 1862, Texas State Archives, Austin, Texas.

45. "Eighth Census of the U.S., Population Schedule," 1860, Angelina County, TX (2nd District), 27, household 219.

46. Lieutenant Anderson became the captain of Company D, 22nd Texas Infantry, mustering in twenty-five of the Angelina deserters as the basis of his unit. CSR, M323, 75–80, Regimental Muster of June 1862, and William R. Anderson, personal papers; Hewett, *Texas Confederate Soldiers 1861–1865*, 2: 520–21.

47. Day, *House Journal, Ninth Legislature*, 48.

48. "Eighth Census of the U.S., Population Schedule," 1860, Tyler County, Texas, household 93; James E. Wheat and Josiah Wheat, *Sketches of Tyler County History* (Bevil Oaks, TX: Whitmeyer Printing, 1986), 92–99; Dean Tevis, "Captain Jack: Tyler County Pioneer," *Beaumont Enterprise*, Mar. 14, 1935.

49. John T. Stark to Martha Stark, Mar. 11, 1862, H. B. Simpson Research Center, Hill College.

50. Governor F. R. Lubbock to Secretary of War J. P. Benjamin, Mar. 7, 1862, O.R., Series 4, I: 977–79.

51. Meiners, "The Texas Governorship, 1861–1865," 128.

52. Adjutant General of Texas, G.O. No. 8, O.R., Series 4, I: 1002-3.

53. Gov. F. R. Lubbock to Sec. of War J. P. Benjamin, Mar. 17, 1862. O.R., Series 4, I: 1006.

54. Lt. Col. Samuel A. Roberts to President Jefferson Davis, Apr. 2, 1862, with undated endorsement by the War Department. O.R., Series 4, I: 1042-44.

55. William J. Cooper Jr., *Jefferson Davis, American* (New York: Alfred A. Knopf, 2000), 382–84.

56. Secretary of War George W. Randolph to Governor Francis R. Lubbock, Apr. 8, 1862, O.R., Series 4, I: 1050-51.

57. CSR, M323-75, Dempsey J. Burton and Robert Burton, and M323-78, James C. Moffatt.

58. Meiners, "The Texas Governorship," 128; Gov. Lubbock to Sec. of War J. P. Benjamin,

Mar. 7, 1862, O.R., Series 4, I: 977-79.

59. "Eighth Census of the U.S., Population Schedule," 1860, Houston County, TX, household 22; Aldrich, *History of Houston County*, 177–78.

60. In June 1860, Houston County reported 23,792 cattle, 26,215 swine, production of 311,030 bushels of

corn and 27,115 bushels of sweet potatoes. Kennedy, *Agriculture of the United States in 1860*, 140–9; the daily ration for horses is based on ten pounds of fodder and 1/6th bushel of shelled corn. Daily soldier rations are based on those published by Brig. Gen.Henry E. McCullough later in 1862 (see Chap. 3, endnote 33.

61. Meiners, "The Texas Governorship, 1861–1865," 128, 133.

62. Lt. Col. Anderson F. Crawford to Department Headquarters, Apr. 10, 1862, CSR, M323-76, A. F. Crawford, personal papers.

63. Lt. Col. Anderson F. Crawford to Capt. Armstead T. Monroe, Apr. 15, 1862, CSR, M323-76, A. F. Crawford, personal papers.

64. Marshall, *Jasper Journal*, 36. Privately owned weapons were required to be inventoried by the counties and reported to the State Troops brigade commanders.

65. B. P. Gallaway, *Texas, The Dark Corner of the Confederacy: Contemporary Accounts of the Lone Star State in the Civil War* (Lincoln: University of Nebraska Press, 1994), 247. The Morse carbine was a breech loading, rolling block rifle produced by the Greenville military works of South Carolina, which fired a .50 caliber brass cartridge. Henry Woodhead, ed., *Echoes of Glory: Arms and Equipment of the Confederacy* (Alexandria, VA: Time-Life Books, 1991), 48–49.

66. Hardison, "Orange County," 4.

67. Elias T. Seale to Lewis Lewtney, Mar. 19, 1862, in Geraldine Primrose Carson, *From the Desk of Henry Ralph* (Austin, TX: Eakin Press, 1990), 73–74.

68. Ibid.

69. *Marshall Republican*, Apr. 12, 1862, 2.

70. This estimate is based on the 13th Cavalry soldiers, without Gould's Battalion, slightly less than 1,200 men, due about $22 for two months' salary.

71. Sec. J. P. Benjamin to Gov. E. Clark, Oct. 13, 1861, O.R., Series 1, 4: 120.

72. *The Confederate States Almanac and Repository for Useful Knowledge for 1862* (Vicksburg, MS: H. C. Clarke, 1862), "Army Wages," n. pg.; CSR, M323-76, Andrew W. Collins, personal papers, "Treasury Department, Final Certificate," Dec. 26, 1864, "for use & risk of horse from 31st of June to 25 July 1862 the date of being dismounted 25 days at 40 c pr day."

73. Carson, *From the Desk of Henry Ralph*, 74.

74. Carson, 37; CSR, M323-77, John M. Hilliard.

75. Carson, *From the Desk of Henry Ralph*, 74.

76. Also known as the 3rd Texas Cavalry Battalion.

77. Wood, *Officers and Men Raised in Leon County*, 5.

78. Hewett, *Official Records Supplement*, pt. II, 67: 767–74.

79. Wood, *Officers and Men Raised in Leon County*, 8.

Chapter 2

The Regiment is Reorganized

"Most of the boys seem to enjoy them selves fine."
—Lt. Andrew Smyth[1]

Early in May 1862, the soldiers of the 13th Texas Cavalry learned that the Confederate Congress had passed the Conscription Act on April 16, 1862. The timing of the Act, one week after the huge losses at Shiloh, also followed declining enlistments. This law made all white males between the ages of eighteen and thirty-five subject to military conscription. Those under eighteen or over thirty-five were exempt from service but could voluntarily become substitutes for someone of eligible age. Existing units were required to discharge exempted soldiers and then "reorganize" with new elections being held for company and regimental officers. Discharged soldiers could not participate in the elections, but they could be kept on active duty for ninety days if the unit was at less than full strength.[2]

The Act had a number of very negative consequences for the 13th Cavalry. Virtually all the enlisted soldiers with combat experience in the Mexican War were lost because of their age. Many family units, which had a stabilizing influence on the organization, were separated. The Confederacy sent an unfortunate and inaccurate message with the discharged soldiers: the army did not have a critical manpower shortage. The Act was amended in September 1862, increasing the upper age limit to forty-five, but this was too late to mitigate the impact the law had on units organizing at the time.[3] Between the initial musters in February and March, and the reorganization May 24, 1862, the assigned strength of the 13th Texas Cavalry declined from 1,125 to 842 soldiers. This loss of slightly more than one soldier in four[4] was due almost entirely to the effect of the Conscription Act.[5]

Misunderstanding of the new law and its provisions was widespread. Some soldiers over the conscription age believed their twelve-month contracts were still in force. Forty-four-year-old Lt. Andrew F. Smyth of Jasper County wrote his wife on May 19, "I have nothing new to write only that I have seen the order of General Herbert [sic] declaring that all twelve months volunteers must serve the time for which they have volunteered."[6] One observer recalled that the companies "were virtually disbanded, for the reason, as the writer remembers, that the enlistments were only for a year, and that the Confederate authorities did not desire to receive, arm and equip such short time men. Whether or not such was the cause, there was a re-enlistment and a new organization of the companies composing the battalion and Burnett's regiment."[7] This confusion was quite widespread. When Brig Gen. Henry McCulloch took command of the District of East Texas in June, one of his first General Orders consisted almost entirely of implementation instructions for the Conscription Act. Section V explained that "all enlisted men under eighteen and over thirty-five years of age, who desire it, will be discharged from the service, and no person who is to be discharged under this order will take part in the reorganization."[8]

TABLE 2
13th Texas Cavalry, Company Assigned Strengths and Ages, March 1, 1862, and Following the Conscription Act Reorganization, May 24, 1862

From Compiled Service Records of Confederate Soldiers Who Served in Organizations
From the State of Texas, Microfilm 323, Rolls 75–80.

UNIT	COUNTY	STRENGTH MAR. 1, '62	MEAN AGE	STRENGTH MAY 24, '62	MEAN AGE	PERCENT LOSS
Co. A	Leon (1)	109	25.5	91	24.8	16.5
Co. B	Houston	120	27.5	98	26.5	18.3
Co. C	Houston	112	28.1	88	26.0	21.4
Co. D	Anderson	129	26.8	90	26.3	30.2
Co. E	Henderson	85	25.9	71	25.0	16.5
Co. F	Angelina	121	28.3	59	26.1	51.2
Co. G	Jasper	105	27.5	87	25.4	17.1
Co. H	Newton	116	29.2	79	25.5	31.9
Co. I	Orange	112	27.1	80	25.1	28.6
Co. K	Tyler (2)	115	27.9	76	25.3	34.0
Regimental Totals		1,125	27.4	842 (3)	25.7	25.3

(1) Leon County totals include volunteers from Polk, Madison, and Trinity Counties.
(2) Tyler County totals include volunteers from Hardin County.
(3) This includes losses to desertion (50), inability (1), disability (17), resignations (3), deaths (4), and civil confinement (2). This amounted to 6.8 percent of the total. Losses directly attributable to the Conscription Act were 18.5%.[9]

A comparison of the experiences of the 13th Texas Cavalry with those of the 28th Texas Cavalry, raised during roughly the same period of February–June 1862, is striking.[10] The differences between Horace Randal's 28th Cavalry and Burnett's 13th Cavalry were based on the timing of their organization. While all of the companies of the 13th Cavalry had mustered by March 1, the 28th Cavalry was mustered nearly two months later.[11] For this reason, the 28th Regiment was not required to undergo reorganization. The effect is illustrated by the mean age of enlistees in the two units. Randal's soldiers averaged 27.1; Burnett's, following reorganization, 25.7.[12] The 28th benefited from the effect of the conscript law to compel older men (from thirty to thirty-four years old) to enlist. The 13th suffered from the loss of volunteers in the over thirty-five age group exempted by the Act. Randal's regiment recruited 177 soldiers in Houston County, which comprised Companies I and L of the 28th. As one might expect, their average ages were greater than those of the 13th Cavalry at 26.6 for Company I and 27.5 for Company L.[13] The data from the 13th Cavalry supports Johansson's conclusion that conscription "was probably an important factor in explaining the [28th] regiment's older mean age."[14] Colonel Randal's recruiting in Houston County in April and May 1862 also meant that Burnett would find it impossible to replace losses from his home county quickly.

An examination of ages of the lieutenants of the 13th Texas Cavalry during and after the reorganization is revealing. Some evidently believed that their duties would be light, and that the labor of the enlisted soldiers would allow them to enjoy an idle, gentlemanly existence. First Sergeant Stark of Newton complained to his wife that "when not on the march, my duties are legion and the balance of the Officers seem willing that I should do it all."[15] At the time of their election, neither the lieutenants nor the soldiers were aware of the additional duties that normally accompanied the positions. The first lieutenant was the commander's representative in his absence, as well as the company adjutant who prepared correspondence and rosters. The second lieutenants were expected to fill the positions of supply officer and commissary officer, as well as serving as officers of the guard.

The median age of the original lieutenants was thirty-four, compared to the overall regimental median age prior to reorganization of twenty-six. The age factor was even more dramatic among the lieutenants of the southern counties of Jasper, Newton, Orange, and Tyler, where the average was over thirty-eight. Not surprisingly, all twelve lieutenants from these counties were dropped.[16] Only one was young enough to require a substitute. By contrast, the companies from the northern counties only dropped one lieutenant each, but in five of six cases, it was the first lieutenant who was dropped, resigned, or arranged for a substitute. The average age of the remaining twelve lieutenants was twenty-nine. Four of the twelve went on to command their companies later in the war.[17]

This can be interpreted as one of the early signs that the enlisted soldiers were breaking with the established local hierarchy by electing officers based on merit or perceived potential rather than social position in the community. Unlike with a lieutenancy in a militia unit, which was often given in consolation after one lost an election for captain, the soldiers of the regiment realized that junior officers would be the managers of their rations, supplies, and duty assignments. By electing the young and energetic, they were voting for their own self-interest. Captain Hanks of Anderson County later had occasion to describe those newly elected as his "three sprightly lieutenants,"[18] an adjective unlikely to have been applied to the original group.

One potentially unpopular aspect of the reorganization was evidently not communicated to the troops. New muster rolls were prepared for the Confederacy on May 24 and for the state adjutant general on May 28. Those prepared by Capt. S. M. Drake, the mustering officer of the Provisional Army of the Confederacy, clearly stipulated that the reorganized units were enlisting "under provisions of the act of Apr. 16, 1862, for the term of three years unless discharged."[19] The officers were aware of this fact. Final statements prepared for soldiers discharged after May included the statement, "joined at the Reorganization for 3 years at Camp Burnett Houston Co Texas 24 May 1862."[20] Subsequent comments make it evident that the enlisted men had not been informed that, by participating in the reorganization, they were making a commitment for "three years or the duration of the war." Thomas J. Rounsaville of Houston County later commented in a letter to his niece, "We had great excitement in our Regiment about furloughs, as the time is about to expire for which we enlisted, 22 of this month [February] the time expires, and the soldiers say if they do not furlough them that they will take an unlimited furlough. I think there is some prospect of our Regiment going back to Texas to reorganize our Regt. as we only enlisted for twelve months."[21] The situation had not improved when he wrote his mother and sisters the day after the twelve months ended. "We have a great deal of dissatisfaction through out our regiment simply because our time is about to expire, & no prospect of going home very soon."[22] Rounsaville's comments make two facts clear. The confusion about terms of enlistment was not limited to his company, and no one in the chain of command came forward to explain the soldiers' three-year enlistment.

Burnett's failure to inform the soldiers of their extended enlistments was understandable in light of even more unpopular news he was compelled to report during the reorganization. As a result of the War Department's requirement for fifteen regiments of infantry, the 13th Cavalry was to be dismounted sixty days after reorganization.[23] Although "the order to dismount was not officially issued until Sept. 28, 1862," the Marshall *Texas Republican* reported the day after the 13th Cavalry was dismounted that all cavalry units on their way to Arkansas would be required to do so.[24] The order to Colonel Burnett was likely verbal, and originated with Brigadier General Hebert, who had a very low opinion of the quality of cavalry being raised. Less than a month later, Hebert wrote General Robert E. Lee, "I would respectfully advise the dismounting of nearly all the troops west of the Mississippi. There is an excess of cavalry, badly mounted and worse armed. As infantry, if not more efficient, [they] would at least be less expensive."[25] Lt. Col. Arthur James Fremantle, a British officer and traveler in the South, commented a year later, "No Texan walks a yard if he can help it. Many mounted regiments were therefore organized, and later dismounted."[26] Burnett downplayed the threat, encouraging hopes that the commander of the Trans-Mississippi Department would need them as cavalry once they arrived at Little Rock.[27] The threat of dismounting did not appear as a serious concern in most soldiers' letters until August 1862.

One soldier who was very concerned was Lt. Edward Currie. Currie, age forty-five, was formerly the commander of Company I, "Currie's Company" of the 1st Texas Infantry Regiment. He wrote to General Hebert on May 28 asking for authorization to raise a company of partisan rangers, since he had fifty men "anxious to take service under me in that branch." He explained, "I feel sure that the Command that I am with [Company D, 13th Texas Cavalry] will be dismounted & the condition of my feet is such that I can [not] do service on foot." Currie concluded that he had commanded an infantry company in Virginia the previous year but had had to resign due to bad health.[28] Colonel Burnett resolved this problem by appointing Currie, who was a physician in civilian life, as the assistant Regimental Surgeon when Dr. Corley declined appointment during the reorganization. Regimental staff officers were allowed to keep their horses.

A substantial amount of the $910,000 in banknotes that the Treasury Department in Richmond had sent to the Texas Department Quartermaster found its way to Camp Burnett about the middle of May. Captain A. T. Monroe, the regimental quartermaster, disbursed roughly $25,000 to company commanders on May 16, to be paid to the men for clothing expenses.[29] Quartermaster funds, exclusively for supplies, could not be used to meet the June 30 payroll.[30] The remainder of the quartermaster funds may have been used to redeem notes that Monroe had given for camp and garrison equipment the regiment required prior to deployment to Arkansas.[31] Limited payroll funds must have been received, since final payments were made to some, but not all, of the men separated as a result of the Conscription Act. Colonel Burnett had sent Sergeant Major Blair to Houston on May 10, 1862, to "superintend the purchase of ordnance & items for the Regt. & see Genl. Hebert relative to pay funds for the Regt."[32]

One very confusing aspect of the reorganization was the redesignation of all the companies. In February and March 1862, the original lettering sequence, established by the order that the units joined the regiment, was: Company A, Capt. James S. Hanks, Anderson County; Company B, Capt. George English, Houston County; Company C, Capt. Hiram Brown, Angelina County; Company D, Capt. William K. Payne, Henderson County; Company E, Capt. Jerome N. Black, Leon County; Company F, Capt. Elias T. Seale, Jasper County; Company G, Capt. William Blewett, Newton County; Company H, Capt. John T. Bean, Tyler County; Company I, Capt. John T. Smith, Houston County; and Company K, Capt. Samuel A. Fairchild, Orange County.[33]

The designations after May 24, 1862, were: Company A, Capt. J. N. Black, Leon County; Company B, Capt. J. T. Smith, Houston County; Company C, Capt. George English, Houston County; Company D, Capt. J. S. Hanks, Anderson County; Company E, Capt. Wm. K. Payne, Henderson County; Company F, Capt. Hiram Brown, Angelina County; Company G, Capt. Elias T. Seale, Jasper County; Company H, Capt. William Blewett, Newton County; Company I, Capt. S. A. Fairchild, Orange County; and Company K, Capt. J. T. Bean, Tyler County. These changes were not considered significant at the time and did not elicit any comment in period correspondence. Most soldiers' letters were addressed to Burnett's Regiment and to the company identified by the commander's name. The company designations were little more than an afterthought. The new sequence was established by the order the companies reorganized and mustered.[34]

A sign that leadership at the higher levels satisfied the soldiers is evident in the reelection of all of the regimental officers and company commanders. Burnett did have nominal opposition. According to then First Sgt. William Wood of Company A, "Captain Black was a candidate for colonel of the regiment, and for this office received a most flattering vote."[35] Following the reorganization, the officers of the regiment petitioned President Jefferson Davis, through Adj. Gen. Samuel Cooper, to promote Colonel Burnett to a brigadier general in the Trans-Mississippi Department.[36] The petition, signed by thirty-six captains and lieutenants of the 13th Cavalry, as well as Maj. Robert Gould's quartermaster officer, was likely authored by Capt. John T. Smith of Houston County.[37] As a historical document, it is important because it shows the level of local confidence and support Burnett enjoyed. In military terms, it was of little significance, since it lacked the favorable endorsement of Burnett's superior officer at that time, Texas Department Commander Brig. Gen. Paul O. Hebert. The petition is also unusual in that it did not suggest that Colonel Burnett command any particular brigade, although that position is implied by the rank.

Politically, the absence of a recommendation by Gov. Francis R. Lubbock would have limited the likelihood of serious consideration. The governor's lack of support for Burnett's ambitions can be explained by the results of the August 1861 election. Of twelve counties in the area in which the 13th Texas was raised, ten had voted against Lubbock in the race for governor.[38] There is no evidence that Lubbock's support was solicited for the appointment.

As the regiment prepared to move to Arkansas, efforts were made to ensure that the unit was familiar with army administration. Each company was required to sign for "an Order Book, a Morning Report Book, a Description Book, and a Clothing Book."[39] At the company level, the order book allowed the commander to track orders received from higher headquarters, as well as recording written orders by the company commander for leaves, passes, and duty details. The morning report book had forms to record the status of the company's personnel strength on a daily basis and to account for the whereabouts of absent soldiers. A copy of the daily accounting was due to the adjutant at regimental headquarters by 9:00 AM each morning. The purpose of the description book was to allow the supply officer to make a record of individual and unit property. It contained listings of the serial numbers of privately owned weapons, unit weapons, and physical descriptions of such army property as draft animals, wagons, and camp and garrison equipment. The supply officer also kept a clothing book, which recorded payments for commutation of clothing, as well as for the actual issue of shoes and other clothing items to individual soldiers.

Colonel Burnett's search for tents was successful, and Captain Monroe issued them to the company commanders beginning on May 1. No physical description of the tents exists, but it is likely they were formerly the property of the state or came from stores captured from surrendered Union garrisons. The basis of issue, one tent for ten soldiers, suggests that they were "wall tents" and not the larger conical

"Sibley" tents designed to accommodate "twenty soldiers and their personal gear with a minimum of discomfort."[40] An indication that the tents were not new was that the number of pole sets was less than the number of tents. For example, Company G received fifteen tents and only one set of poles. Less than a year later, commanders were turning in the tents as unserviceable, probably because of dry rot or mildew.[41] They were replaced with newer tents from the depot at Little Rock.[42]

Company drill had evidently progressed to the point that Colonel Burnett decided to invite his neighbors to witness a regimental drill. Lieutenant Smyth of Company G told his wife, "I can't write you much at present[.] I will write again before we leave Crockett. The most of the boys seem to enjoy them selves fine. . . . We had a Regimental drill yesterday and the Prairie was full of spectators. There was more Ladies on the Prairie than I have seen together in a long time."[43] Such events often concluded with a barbecue and farewell speeches by the ladies, as well as the presentation of company and regimental flags. The first regimental color bearer of the 13th Texas Cavalry was nineteen-year-old Pvt. George A. Hadon of Houston County.[44] A witness to a similar regimental parade said the soldiers were "dressed in every variety of costume, and armed with every variety of weapon."[45] Lieutenant Colonel Crawford's wife Elizabeth came to see her husband off and stayed with Colonel and Catherine Burnett. She left to return to Jasper on Sunday with Judge Gray.[46]

A final supply issue was addressed the third week in May. One soldier reported, "we are going a few miles above Crockett and there remain a few day's [sic] for the purpose of fiting [sic] up wagons, etc."[47] Each company had two freight wagons for hauling supplies and personal baggage beyond what could be carried by soldiers on horseback. One or two pairs of oxen or mules drew each wagon. Some companies may have arrived with their own wagons. Captain Black of Leon County signed a receipt for replacement harness items for a wagon from the quartermaster on May 1.[48] Once the regiment was dismounted, the issue of the number of wagons allowed to a company became highly controversial, since the men had to carry all the excess baggage.

The date for departure for Arkansas by way of Tyler and Smith County was set for June 7, 1862. The task at hand for the regiment was to move the camp, the equipment, tents, wagons, and provisions for the first time. Over three months, cots had been constructed from poles, mattress ticks stuffed with straw, camp chairs made, and innumerable empty boxes and barrels converted to furniture. It was soon discovered that this would not all fit in the wagons available to each company. The hard lessons of unit movement were being learned. The staff planned the movement, commanders gave orders, and sergeants tried to carry them out. The last night at Camp Burnett was spent around campfires cooking beef or salt pork and sleeping without tents. The horses were picketed near their riders and ate discarded mattress straw.

The morning of the seventh began very early. Dawn found the first companies already on the road from Porter's Springs to Crockett. The route was roughly north, passing through Palestine in Anderson County and fording the Angelina River twenty-five miles further north. Captain William Blewett of Newton wrote his wife Nancy on June 11.

> I am at this time 8 miles below Tyler awaiting for dinner. The Regiment Camped 3 miles above here last night and will go about 15 miles To day and if nothing prevents we will overtake them Tonight. This is Wednesday and I have been 4 ½ days getting here which is about 140 miles[.] I have had to Travel Slow on account of My mules getting Lame the second day after I Started, but She is improving So that I shall make a good ride today. The people on the road Say the Regiment is in good health and are getting along verry well . . . We are now on our march to Little Rock Arkansas. The Federals have not taken it as we heard but are retreating to Missoura. My ink is so bad I can Scarcely write so it Can be read So you must excuse this Short note. Direct your Letters to me at Little Rock Arkansas Company .G. 13th Texas Mounted Regiment.[49]

The next day, June 12, 1862, Brig. Gen. Henry E. McCulloch, a veteran of the Mexican War and former commander of the First Regiment of Texas Mounted Rifles, took command of all troops "east of the Brazos River and north of the old San Antonio road."[50] His first visitors at the new headquarters near Tyler were Burnett's regiment, stragglers, lame mules, and all. The general was not favorably impressed. Captain Blewett reported, "We are at this place 12 miles north of Tyler in Smith County and will probably remain here for several days. We were stopped here by Gen McCullogh [sic] and [he] has put us under pretty Strict Discipline. I arrived at Camp on the 11th and have not been out Side of the Lines except on duty Since my arrival."[51] General McCulloch's concerns about discipline were not without a sound basis. Confederate officers in the east had already experienced botched operations due to "green troops who insisted on shooting their rifles at every passing rabbit."[52] Partly trained volunteers were a danger to themselves and to their commanders.

Never one to waste a training opportunity, McCulloch spent considerable time with the 13th Texas that month. His General Order No. 5 required the regiment to submit reports of "arm of service, strength of command, character, quantity, and condition of arms, ammunition, camp and garrison equipage, hospital and medical stores, and transportation."[53] These administrative reporting requirements would have placed a considerable burden on Burnett's inexperienced regimental staff. The delay at Camp McCulloch may also have been made necessary by the number of stragglers and others who had overstayed leave at home.

As drill and training continued, it became clear that some of the soldiers were unable to meet the physical demands required. Captain Bean's Company K, probably typical of most units, lost five men during its time at Camp McCulloch.[54] All were discharged because of disability. No meaningful physical evaluation had been conducted prior to their enlistment. On the frontier, heavy labor and injuries resulting from working with large animals and the lack of skilled medical treat-

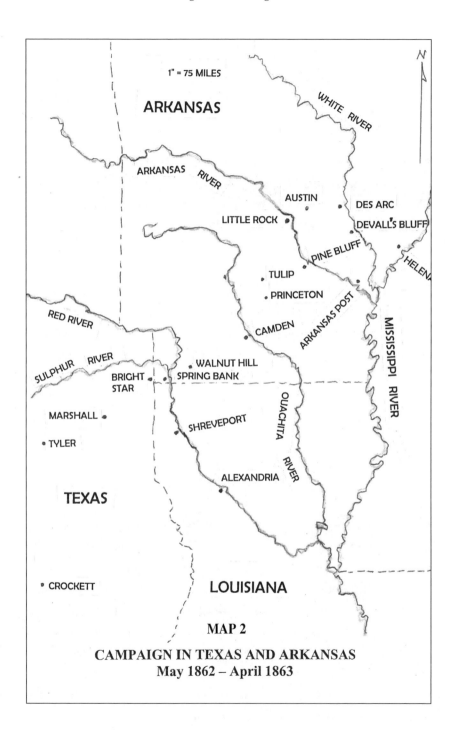

1" = 75 MILES

ARKANSAS

WHITE RIVER

ARKANSAS RIVER

AUSTIN

DES ARC

LITTLE ROCK

DEVALL'S BLUFF

PINE BLUFF

HELENA

TULIP

PRINCETON

RED RIVER

CAMDEN

ARKANSAS POST

MISSISSIPPI RIVER

SULPHUR RIVER

WALNUT HILL

SPRING BANK

BRIGHT STAR

OUACHITA RIVER

MARSHALL

SHREVEPORT

TYLER

ALEXANDRIA

TEXAS

CROCKETT

LOUISIANA

MAP 2

CAMPAIGN IN TEXAS AND ARKANSAS
May 1862 – April 1863

ment meant that many soldiers simply could not meet the demands placed upon them. Hernias, badly healed broken bones, and joint injuries were common. Untreated intestinal parasites from improperly prepared food and contaminated water added to the poor condition of others. "That old boy moves like he's got the worms" was a common criticism of someone with limited energy. Previously undiagnosed tuberculosis was also a frequent cause for a medical discharge.[55]

According to all accounts, the summer of 1862 was very hot. J. P. Blessington of Company H, 16th Texas Infantry, mentioned days of intense heat when "the thermometer stood at 110 degrees, and the breeze was as refreshing as steam from an escape-pipe."[56] Drill under such conditions was exhausting but did much to prepare the soldiers for even more difficult times to come. The regiment spent four hours a day practicing close order drill, both mounted and dismounted. Once trained, each company was able to perform such complex tasks as maintaining a continuous volley of rifle fire, if necessary, without orders. Most importantly, it taught the high degree of self-control needed to be a unit, not individuals, in battle. That did not prevent the soldiers from roundly cursing "old Mister Hardee," the author of an infantry handbook carried by the officers.[57] Officers were expected to master and memorize such instructions as, "At the second command, the covering sergeants, and the sergeant on the left of the battalion, will place themselves four paces in rear of the front rank, and opposite their places in line of battle, in order to mark the new alignment of the rear rank."[58] Some officers made no effort to learn their infantry drills until threatened later with the loss of their commissions. Of their cavalry drills, no information remains. The foremost reference on the subject would have been a work first published in November 1861 by the former commander of the Utah Mormon Battalion, Brig. Gen. Philip St. George Cooke's, *Cavalry Tactics: or Regulations for the Instruction, Formations, and Movements of the Cavalry of the Army and Volunteers of the United States.* It is more likely cavalry training was based on fragmentary memories of the few veterans of the Mexican War who remained in the regiment.

Captain Blewett of Company H gave a positive report on conditions at Camp McCulloch.

> The health of the Company and Regiment is tolerable good at this time there were about 40 reported not able to do duty this morning. We are camped in a bountiful Country with plenty of Good water. Our stock is all in good order and improving So that we will be in a good Condition to Travel soon. Our orders are now to Little Rock Ark at which place you will direct your letters. The beef to feed us to Arkansas will be delivered to us on the 24th and I presume we will leave for Little Rock on the 25th.[59]

The 13th Texas Cavalry and Gould's Battalion left Smith County on July 2, 1862.

Although it may appear that Burnett's regiment was slow in departing for Arkansas, it was on the road eight days before Horace Randal's 28th Cavalry left Marshall, Texas.[60] During the time Burnett's Regiment spent near Tyler, Union naval forces were tightening the blockade of the Texas coast. Shortages of coffee, medicines, and manufactured goods soon resulted. Union Captain Henry Eagle had demanded the surrender of Galveston in May. General Hebert, sensing a bluff, refused to capitulate but did order the evacuation of civilians, livestock, and supply stocks beyond those necessary for the Confederate garrison. It was a matter of concern for the soldiers of the 13th Texas that they were ordered to Arkansas despite the dangers facing their own state.

TABLE 3
BURNETT'S 13th TEXAS CAVALRY
REGIMENTAL SUMMARY OF ISSUE
Camp & Garrison Equipment, Issued by Capt. A. T. Monroe, A.Q.M., May – June 1862

	Co C	Co E	Co F	Co G	Co I	Co K	F&S	Total
Item								
Tents	10	10	10	15	10	10	4	69
Tent Poles	10	10	10	1	10	10	4	55
Spades	0	0	1	2	0	0	0	3
Axes	4	2	3	4	4	2	1	20
Pickaxes	1	1	1	1	1	1	0	6
Hatchets	0	1	0	0	0	0	0	1
Camp Kettles	4	4	4	4	4	4	0	24
Mess Pans	0	24	0	10	0	0	0	34
Iron Pots	5	0	5	0	6	0	0	16
Kettles	1	9	6	1	1	1	0	19
Ovens & Lids	0	11	0	8	28	2	0	49
Skillets	17	1	9	17	0	2	0	46
Frying Pans	1	10	9	1	11	1	0	33
Tin Pans	10	18	9	2	0	0	0	39
Buckets	10	12	12	3	12	0	0	49

Note: Data from Companies A, B, D, and H is missing. All other requisitions are filed with the personal papers of the company commanders in the Compiled Service Records, National Archives Microfilm M323, rolls 75–80.

1. Andrew F. Smyth to Emily Smyth, May 19, 1862, Papers of William Seale, Bevilport, Texas.

2. O.R., Series 4, I: 1095–97.

3. Cooper, *Jefferson Davis*, 445.

4. Losses amounted to 25.2%.

5. Data from Compiled Service Records is summarized in Table 2.

6. Andrew F. Smyth to Emily Smyth, May 19, 1862, Papers of William Seale, Bevilport, TX.

7. Wood, *Officers and Men Raised in Leon County*, 24. Wood's comment concerning "short time men" was quite accurate. On Apr. 15, 1862, Gen. Samuel Cooper, the Confederate Adjutant General, published General Order No. 23, which said, in part, "Parties who have been authorized by the War Department to raise troops in Texas are prohibited from enlisting or receiving twelve-months' men," O.R., Series 4, I: 1059.

8. Headquarters, District of East Texas (North of the Old San Antonio Road and East of the Brazos), General Orders No. 5, Jun. 12, 1862, O.R., Series 1, 9: 718.

9. A large number of desertions and resignations may have been a direct result of the reorganization as well. Significant numbers of "desertions" can be documented as unauthorized transfers to other units.

10. In her work *A Peculiar Honor: A History of the 28th Texas Cavalry, 1862–1865* (Fayetteville: University of Arkansas Press, 1998), M. Jane Johansson provides clear data for comparison.

11. Johansson, *Peculiar Honor*, 13. The initial organization date of the first companies is given as May 17, 1862.

12. Johansson, *Peculiar Honor,* 17. (See Table 2 for data for the 13th Cavalry.)

13. Ibid., Table 1, 12.

14. Ibid., 17.

15. John T. Stark to Martha Stark, Mar. 11, 1862, Hill College, Confederate Research Center files.

16. Hewett, *Official Records Supplement*, pt. II, 68: 3–19.

17. Granderson M. Nash of Leon County (Co A), Joshua Young of Houston County (Co B), John Long of Houston County (Co B), and Crockett English of Houston County (Co C). Hewett, *Official Records Supplement*, pt II, 68: 3–4.

18. Capt. James S. Hanks to Gen. Samuel Cooper, Apr. 14, 1863, CSR, M323-77, James S. Hanks, personal papers.

19. Hewett, *Official Records Supplement*, pt. II, 68: 4-19. Three-year obligations are missing in the files of the companies of Capt. John T. Smith (Co B), and Capt. Samuel A. Fairchild (Co I).

20. CSR, M323-79, H. Jackson Rawls, Jul. 29, 1862.

21. Thomas Rounsaville to Mattie H. Bond, Feb. 8, 1863, in United States Army Military History Institute, Carlisle, Pennsylvania, papers of James Rounsaville.

22. Thomas Rounsaville to his mother Lucy and sisters, Narcissa and Salitha, Feb. 23, 1863, James Rounsaville papers.

23. CSR. Many documents indicate "cavalry pay" ceased on July 25, 1862.

24. Johansson, *Peculiar Honor,* 26.

25. Brig. Gen. Paul O. Hebert to Gen. Robert E. Lee, Jun. 16, 1862, O.R., Series I, 9: 719.

26. Walter Lord, ed., *The Fremantle Diary* (Boston, MA: Little, Brown, and Company, 1954), 58.

27. Colonel Burnett and Lieutenant Colonel Crawford left the regiment Jul. 14, 1862 to visit Little Rock and discuss the issue with Maj. Gen. Thomas C. Hindman, and later Maj. Gen. Theophilus H. Holmes. John T. Stark to Martha Stark, Sept. 2, 1862; Carson, *Desk of Henry Ralph,* diary entry, Jul. 14, 1862, 75.

28. CSR, M323-76, Edward Currie, personal papers.

29. CSR. Five of the receipts for about $2,500 each survive in the personal papers of J. S. Hanks, W. K. Payne, H. Brown, W. Blewett, and S. A. Fairchild for six months' "commutation for clothing."

30. CSR. The annotation "paid through Jun. 30th, 1862" first appears on the October 1862 muster.

31. Table 3, Camp & Garrison Equipment, Summary of Issues.

32. CSR, M323-75, Riley J. Blair, personal papers, travel voucher and authorization dated May 10, 1862.

33. Hewett, *Official Records Supplement*, pt. II, 68: 4-19.

34. CSR. The U.S. War Department filed all personnel documents by the later company designations.

35. Wood, *Officers and Men Raised in Leon County, Texas*, 30.

36. National Archives and Records Administration, Washington, Records Group 109, Document 3229 ½, undated.

37. CSR, M323-79, John T. Smith, personal papers. See Smith's later correspondence with John H. Reagan and Congressman Franklin B. Sexton.

38. Day, *House Journal, Ninth Legislature, Regular Session*, 5–7. Only Leon and Orange Counties had solid Lubbock majorities. Anderson, Angelina, Cherokee, Henderson, Jasper, Newton, Trinity, and Tyler Counties voted overwhelmingly for Edward Clark. Houston and Polk Counties had majorities for perennial candidate Thomas Jefferson Chambers of Anahuac.

39. CSR, M323-75, Lt. David T. Arrington, receipt in personal papers.

40. Patricia L. Faust, ed., *Historical Times Illustrated Encyclopedia of the Civil War* (New York: Harper & Row, 1986), 687–8, cited in M. Jane Johansson, ed., *Widows by the Thousand* (Fayetteville: University of Arkansas Press, 2000), 270n 5.

41. CSR, M323-80, Thomas F. Truett, personal papers include a turn-in document for five unserviceable tents on Apr. 25, 1863. A number of other commanders turned in tents at that time as well.

42. Joseph P. Blessington, *Campaigns of Walker's Texas Division* (Repr., Austin, TX: State House Press, 1994), 76.

43. A. F. Smyth to Emily Smyth, May 19, 1862, in the Seale family papers.

44. CSR, M323-77, Private Hadon, of Company B, died during the epidemic at Camp Nelson, Jan. 23, 1863.

45. Lord, *The Fremantle Diary*, 58.

46. A. F. Smyth to Emily Smyth, May 19, 1862.

47. Ibid.

48. CSR, M323-75, Jerome N. Black, receipt for "2 pair hip straps for harness, 1 stretcher & 2 thigh truss, and 4 blind bridles," May 1, 1862, in personal papers.

49. William Blewett to Nancy Blewett, Jun. 11, 1862, in Whitmeyer family papers.

50. Brig. Gen. Henry E. McCulloch, General Orders No. 5, Tyler, Texas, Jun. 12, 1862, in O.R., Series 4, I: 718. This area was known as the District of East Texas.

51. William Blewett to Nancy Blewett, Jun. 19, 1862. Capt. Blewett addressed his letter from "Camp McCulloch," the campsite of Gould's Battalion nearby was known as "Camp Lubbock." Both were at the same location, ten miles north of Tyler in Smith County.

52. John Elsberg, ed., *American Military History* (Washington DC: Center for Military History, United States Army, 1989), 213.

53. O.R., Series 4, I: 718.

54. Thomas R. Reid, *Captain Jack and the Tyler County Boys* (Woodville, TX: Heritage Village Museum, 2000), 13.

55. Recorded in period diagnosis as *phthisis pulmonarialis.*

56. Blessington, *Campaigns of Walker's Texas Division,* 33.

57. Brevet Lt. Col. William J. Hardee, *Rifle and Light Infantry Tactics: for the Exercise and Manoeuvres,* Vol. 1, School of the Company (1855, Repr., n.p., James R. Gunn, 1991).

58. Lt. Col. William J. Hardee, *Rifle and Light Infantry Tactics; for the Exercise and Manoeuvres of Troops When Acting as Light Infantry or Riflemen,* Vol. 2, School of the Battalion (Philadelphia, PA: J. B. Lippincott & Co., 1861), 9.

59. William Blewett to Nancy Blewett, Jun. 19, 1862, in Whitmeyer family papers, Colmesneil, Texas.

60. Johansson, *Peculiar Honor,* 26. Colonels Edward Clark, Horace Randal, Richard Waterhouse, and William Ochiltree were all directed to "take up the line of march, with as little delay as possible, for Little Rock, Ark." on June 12, 1862 by Brig. Gen. Henry McCulloch's G.O. No. 5., O.R., Series 4, 1: 718. The 28th Cavalry, along with Colonel G. W. Carter's 21st Cavalry, would spend nearly two more weeks in Shreveport, Louisiana, fitting out wagons and attempting to have all their mounts shod.

Chapter 3

From Red River to White River

"We was compelled to take it afoot."
— Pvt. Thomas Rounsaville[1]

Leaving Camp McCulloch on July 2, the 13th Cavalry traveled through Gilmer in Upshur County and spent the Fourth of July in camp four miles north of Coffeeville on Cypress Bayou. By July 8, the regiment had passed Hickory Hill and Linden in Cass County on the way to the Texas state line. The weather was hot, but not excessively so. In the afternoons, breaks were called every hour or so, to take advantage of roadside shade. Capt. William Blewett of Company H wrote,

> Several of the boys are complaining but all of them are able to ride . . . we are traveling from fifteen to twenty miles a day which will reduce our horses but very little. So far we have found plenty of corn but the probability is that in some places between this and Little Rock we will be scarce. Our stock are generally in fine order at this time and the only difficulty now is to get them shod, a great many of them being tender footed and the roads are rocky and very rough.[2]

Typically, campsites were selected near creeks or springs or on higher ground to take advantage of the shade and breeze.

The supply of corn was not as dependable as Captain Blewett believed. Later that evening, his second in command, John Stark, wrote, "We must grumble this evening by fault of one man, the forage master, we are without feed for our horses, but maybe we will get some yet."[3] The next day Colonel Burnett relieved Pvt. Philepus Finch of his duties and sent Lieutenant Stark of Company H ahead along the route of march to buy horse feed. This arrangement was highly satisfactory to Stark, who remarked, "I like my present appointment better than having to ride along in the dust. I believe I get 75 cents a day extra of my pay and my expenses paid and [sic] when on the march. I keep two days or one or two ahead of the troops so as to have the corn & fodder on the ground by the time they get up."[4] Lt. Edward W. Cade of the 28th Texas Cavalry, who performed similar duties in that unit's advance camps, estimated that the daily requirement for his regiment was "250 bushels of corn and 9000 [pounds] of fodder to do them of a night."[5]

The 13th Texas crossed the state line into Arkansas on July 7, 1862, near the town of Bright Star, riding another ten miles before they camped near Spring Bank at the confluence of the Red and Sulphur Rivers. The selection of a campsite for the regiment, named Camp Blair after the sergeant major, was unfortunate. An outbreak of measles was soon aggravated by contaminated water that caused typhoid fever. Pvt. Henry Ralph of Company G returned from a visit to his brother in northern Louisiana to note, "the crops on the hills are suffering very much for rain, in fact they are very nearly ruined. I write this while on guard in red river swamp July 14th 1862 . . . ther is but little making in this State, the wheat Being ruined by rust & corn by drought."[6] Lieutenant Stark of Burkeville wrote, "There is no telling how long we will stay here as we have the measles and may have to remain here till they get better. Our leaders are very notionate and changeable."[7] The Compiled Service Records indicate nineteen soldiers of the 13th died in the Lafayette County swamps near the river during the month of July.

E. P. Burnett, Colonel Burnett's older brother, lived not far from Spring Bank near Rondo in Lafayette County, where he had a large plantation.[8] Colonel Burnett, Lieutenant Colonel Crawford, and Capt. A. T. Monroe left the plantation bound for Little Rock on the 14th. Burnett's younger brother James, formerly a captain in the Arkansas infantry, volunteered to act as the colonel's aide and joined them.[9] There were several pressing matters that Colonel Burnett wanted to discuss with Maj. Gen. Thomas Hindman and his staff.[10] The order to dismount the regiment could be countermanded and the loss of cavalry pay to the men could be avoided.[11] Captain Monroe needed payroll funds, both to make final payments to soldiers separated by the Conscription Act, and to pay what was owed to the soldiers through June 30. Burnett also reported the regiment's delay caused by the measles epidemic.

Colonel Burnett was too late to discuss the issue of dismounting with General Hindman. On July 10, 1862, Hindman had issued Special Order No. 26, which directed, in part, that "commanders enroute to these Headquarters from Southern Arkansas and Texas, upon seeing this order, are required to dismount their men before proceeding farther, and send the horses with suitable details home, and move forward as infantry." The reason for the order to dismount was the "impossibility to maintain a large mounted force, without causing distress, if not actual starvation, among the troops and poorer people of the country. . . . The imperative necessity of the case admits of no exception whatever, and it is hoped that a proper degree of patriotism will ensure a ready obedience."[12] Colonel Burnett remained in Little Rock until Maj. Gen. Theophilus Holmes replaced Hindman, perhaps believing that Holmes would be more receptive to mounted troops.

Shortly after the commander left, a decision was made to move the regiment's camp to the hills overlooking the flat, swampy floodplain of the river. John Stark wrote that the regiment relocated twelve miles east of "our last camp and are now in what has every appearance of a healthy location. We still have a great many sick and two more deaths in our company [H] Charles L. Potter died on the 6th and Wynant Dehart on the 7th. I think both of Typhoid fever."[13] The new location was called Camp English after the commander of Company C, a veteran of the Texas Revolution.[14] Colonel Randal's 28th Texas Cavalry passed by on its way north from Shreveport. Captain Perry wrote home on July 23, "Burnett's regiment & [Gould's] battalion is encamped near us. He has dismounted his men. The measles is annoying them."[15] The new camp was near Walnut Hill, the plantation of James S. Conway, the first governor of Arkansas. Jackson Thomas of Bradley, Arkansas, the closest town, operated a sawmill on a nearby stream. He is said to have produced ninety coffins during this period for "Confederate soldiers who died of measles there." The cemetery on the high ground near the earlier location of the sawmill is still known as "Soldiers' Ridge."[16]

Private Ralph's observations of failing crops were symptomatic of a second bad year in Arkansas. Said by the natives to be the "manifest evidence of the displeasure of God," the corn was destroyed by drought, the acorns that fattened the pigs were blighted, the wheat rusted, and oats were diseased. Compounding the bad harvest, an epidemic of swine cholera destroyed the people's primary source of meat.[17] Fifteen miles southeast of Camp English, in Spring Hill, Louisiana, Louisa Perry wrote, "hogs have been dying up very bad with the cholera."[18] Sweltering in the August heat, the soldiers of the 13th Texas, sick and ill-fed, may well have felt that they had crossed into a land cursed by Providence. Added to their discomfort was the loss of their horses. Capt. W. D. Wood of Gould's Battalion remembered, "On the road there, at Walnut Hills, La. [sic], the regiment, by order of Gen. Holmes, was dismounted and the horses sent home."[19] A lieutenant and several men from each company were selected to return the horses to their home counties. Those fortunate enough to be chosen for the task did gain a few days with loved ones at home but faced a march of over one hundred miles to return to Walnut Hill.

The long delays at Camp English had a serious impact on unit morale. First Lieutenant Stark of Newton County wrote:

I have never been so low spirited in my life. I see no prospect of being able to do any good here and to think of all I have sacrificed and of where and how I am now situated is hard indeed. . . . I shall perhaps send my horse by Mr G W Layton the bearer of this [letter]. I cannot tell you what to do with him I am too down hearted to look ahead or to be able to see what is best and cannot sell him here for any thing like a fair price. tell my boys to take good care of Turk for my sake. he has borne me thus far faithfully and has taken a great liking for me. I shall feel sad at parting from him but cannot keep him here. we are all studying our infantry tactics hard and trying to qualify ourselves for our new position. it has been said that Genl Hindman who commands at Little Rock has appointed a board of military Officers who examine all the officers of the Volunteer Regts and those who are not able to pass are reduced to the ranks, whether true or not, some of our Officers are a great deal more industrious then they have ever been before. it will thus be of great benefit to us. our company is now reduced to 69 in all and only 10 or 12 able to do duty. this looks bad indeed. . . . time has passed very heavy on my hands since we have been dismounted.[20]

Dr. Edward Currie, the regimental surgeon, and Dr. Shadrach Collins, the assistant surgeon, treated the troops during the epidemic of measles and typhoid. Dr. (2nd Lt.) John J. Burroughs of Company K assisted them, and a number of soldiers were detailed as nurses.[21] The medical staff not only treated the symptoms of typhoid fever and measles but also took preventive measures. One soldier reported, "I have been a little sick myself for a day or two arising from being vaccinated [for smallpox.] I was vaccinated first when a little boy but for fear of accidents I tried it again. It took finely and is now a very fine sore most of our men are trying it as fast as they get well enough."[22]

The march through Arkansas resumed Friday, August 22, 1862, with slightly cooler temperatures. Leaving many of the sick at Camp

English, the column moved north through Columbia County toward Camden, Arkansas.[23] Pvt. James Mann of Company K wrote his sister Mary from "Columbus County" on Sunday, "Dear Sister, I seat myself on an old log—soldier like—to let you know that we are all well at this time and hope these few lines will find you all enjoying the same. . . .We are now on our way to Little Rock and will not stop until we get there and they say we will have something to do but I hope not." In spite of the heat, he and his brothers, John and David, were thinking about winter. "Mary, I want you to make us some good warm clothes and send them by [Lieutenant] C. H. Jones."[24] The soldiers knew that once they reported to Little Rock, several of the officers would be going back to their home counties to recruit and to collect winter clothing. Captain Bean of Company K had been recruiting in Tyler County since early June and returned with six new soldiers.[25] They arrived just as the regiment was preparing to leave Camp English. The companies were all seriously reduced in numbers due to the reorganization and losses to disease.

During the next two weeks, the regiment crossed the Ouachita River at Camden, marched through Princeton and Tulip, and waded the Saline River near Benton. On September 2, the regiment was twenty-eight miles south of Little Rock. Word would have reached the men that Confederate forces commanded by Maj. Alfred Hobby had repulsed a Union attempt on August 16 to take the city of Corpus Christi on the south Texas coast. Colonel Burnett had returned from his visit with the new department commander, and mentioned that the General "holds out some slight hopes that we may be remounted."[26]

About four miles short of Little Rock the column turned east and arrived at Camp Texas thirty minutes later.[27] The purpose of this detour was to give the troops a much needed opportunity to clean up prior to being scrutinized by Maj. Gen. Theophilus H. Holmes, the new commander of the Trans-Mississippi Department, and Henry M. Rector, the governor of Arkansas. Friday the fifth dawned clear and cooler. Quantities of clay and mud had to be removed from practically everything.

The afternoon included several hours of close order drill to ensure that the unit would not be an embarrassment to the Army of the Confederacy. At the formation or "dress parade" that evening, orders were read from General Holmes, naming Brig. Gen. Henry E. McCulloch the new commander of a "Texas" division, then consisting of Col. Horace Randal's and Col. Edward Clark's brigades.[28] Traditional military priorities dictated that weapons cleaning and maintenance of other equipment would have been foremost.

The men of the 13th Texas Cavalry no doubt tried to look their best as they passed in review for those on the steps of the State House. Pvt. Joseph P. Blessington of the 16th Texas Infantry described a similar experience two weeks later. "The men were in fine spirits, and marched through the streets of Little Rock with a firm and regular step. They attracted universal attention and received a perfect ovation, the streets being crowded with men and fine ladies, who greeted them most enthusiastically."[29] Little Rock was an impressive capital with many imposing public buildings and private homes with landscaped gardens. Churches and some homes were built of brick. Even the humbler sort of houses were framed of sawed lumber and painted. There was not a log house to be seen. The men continued their march through the principal streets of the city, finally turning onto the road to St. John's College two miles from town. The buildings of the college were being used as a hospital and convalescent camp.[30]

The regiment camped on the college grounds that night and continued north on Sunday, September 7, when overcast skies began to produce a steady drizzle. Dusty roads quickly changed to sticky clay. Captain Blewett of Company H had recovered from measles at Camp English but had been suffering from an intermittent fever for several days. Maj. Charles Beaty, his brother-in-law, found a place for him to convalesce at the home of Mr. John Robbins in Little Rock, before continuing to Camp Holmes.[31]

When time came to camp, tents were quickly unloaded and pitched. As the night progressed, the rain became a downpour. Campfires were extinguished and drenched sentries waited for guard changes. Dawn broke, the tents were loaded on the supply wagons, and the regiment resumed its march to the northeast. Light rain continued throughout the day. They arrived near Austin, Arkansas, at Camp Hope known in some documents as Camp Holmes, on the ninth, and remained several days waiting for further orders. Thomas Rounsaville of Company C wrote his niece on Sunday, September 14, 1862:

> [It] is with pleasure that I take the present opportunity of writing you a few lines this beautiful and bright Sabbath morning after a long and fatiguing travel of about three months. We left home the seventh of June and arrived at this camp the ninth of September, which was three months we was on the road. We was dismounted some two hundred miles from this place. Matt, we had a long and wearisome trip of it since we left home. When we was dismounted we was sadly disappointed for we was compelled to take it afoot and we walked about two hundred miles and our feet was blistered considerably. Some of our boys entirely gave out. We are at this time twenty five miles north of Little Rock near White River.[32]

Conditions were already bad at the camp near Austin, Arkansas, when the 13th arrived. James Rounsaville of Company C wrote, "We number at this place I suppose about 20,000 strong, though there is a great deal sickness in different Regiments from 4 to 6 buried every day. . . . The poor people in this country are about to starve, provision is so scarce, we get about half rations of poor beef once a day & musty meal, also have some molasses occasionally."[33] The extreme scarcity of food was the result of crop failures in Arkansas in 1861 and 1862, as well as thriving speculation and a black market in Little Rock. In addition to crowded conditions, one soldier observed, "There is an odor about camps, that is sickening after one has been absent from there awhile. I do not care how nice they are kept they will smell badly. And any thing that is cooked taste[s] like the camps smell. It is a disagreeable Kitchen smell, that I cannot describe."[34]

Sanitary conditions in camp were not as bad as the odors indicated, and the regiment had no fatalities in September after arriving at Camp Holmes.[35] Capt. William Blewett, after sitting up in bed and being told by the doctor that "he needed no more medicin" on Wednesday, died of a hemorrhage of the bowels early Friday morning, September 19. Both the regimental chaplain John B. Renfro, and Blewett's brother-in-law Maj. Charles Beaty were with him in Little Rock when he died. Beaty wrote Blewett's widow, "he was not able to talk any after I reached him . . . the Chaplain of the Regiment was with him, and asked him if he was willing to die. [H]e answered he was. [H]e was buried in the same Enclosure where your brother John lies."[36] Chaplain John Renfro wrote a eulogistic poem that appeared in a local paper. Part of it is quoted here:

> 'Twas on a bright autumnal day,
> His troubled spirit passed away,
> And sought in boundless realms on high,
> Substantial joys that never die.
>
> A Christian soldier! Brave and true,
> As e'er the gleaming sword drew,
> With patriotic zeal he sought "the right,"
> And gave to freedom all his might.
>
> Yes, freedom's flag he raised on high,
> Then came the shout and battle cry:
> While Texas poured her legions forth,
> To oppose the vandals of the North.
>
> With Spartan band he left his home,
> For martial fields, till peace should come,
> To light, with smiles, war's sullen brow,
> And realize his country's vow.

> But fate had not reserved for him,
> The clash of arms and battle's din;
> The hero's fame and laurel green,
> That render dear each warlike scene.[37]

John Stark wrote his wife, "I am now Captain of the Company, but God knows that I do not seek for promotion in this way. T. J. Brack is 1st and G. W. Hanson 2nd Lt. we have had no election yet to fill the vacancy—we are waiting till the men all get up. The men we left at Camp English have not got up yet. [T]wo we left on the road and three men sent home with the horses not in yet. [W]e still have a good deal of sickness in camp."[38]

On Tuesday, September 23, the regiment participated in its first brigade review. The 13th Cavalry (dismounted) was assigned to the First Brigade of the Texas Division along with Col. Overton Young's 8th Texas Infantry,[39] Col. William B. Ochiltree's 18th Texas Infantry, and Col. Richard B. Hubbard's 22nd Texas Infantry. Capt. Horace Haldeman's four-gun battery was assigned as the First Brigade's artillery. General Holmes named Colonel Young as the brigade commander. John Stark remarked that the 13th Texas "made quite a display for an hour or two. The Genl and his staff were out in force and we had a fine time generally. Some of our boys said they had never seen so many men together in their lives."[40] While the regiment had no musical instrument other than "the old stage horn that our company [H] took out," at least one regiment had an accomplished brass band. The military music had a "very inspiring effect[,] even our boys walk prouder when the different bands are playing around them."[41]

There was some contention and squabbling among the regimental commanders following their assignments to brigades in September. On September 21, 1862, Capt. Theophilus Perry of Randal's 28th Cavalry wrote:

> Gen. Holmes was at Col. Randel's Headquarters a few days
> ago for the purpose of settling the rank of the Colonels. . . . The

old General assembled all of the Colonels around him & told them that he had come to settle the question of rank between them, and that they must submit in spirit as well as deed. That if there was any faction discontented, he would find it out, and crush it out. [Col.] Ochiltree made some remark in opposition to Col. Randol, but I could not hear them good. It was the place of inferior officers to stand off in the back ground. The Gen. reprimanded Col. Randol right severely. He began by telling him that he was young, enthusiastic, & capable but not conciliatory enough, and then counseled him in regard to the absolute necessity of gaining the esteem & love of his Men, and officers. There is a great opposition towards Randol, by Burnet & Ochiltree particularly. I do not know to what single fact to attribute it. If any one fact more than another accounts for it. I am disposed to say it is irritation & jealousy, though I dislike to attribute such motive[s] to men.[42]

There was more to this disagreement than "irritation & jealosy," but little of real substance. The dates of rank of four of the colonels were the bone of contention. Col. Horace Randal's commission was the senior one dating from February 12, 1862.[43] Colonel Burnett's dated from his election at the final muster of the 13th Texas on March 1, 1862.[44] Col. William B. Ochiltree's commission dated from May 13, 1862,[45] and Col. Oran B. Roberts's of the 11th Texas Infantry was February 24, 1862.[46] A more pertinent source of friction was the background of the four officers. William Ochiltree had served as a brigadier and adjutant general of the Republic and State of Texas in 1845. John Burnett had been commissioned a colonel in the Georgia militia when he returned from the Mexican War at about the age of twenty-one. Oran M. Roberts, at forty-seven, had served as a justice of the Texas Supreme Court and had been president of the Secession Convention that removed Texas from the Union in January 1861. Horace Randal's permanent rank in the United States Army had been first lieutenant. Before returning to

Texas from Virginia to raise his regiment, he had applied to President Davis for a captain's commission but without success.[47]

In practical terms, Randal, as a United States Military Academy graduate and a professional soldier, would have been the obvious choice for acting brigade command. His disciplinary attitudes would have been more likely to establish good order, and his staff experience made his actions more in keeping with what the Department wanted and expected. But as General Holmes forcefully pointed out, his relations with his peers would have to be more collegial than dictatorial. In short, he was "not conciliatory enough" to work with those around him. The other three regimental commanders had held political offices. Colonel Roberts had been a justice of the Texas Supreme Court and president of the secession convention. Colonel Ochiltree had resigned as a Confederate Congressman to raise his regiment, and Burnett had resigned from the Texas Senate. It was also the case that standing armies and professional soldiers had always been mistrusted in Texas.

Because of the friction between Burnett and Randal, Capt. John T. Smith of Company B decided that a political solution was best. He wrote to his friend, Postmaster General John H. Reagan, at Richmond on September 15, 1862, and recommended "our mutual friend" Col. John H. Burnett for promotion to brigadier general.[48] His justifications for the promotion were very similar to those in the petition of the previous June, but he also reminded Reagan that Burnett had been "among the very first to take part in the great revolution now going on." Smith noted the confidence Burnett inspired in the men and his great energy. In a more political vein, Smith pointed out as one East Texan to another, that in the past "Western Texas seems to get all the appointments. I suppose from the fact that all our military operations have heretofore been conducted at San Antonio." To correct this imbalance, Smith asked Reagan "to use your influence with the proper offices at Richmond."[49]

Reagan submitted the recommendation on October 8, 1862, with the rather neutral endorsement "respectfully referred to the Secretary of War." His other actions on behalf of Burnett were more supportive.

On the evening of October 7 he went out horseback riding with Congressman Franklin B. Sexton of San Augustine and discussed the matter.[50] Sexton wrote a personal letter to President Davis on October 8.[51] That same day, a petition to the President recommending Burnett's appointment was prepared and signed by five of the six congressmen in the Texas delegation.[52] The petition mentioned that Burnett had raised sixteen companies for the service and that he had served in both the Texas House and Senate. Sexton added, "he is highly recommended by the officers of his own and several other regiments and we doubt not his appointment would be highly satisfactory to them."[53]

This lobbying for Col. John Burnett's promotion finally came to naught. Congressman Franklin B. Sexton broached the subject again in a meeting with President Davis in January 1863 but without result.[54] Col. Horace Randal survived the assaults on his brigade command, and his rank was confirmed by the War Department early in 1863.[55] General Holmes is credited with very few sound decisions during his tenure as commander of the Trans-Mississippi Department; his appointment of Colonel Randal to brigade command was an exception. The challenges to Randal by the other regimental commanders are best understood in the terms of their political experiences, not military ones. In the political world, the others were accomplished and prominent members, but in the military establishment they were newcomers.

The junior officers and enlisted men of the 13th Texas were either unaware of or had little interest in the wrangling of the regimental commanders. Their correspondence indicates that their primary concern was in closing with and destroying the enemy. One soldier from Company H wrote that camp life was prevented from becoming dull by the proximity of the enemy. "Every day or two our pickets bring in a straggler or spy from the federal camp at and around Helena. . . . our spies go into their camp also and say that there are not over 6000 yankees at Helena but they could reinforce very easily so long as they command the Mississippi but we hope they will not be able to hold it long."[56] Pvt. James B. Rounsaville of Company C reported that Brig. Gen. Mosby

M. Parsons had taken Union General Samuel Curtis' adjutant prisoner "and sent him down to Little Rock for Safe Keeping, but he made his escape some how."[57]

The brigade received orders directing movement of some regiments to DeVall's Bluff on the White River and later orders directing others to Clarendon Heights, about ten miles downriver. Its march on October 2, under increasingly overcast skies, was uneventful. After the men arrived in camp that evening, light rain soon became a downpour. Prairie County, Arkansas, is very flat and poorly drained. The field where they camped was already flooded by morning. The downpour continued as the columns formed in the morning and moved slowly for twelve more miles. The men soon began to suffer from immersion foot, leading in many cases to blisters and infections from water contaminated by animal manure and urine. As rain continued through the night of October 3, the soldiers of the 13th Texas Cavalry huddled under soaked blankets, unable to build campfires. On the fourth, they marched a final twelve miles, often through water and mud that was knee deep. Adding to the confusion, some soldiers from Colonel Parsons' Cavalry spread inaccurate rumors of enemy activity in the area.[58]

The regiment camped the night of October 4 near DeVall's Bluff overlooking the White River. Supply wagons finally caught up with the troops, and rations were prepared around campfires as the rain came temporarily to an end. No tents had been brought, so officers and men slept around the fires and tried to dry their clothing and blankets. The camp was in a scrubby pine forest on top of a bluff, which provided little protection from the wind. They stayed in the camp at DeVall's Bluff for one day. Pvt. Henry Ralph of Captain Seale's Jasper County company, who had been recovering from "measles & flucks" with relatives in Camden, Arkansas, noted in his diary, "We came up with them at Duvalls [sic] on White river [,] from thence we marched to Des Arc."[59] Rain continued to fall intermittently, adding to the muddy conditions. Capt. John Stark wrote his wife October 9, "We are marching and countermarching our army from one place to another, one day on a forced march and another lying by and all the time knowing no more where we are going than a drove of beeves. The whole country seems to be covered with troops moving in different directions."

The 13th Cavalry camped one mile from the village of Des Arc on the seventh or eighth. Confederate pickets captured Union deserters and spies almost daily. Captain Stark noted that they "have a whole-some dread of the Texians. Some of them seem to think that we would murder them as fast as we could lay hand on them." Soldiers guarding the prisoners found that the Yankees, once recovered from their fear of "Texians," were not actually dissatisfied with their situation. They seemed sure that they would be paroled soon and then could go home to wait for the formalities of a prisoner exchange before returning to their units.[60]

As an unusually early winter began to grip Arkansas, it was not the dispirited Yankees at Helena that posed the greatest threat to the soldiers of the Texas division. Disease was already producing many casualties in the poorly fed and clothed 13th Texas and the other regiments. Company H was not unusual with "thirty-five of our Company present but all of them are not able for duty . . . our company keeps getting less and less every day almost." The regiment lost another officer when 2nd Lt. George W. Hanson of Company H died "of congestion brought on by exposure and hard marching when he ought to have been in bed . . . he died out of his senses and did not know anyone. We buried him with military honors. The funeral volleys over a brother soldiers grave have something peculiarly solemn about them [,] it is a loud toned farwell."[61] Losses to disease would only increase as the fall turned into a bitter winter.

The news from Texas was also disturbing. Following a four-day truce to evacuate civilians, Gen. Paul Hebert was forced to surrender Galveston on October 8, 1862. He had believed that an effective defense of the city was impossible and had removed to the mainland all but one of the heavy cannons in the Confederate positions on the island. Late in September three Union warships attacked Confederate forces defending Sabine Pass. The defenders withdrew, and nine days after the fall of Galveston, U.S. Marines returned and destroyed fourteen barracks and stables on the Texas side of Sabine Lake. General John Magruder replaced Hebert as commander of the District of Texas shortly after the loss of Galveston.[62]

1. Thomas J. Rounsaville to Mattie H. Bond, Sept. 4, 1862, papers of James B. Rounsaville, United States Army Military History Institute, Carlisle, Pennsylvania.

2. William Blewett to Nancy Blewett, Jul. 4, 1862, Whitmeyer family papers, Colmesneil, Texas.

3. John T. Stark to Martha Stark, Jul. 4, 1862, H. B. Simpson Research Center, Hill College.

4. John T. Stark to Martha Stark, Jul. 9, 1862.

5. Edward W. Cade to Allie Cade, Jul. 21, 1862, Anderson Collection, in Johansson, *Peculiar Honor*, 28.

6. Carson, *Desk of Henry Ralph*, 77, diary entries, Jul. 14–15, 1862.

7. John T. Stark to Martha Stark, Jul. 9, 1862.

8. Aldrich, *History of Houston County*, 135.

9. Ibid. Following the battle of Shiloh, the surviving troops of (old) Company F (La-Fayette Guards), 6th Arkansas Infantry, elected Lt. James Russell Burnett their Captain. The soldiers were later assigned to fill other companies, and Captain Burnett was discharged for disability.

10. Colonel Burnett went to see Maj. Gen. Thomas Carmichael Hindman, commander of the Department of the Trans-Mississippi. Hindman was relieved by the War Department and replaced by North Carolina native Maj. Gen. Theophilus Hunter Holmes on July 16, 1862. See Michael B. Dougan, *Confederate Arkansas: The People and Policies of a Frontier State in Wartime* (University, AL: University of Alabama Press, 1976), 92–93. Holmes, however, did not arrive in Little Rock until Aug. 10, 1862; *Little Rock Democrat*, Aug. 13, 1862, cited in *The Tyler (Texas) Reporter*, Aug. 28, 1862.

11. In an unnumbered special order dated July 19, 1862, Brig. Gen. Henry E. Mc-Culloch gave orders that units enroute to Arkansas could remain mounted only until they reached the Red River. By that time, Colonel Burnett was already in Little Rock, and would have been unaware of the directive. *The Tyler (Texas) Reporter*, July 24, 1862.

12. *The Tyler (Texas) Reporter*, July 24, 1862. Brigadier General McCulloch called upon his men "as Texians, to yield cheerful obedience to the necessities of our struggling country."

13. John T. Stark to Martha Stark, Aug. 9, 1862, H. B. Simpson Research Center, Hill College.

14. Capt. George English of Houston County; Tyler, *New Handbook of Texas*, 2: 456.

15. Theophilus Perry to Harriet Perry, Jul. 23, 1862, in M. Jane Johansson, ed., *Widows by the Thousand: The Civil War Letters of Theophilus and Harriet Perry, 1862–1864* (Fayetteville: Univ. of Arkansas Press, 2000), 7.

16. Papers of John A. Manry, Louisiana State University, Noel Memorial Library, collection 215. Only 31 deaths are recorded in the Compiled Service Records for the 13thTexas; however, large numbers of discharged soldiers were present waiting for their final pay. A number of soldiers who received medical separations were also reported as too ill to travel when the regiment departed. Gould's Battalion remained with the 13th Texas at Camp English until Jul. 30, 1862. The number of total deaths was likely near ninety.

17. Judge Brown's Diary, in Dougan, *Confederate Arkansas*, 106.

18. Louisa Perry to Theophilus Perry, Nov. 15, 1862, in Johansson, *Widows by the Thousand*, 60.

19. Wood, *Officers and Men Raised in Leon County*, 30. Wood was incorrect; Major General Hindman, not Major General Holmes, had issued the order.

20. John T. Stark to Martha Stark, Aug. 9, 1862, H. B. Simpson Research Center, Hill College.

21. Hewett, *Official Records Supplement*, pt. 2, 68: 3; CSR, John J. Burroughs and John H. Burnett. Dr. John Burroughs was authorized to travel to Little Rock during July to purchase medical supplies.

22. John T. Stark to Martha Stark, Aug. 9, 1862, H. B. Simpson Research Center, Hill College.

23. John T. Stark to Martha Stark, Sept. 2, 1862, H. B. Simpson Research Center, Hill College.

24. James Mann to Mary Mann, Aug. 24, 1862, in Lou Ella Moseley, *Pioneer Days in Tyler County* (Fort Worth, TX: Miran Publishers, 1979), 92.

25. CSR, M323, 75–80. Soldiers recruited for Company K in June included Arch Burk, R. G. Foster, Isaac Futch, Jacob Gilder, William Manley, and John Parr.

26. John T. Stark to Mary Stark, Sept. 2, 1862, H. B. Simpson Research Center, Hill College.

27. Blessington, *Walker's Texas Division*, 38. "We arrived [Sept. 22, 1862] at an old campground, known by the name of 'Camp Texas,' where all Texas troops had to go through the etiquette of military tactics, previous to paying their respects to . . . General Holmes."

28. Ibid, Special Order No. 19, Sept. 6, 1862, Headquarters Trans-Mississippi Department, Little Rock, Arkansas.

29. Blessington, *Campaigns of Walker's Texas Division*, 38–39.

30. Ibid; CSR, M323-75, Owen W. Butler, personal papers. The convalescent camp at St. John's College was later called Camp Terry, and was commanded by Col. Oran M. Roberts of the 11th Texas Infantry.

31. Charles R. Beaty to Nancy Blewett, Sept. 24, 1862, in the Whitmeyer family papers, Colmesneil, Texas. Billeting the sick in private homes was a common practice in the Confederacy; enlisted soldiers were reimbursed for the expense with payment of "separate rations."

32. Thomas J. Rounsaville to Mattie H. Bond, Sept. 4, 1862, papers of James B. Rounsaville, United States Army Military History Institute, Carlisle, Pennsylvania (hereafter USAMHI.).

33. James B. Rounsaville to Narcissa Rounsaville, Sept. 12, 1862, USAMHI. The normal ration, published by Brigadier General McCulloch in General Order No. 6, paragraph VII, June 14, 1862, was "one pound of fresh beef or half pound of bacon or pork, [and] not more than one and a half pounds of flour or corn meal will be issued to the ration. Commissaries are required to issue fresh beef five days out of seven, and bacon or pork for the remaining two days;" *The Tyler (Texas) Reporter*, June 19, 1862.

34. Theophilus Perry to Harriet Perry, Sept. 23, 1862, in Johansson, *Widows by the Thousand*, 35.

35. Pvt. Martin W. Berry of Company D died on Sept. 8, 1862, on the way from Little Rock; CSR, M323-75.

36. Charles R. Beaty to Nancy Blewett, Sept. 24, 1862, Whitmeyer family papers, Colmesneil, Texas.

37. In a clipping from the *Little Rock Gazette*, Sept. 1862, Whitmeyer family papers, Colmesneil, Texas.

38. John T. Stark to Martha Stark, Sept. 24, 1862, H. B. Simpson Research Center, Hill College.

39. Later known as the 12th Texas Infantry Regiment.

40. John T. Stark to Martha Stark, Sept. 24, 1862, in H. B. Simpson Research Center, Hill College.

41. Ibid.

42. Johansson, *Widows by the Thousand*, 32–33.

43. Johansson, *Peculiar Honor*, 13, 45; in Tyler, *New Handbook of Texas*, Randal's date of rank is given as Feb. 12, 1862.

44. CSR, M323-75, John H. Burnett's date of commissioning as colonel is noted as Mar. 1, 1862, in Special Orders 83-13, Adjutant and Inspector General's Office, dated Apr. 11, 1862.

45. Tyler, *New Handbook of Texas*, 4: 1103.

46. Ibid., 5: 611–12.

47. Johansson, *Peculiar Honor*, 7–8.

48. Capt. John T. Smith to John H Reagan, Sep. 15, 1862, in CSR, M323-75, John H. Burnett, personal papers.

49. Ibid.

50. Mary Sexton Estill, "Diary of a Confederate Congressman," *Southwestern Historical Quarterly* 38 (Apr. 1935): 288.

51. The ink of this letter is faded to such an extent that the microfilm is largely illegible. CSR, M323-75, John H. Burnett, personal papers.

52. Franklin B. Sexton, *et al.*, to President Jefferson Davis, Oct. 8, 1862, CSR, John H. Burnett, personal papers. Texas Confederate Congressmen Malcom D. Graham, Peter W. Gray, John A. Wilcox, William B. Wright, and Franklin B. Sexton signed the petition; Ezra J. Warner and W. Buck Yearns, *Biographical Register of the Confederate Congress* (Baton Rouge: Louisiana State University Press, 1975).

Chapter 3

53. F. B. Sexton, *et al.,* to Pres. Davis, Oct. 8, 1862.

54. Estill, "Diary of a Confederate Congressman," 291. Sexton discussed Burnett's appointment with President Davis on January 20, 1863.

55. Johansson, *Peculiar Honor,* 45; the conditions of Randal's commissioning as a colonel differed from the others in that he had an existing Confederate commission, and Colonels Burnett, Ochiltree, and Roberts did not. Randal was promoted to colonel with the proviso that he had to muster a regiment within four months; the others, having no existing commissions, became colonels only when their regiments were mustered and they were affirmed by election. This accounted for the confusion in establishing the date of rank of the four officers.

56. John T. Stark to Martha Stark, Sept. 24, 1862, H. B. Simpson Research Center, Hill College.

57. James B. Rounsaville to Narcissa Rounsaville, Sept. 12, 1862, U.S. Army Military History Institute. Gen. Samuel Curtis had withdrawn his harassed Union forces into defensive positions at Helena in the summer of 1862, Dougan, *Confederate Arkansas,* 91.

58. Blessington, *Campaigns of Walker's Texas Division,* 40-41.

59. Carson, *The Desk of Henry Ralph,* 77, diary entry of Oct. 28, 1862.

60. John T. Stark to Martha Stark, Oct. 9, 1862, H. B. Simpson Research Center, Hill College.

61. Ibid; CSR, M323-77, George W. Hanson died "enroute to Duvall's [*sic*] Bluff," Oct. 6, 1862.

62. Ralph A. Wooster, *Civil War Texas* (Austin: Texas State Historical Association, 1999), 13–16.

Chapter 4

The Trials of a Bitter Winter

"We have had a cold time lying on the ground and eating pore beef."—Pvt. Sherwood F. Spivey[1]

The 13th Texas Cavalry was ordered back to Camp Hope on October 10. Joined by the other regiments of their brigade, they marched about seventeen miles that day. The night of the tenth was marked by hail, and in the morning the sleepless men were greeted by cold rain that turned to sleet. The north wind gained force, the temperature dropped below freezing, and the rain still fell. Numbed by cold, marching across a partially flooded prairie, many of the sick were unwilling or unable to go on. The healthy soldiers had to help them on foot because the supply wagons were already finding it nearly impossible to get through the mud and could carry no more weight. After fourteen miles, some higher ground was located, and large fires were built. The sick huddled around them listlessly, more dead than alive. It was impossible to prepare any food as the rain continued and the freezing wind blew.[2]

The next day as the rain continued and the north wind blew, the Texans returned seven miles to Brownsville, Arkansas. Here they camped for two days, while winter quarters were being organized near Austin thirteen miles away. The rain abated on Sunday, but the overcast skies and the north wind remained. Temporary shelters were made for the sick from blankets, old canvas, or tree branches. Beef was boiled into broth and cornmeal into mush for the many who could not keep down solid food. Blessington recalled, "The fever and ague, having broken out among the troops, spread to an alarming extent; more than half of the Division was confined with them, and amongst the members of several regiments there was not a sufficiency of men well enough to do guard duty."[3] First Sergeants tried to meet the brigade's demands for soldiers for duty, as well as for teamsters, blacksmiths, gunsmiths, nurses, and other details and detachments from a smaller and smaller pool of healthy soldiers. The physical impact of the White River movements on the soldiers of the 13th Texas Cavalry was disastrous; scores of men never recovered fully and were later discharged. The psychological impact on the remaining soldiers seems to have been less negative and in fact led to an increased trust in the regiment's leadership which had kept the men together and done what they could to make the best of a truly bad situation. One begins to see a pattern of respect for their leaders and a dedication to their cause after White River that would abide through the war and beyond. None of the remaining letters or diaries has any entries critical of the regiment's senior leaders or the company commanders. The soldiers saved their invective for Gen. Theophilus Holmes and the state of Arkansas, both of which they held in particularly low regard.

After the miseries of the White River campaign, the prospect of moving to winter quarters was probably appealing. The 13th Texas left Brownsville, Arkansas, on Tuesday, October 14, 1862, and camped near Austin, Arkansas, late that evening after a march of thirteen miles. Blessington described the campsite as being several narrow dark valleys between ridgelines running east and west. It was a thin forest of leafless white oaks and some scrub pines. He said, "this camp was to be our winter quarters, and to be known by the name of Camp Nelson, in memory of General [Allison] Nelson, who died a few days previously."[4] Pvt. Sherwood Franklin Spivey, formerly of Company F, was less charitable in a letter to his wife written on October 18, 1862. "We are camped 26 miles from Little Rock. [This is] the poorest country in the world." Three days later, he complained, "I offered $4.00 for one chicken & couldn't get it at that price . . . we have had a cold time lying on the ground and eating pore beef and sole leather [salted beef and beef jerky]. We have the tightest orders here that you ever heard of."[5]

Most commanders did whatever they could to make their men more comfortable, but with an entire division encamped in an already poor area, little could be done. Staff duties delegated to company commanders and lieutenants, probably nominal at first, increased due to illnesses among the staff. Quartermaster A. T. Monroe, Chaplain John B. Renfro, Commissary Wilson E. Hail, Adjutant James Burnett, and Regimental Surgeon Edward Curry were all incapacitated and resigned their commissions before the 13th Texas left Camp Nelson. Colonel Burnett appointed Lt. John J. Burroughs of Company K as the acting Regimental Surgeon on October 29, 1862. Burroughs selected a site and set up an improvised hospital. Four or five soldiers from each company were detailed as nurse orderlies. Dr. Burroughs' difficulties were compounded in mid-November when his Assistant Surgeon, Dr. Shadrach Collins, was relieved of duty, probably for failing to appear for a required professional examination.[6]

It was recorded that "dysentery and fevers of various kinds made many victims. The hospital was filled with sick . . . owing a great deal to the impure water we had to use."[7] The porous nature of the limestone in the valleys sent all latrine effluent and animal waste directly into the groundwater. One recent analysis suggests, "Of all the adversities that Union and Confederate soldiers confronted, none was more deadly or more prevalent than contaminated water. . . . Few physicians or commanders recognized the importance of placing latrines downstream from camp."[8] A few months later an army surgeon at Vicksburg observed, "Men were in the habit of going out into the bushes, and not infrequently some 30 or 40 feet from some of their tents and relieving themselves; in fact, human excrement has been promiscuously deposited in every direction, until the atmosphere . . . is so heavily loaded with effluvia that it is sickening."[9] Habits that the young soldiers had acquired living in the wilderness were deadly in the crowded conditions of a camp.

At about the same time, Lt. C. H. Jones of Company K returned from Tyler County with eight recruits, mostly boys just turned eighteen. New recruits also arrived in smaller numbers from Leon, Houston, Anderson, and Jasper Counties. These newest soldiers were the most likely to become disease casualties. Most of the companies had sent soldiers home to collect winter clothing, often in conjunction with the officers returning to recruit. Supply wagons began returning in late November. Parcels and letters from home were handed out around campfires, temporarily brightening the prospect of Camp Nelson. Smoked pork and fresh tobacco broke the monotony of army rations. The winter clothing was a blessing, but the food was not enough to make any lasting difference. A few days later one soldier wrote, "the beef we have to eat won't raise one eye of grease on the pot, we have to eat flour without any grease . . . I go to bed hungry every night, it gets worse every day."[10] The weather stayed cold, the ground was wet, and more soldiers reported to sick call every morning. On November 2, Company H of Newton County lost Lt. Creed M. Collins, its third officer in five weeks.[11]

One unfortunate result of Lt. Charles H. Jones' recruiting that fall was later reported in an article by the Reverend A. C. Sims, a veteran of Gen. John Bell Hood's Brigade. He wrote:

> There were recruiting officers in the land calling for men to join the army and my twin brother, Albert Hubert Sims, although under age, quit the school room at Woodville and volunteered to join the Thirteenth Texas Regiment [Company K] which was then in Arkansas. This was in October 1862. I endeavored to dissuade him from his purpose, and told him that if he would wait until spring I would go with him anywhere he might wish, but he would not consent. I told him that if he went into Arkansas that late in the fall he would die before spring. His reply

was that he did not care if he did. He was determined to go. No prophet ever spoke more truly than I did on that occasion, for on the 19th of February, he died in a hospital at Little Rock.[12]

Another recruit from that Woodville schoolroom, Pvt. Edward Turner Ratcliff, no older than seventeen if the 1860 census is correct, was discharged that same month due to chronic illness.

On Thursday, October 30, 1862, first sergeants spent several hours preparing the muster roll for payday. Men were recorded "present for duty" or "sick in hospital." No one was "absent without leave," but those absent for details included Lieutenant Burroughs as acting surgeon, approximately forty soldiers as nurses, and another twenty skilled workmen at the supply depots and factories in Tyler, Marshall, and Jefferson, Texas. Lieutenant Jones of Company K, now the acting regimental quartermaster, held the muster formations and pay call that day.[13] As usual, there was little for the soldiers to buy. An enterprising local farmer may have offered some sweet potatoes or salt pork at an inflated price. The commissary sergeants offered "Confederate coffee" made from scorched cornmeal, barley, and peas.

On Saturday, November 1, commanders were able to sign requisitions for twelve pounds of bedding straw for each junior officer, enlisted soldier, and servant present for duty.[14] The straw was intended to stuff mattress covers, but many probably discarded these on the long march. In Company K, only thirty-eight soldiers and two servants remained of the one hundred and fifteen men who originally left Tyler County. After accounting for those discharged or detailed, nearly twenty must have been hospitalized. Most companies were at less than forty percent of required strength. Company C of Houston County drew straw for only twenty-seven men and one servant. Company H of Newton was in slightly better health with thirty-eight men. Between June 1862 and February 1863, Company A of Leon County was hardest hit, with thirty-three men lost; Company E of Henderson County followed with thirty-one.[15] Later records indicate that the companies seldom exceeded sixty percent present for duty for the duration of the war. It was estimated that the division lost nearly fifteen hundred men during this period, with not a single casualty from enemy action.[16]

The following weeks saw no improvement. On Monday, November 3, 1862, Lieutenant Jones of Company K was officially detailed to regimental staff as the acting quartermaster officer, leaving the first sergeant to command the company. A few weeks later, on November 22, Ernest Geisendorff, a young clerk from Woodville, was elected as the junior 2nd lieutenant, replacing Lt. Matthew L. McAlister, who had been discharged for disability. Colonel Burnett returned to Houston County in an effort to replace his heavy losses by recruiting and ensuring that conscripts were assigned to the 13th Texas Cavalry. Many of the men on picket duty had fevers, chronic coughs, or diarrhea. Young Texas volunteers reported to the regiment after processing at the depot in Little Rock and became sick almost at once. The cold, damp weather continued, and wood for campfires was rationed. Most companies had only six or seven cords of wood for the month.[17] Men not on duty hunted for something to eat or lay listlessly in their tents. If there was a raccoon, opossum, shoat, or chicken living within two miles of camp, it was a very wily or fortunate animal indeed.

The physical conditions endured by the soldiers of the Texas Division at Camp Nelson are difficult to imagine. The following notice appeared in a Texas newspaper under the heading "Wants of the Texas Troops" and was based on a letter written from LaGrange, Texas, on November 24, 1862. "A citizen of this county has just returned from our army in Arkansas, and the news that he brings is bad enough, not that our army has been whipped, but that our army is naked and shoeless, and from the fact that they are without clothing and in a colder climate than our own, there is much sickness and many deaths. Texas will lose more men this winter for the want of good warm clothing than she has lost in every battle since this war commenced."[18] Capt. John T. Stark had mentioned the problem earlier while the regiment was at Camp English, saying, "some of the boys are nearly naked now, and some barefooted."[19]

To gain a clearer understanding of some of the causes of the East Texans' problems, one has only to read Capt. William Blewett's sister's description of the young men of Jasper County ten years earlier. "If a man has but one pair of pants and the whole seat patched with buckskin and no shoes he will be certain to have on a linen bosom shirt."[20] The demands of fashion and a complete disregard for the future evidently led many soldiers to leave home quite poorly equipped. Pvt. Andrew W. Collier of Company H, who died of "typhoid pneumonia" at Camp Nelson on November 29, 1862, had in his personal effects no clothing other than what he was wearing, but he did have $149.00 in cash on his person.[21] That was more than a year's salary for a private in the Confederate Army. Pvt. William H. McWilliams Jr. also of Company H, died of pneumonia on November 9, 1862. Unlike Collier, he owned two extra pairs of woolen trousers in addition to the clothing he was wearing. McWilliams had no change of undergarment, no socks, and no clean shirt. In his saddlebags, he had a half quire of paper, twenty envelopes, and a wallet containing $226.50.[22] The clothing shortages resulted, in part, from the plan by the Confederate Congress to give soldiers cash instead of a standard clothing issue. For those officers responsible for caring for the soldiers, the clothing problem was a lost battle, which was already producing casualties.

Gen. Richard Taylor commented in his memoirs that Confederate soldiers were "drawn almost exclusively from rural districts, where families lived isolated, the men were scourged with mumps, whooping-cough, and measles, diseases readily overcome by childhood in urban populations."[23] In addition to these childhood diseases, probably overcome by many of the men of the 13th Texas Cavalry during their stay at Camp English, the soldiers at Camp Nelson suffered a second wave of disease. Epidemic levels of such respiratory infections as pneumonia and tuberculosis, as well as typhoid fever from polluted groundwater and bacterial skin infections such as erysipelas spread through the camps.[24] This deadly mixture was aggravated by a diet consisting primarily of coarsely ground cornmeal and often putrid lean beef that failed to meet minimal dietary requirements and weakened the soldiers' immune systems. Virgil S. Rabb of Company I, 16th Texas Infantry, wrote, "The Government tries to feed us Texians on Poor Beef, but there is too Dam many hogs here for that, these Arkansaw hoosiers ask from 25 to 30 cents a pound for there Pork, but the Boys generally get [it] a little cheaper than that. I reckon you understand how they get it."[25]

TABLE 4
13th Texas Cavalry, Losses to Disease and Disability
June 30, 1862, to February 28, 1863
Based on Company Assigned Strength*

Unit	6.30.62	8.30.62	12.31.62	2.28.63	% Loss
Company A	91	76	64	58	36.3
Company B	98	87	75	69	29.6
Company C	88	78	73	69	21.6
Company D	112	90	79	76	32.1
Company E	85	71	64	54	36.5
Company F	59	57	50	46	22.1
Company G	87	82	79	73	16.1
Company H	79	71	60	59	25.3
Company I	80	62	56	51	36.2
Company K	76	69	66	60	21.1
Total Assigned	855	743	666	615	28.1

* From National Archives, "Compiled Service Records, " microfilm M323 rolls 75–80.
Note: Soldiers on medical leave who did not return after sixty days were categorized as absent without leave or deserted.

Many of the better-educated East Texans would have been reminded of the lessons of classical history, particularly the writings of Xenophon, who was quite popular in the antebellum South, on the education of the Spartan youth. "[Lycurgus] allowed them to alleviate their hunger by stealing something. . . . There can be no doubt then, that all this education was planned by him in order to make the boys more resourceful in getting supplies, and better fighting men."[26] It is unlikely that the Spartan lawgiver had stealing full-grown hogs in mind.

As malnutrition and disease took their toll on Confederate forces in Arkansas in the early winter, Union commanders were completing plans for a major campaign to seize control of the Mississippi River. Two major obstacles stood in their way. Commanded by Lt. Gen. John C. Pemberton, the Confederate fortifications at Vicksburg and Port Hudson prevented the Union forces from dominating the entire length of the Mississippi River. Strongly supported by General-in-Chief Henry W. Halleck, and later President Lincoln, Maj. Gen. Ulysses S. Grant was given command of the forces attacking Vicksburg from the north. Maj. Gen. Nathaniel P. Banks led the attack on Port Hudson from Union-occupied south Louisiana. The preliminary phase of the operations began in December 1862, with Maj. Gen. William T. Sherman's initial failed attacks on Vicksburg's northern lines of defense, as well as Grant's repulse in north Mississippi.[27]

By early December 1862, the 13th Texas Cavalry was on the verge of its first major campaign. It was reduced by disease to an effective strength of less than fifty percent. During the months of November and December, 237 soldiers remained hospitalized, and twenty-five died in November alone.[28] November marked the worst mortality among the soldiers stationed at Camp Nelson. In early December, medical authorities began to move recovering and ambulatory patients to Camp Terry convalescent camp at St. John's College and to existing or newly organized hospitals in Little Rock. Typical of these experiences were those recorded in the diary of Pvt. Milton P. Gaines of Capt. James S. Hanks' Company D. "October 17—Got back to Camp Nelson, thirty miles Northeast of Little Rock, Arkansas. October 20—Took pneumonia and was sent to Camp Hospital. November 11—Sent me to Little Rock Hospital. January 11—Left Little Rock on a steamboat and went down the Arkansas River. Landed near my command [at Pine Bluff]."[29] The experiences of the acting regimental surgeon, Lt. John J. Burroughs of Woodville, were similar. He moved with the last soldiers from Camp Nelson in December to Little Rock and did not rejoin the regiment until January.[30]

On Monday, November 24, 1862, Brig. Gen. McCulloch began moving those of the Texas Division still able to perform duty away from Camp Nelson. Over a period of several days, the 13th Texas Cavalry and the other units were marched about twenty miles to a campsite near Bayou Meto, a northern tributary of the Arkansas River. Moving the heavily laden supply wagons over the prairie required that the unpaved roads be "corduroyed" over much of their length with a bed of cut saplings and timber. Once in camp, heavy frost did not deter McCulloch from ordering a division review for departmental commander Lt. Gen. Theophilus Holmes on Thursday the twenty-seventh. He also issued a standing order for four hours of company drill each day. The review was evidently quite impressive to Private Blessington, "the columns extending about two miles marching along with their guns and bayonets glittering in the morning sun, and their gay flags and banners flaunting in the breeze." The camp, initially situated on the prairie, was relocated a few days later to higher ground several miles to the west. Considerable snow fell at their new campsite on the night of December 4, a novel, if uncomfortable event for many of the young Texans.[31]

Orders came for the division to prepare for a deployment to assist in the defense of Vicksburg, threatened by Grant's Federal forces. On December 13, the division marched about eighteen miles to the east. The next morning, the destination was changed to Van Buren, Arkansas. The division followed the tracks of the Memphis & Little Rock Railway eight miles. On Sunday the troops rested and cooked rations. Monday morning found them back on the road to Little Rock, marching nineteen miles and camping near the city. Here they remained through Christmas Day, which was celebrated without the traditional eggnog and toddy. On Friday, December 26, 1862, they were redirected to Pine Bluff, one hundred miles to the southeast. These seemingly aimless wanderings were disconcerting to the soldiers. Several comments by soldiers of the Texas Division indicated they had doubts about the mental state of General Holmes.[32] The division had returned to its camp four miles from Little Rock and learned at the evening formation that its new division commander was Maj. Gen. John G. Walker, replacing Brig. Gen. Henry E. McCulloch, who was given command of the third brigade.[33] Walker was a native of Missouri with a spotless record in both the Mexican War and with the armies of Lee and Beauregard in the east. At five-feet, ten inches tall and 140 pounds, he was described as "small" by one of the Texans present at the change of command ceremony.[34] President Jefferson Davis had personally selected him to command the division. The men soon developed a real affection for Walker, who took time to meet with each company commander as he conducted his initial inspection.

The next morning the division embarked on a three-day march on the Pine Bluff road, which took the Texans over increasingly stony paths that, rose and fell over a seemingly endless progression of ridgelines. After moving almost forty miles, they reversed course on New Year's Eve and marched fifteen miles back toward Little Rock. Later that night the tents were shaken by the passage of an extremely strong norther. North winds were frigid and strong as the soldiers changed directions again and covered twelve miles that day and six miles the next.[35]

On Monday, January 5, 1863, the Texans broke camp once more with orders directing them to Pine Bluff. On Thursday they arrived near the city and camped that evening on a high bluff overlooking the river five miles west of town. To the south, miles of fertile farmland could be seen. The historian of Walker's Division recorded, "at this camp the division was formed in line of battle to witness three soldiers belonging to McCulloch's Brigade, drummed out of camp for 'hog-stealing'. The bands played 'The Rogue's March' along the line. The three soldiers marched along the entire line, followed by a file of soldiers with fixed bayonets. This kind of punishment, inaugurated by General Mc-Culloch, seemed to be a novelty to the Texas boys, and it created roars of laughter amongst the troops."[36] Given the Texans' affection for pork, however acquired, there may have been some burying of bones and other evidence when they returned to their company areas.

Trouble was brewing for the fourth brigade of Walker's new division. Immediately after the division's formation, the brigade had been sent to man Fort Hindman, a heavily fortified bluff on the Arkansas River usually known as Arkansas Post or the Post of Arkansas. This defensive work commanded the Arkansas River about forty miles from the Mississippi River. Shortly after December 20, 1862, a Confederate vessel captured an unarmed Union steamboat, the *Blue Wing*, loaded with ammunition and towing barges of coal for Grant's Vicksburg Campaign. Maj. Gen. William T. Sherman, second in command of the Union forces, learned of the incident from a boy who had escaped after the Rebels captured the ship. Sherman concluded, "We could not carry on operations against Vicksburg as long as the rebels held the Post of Arkansas, whence to attack our boats coming and going without convoy."[37] Sherman convinced Maj. Gen. John A. McClernand, commanding in Grant's absence, as well as Rear Adm. David D. Porter, the naval commander of the Vicksburg operations, of the dangers of the situation. As a result of Sherman's arguments, the entire Federal task force took ship from near Milliken's Bend on the Mississippi north of Vicksburg and proceeded north to Arkansas Post, arriving on January 9, 1863.[38]

In the early morning hours of Sunday, January 11, orders arrived that the 13th Texas and other regiments of Walker's Division were to reinforce the garrison at Arkansas Post. A forced march took them nearly twenty-five miles, but the next day after a five-mile march, they learned that the post had surrendered. General Sherman reported that 4,791 prisoners had been loaded onto transports for shipment to St. Louis, Missouri; he was also gratified to recover the ammunition from the *Blue Wing* from the magazine at Arkansas Post. After an intense bombardment by Porter's gunboats on January 10, the Union forces had begun an assault on the fortifications the next day that was cut short in mid-afternoon by the unfurling of a white flag of surrender. The Confederate garrison commander later said that he had not ordered this signal, and it was assumed by the troops of Walker's Division that the surrender was the result of conspirators.[39]

Pvt. Tom Rounsaville of Captain English's Company C, Houston

County, reported on the aftermath of the Union victory in a letter to his mother and sisters on January 15:

> My dear ma & sisters
> Once again I am permitted to address you through the dull medium of pen and ink. . . . Ma I am in the hospital at this time in the town of Pine Bluff this is located on Ark[ansas] River about forty or fifty miles from Little Rock. We left Little Rock about two weeks ago for Ark[ansas] post & when we left Little Rock I was very sick and had to be hauled in the ambulance and on our company wagon, and when we got to this place, I concluded that I would stop at the hospital as it is a very nice one. I have improved everyday since I stopped here. Jim could not stay with me & went on with the command and our brigade. Col Randals & Gen McCulloch is about twenty-five miles from here. They left here for Arkansas post & before they could get there the Yankees came up the River in their gun boats to Ark post & they had a bloody battle, the fight commenced on Friday evening & ended on Sunday evening. they gave us an awful whipping & taken the post, they had our men completely surrounded. . . . I never saw so much excitement in my life, as there is now in this town. All of the citizens, are leaving as fast as they can get away, & taken all of their furniture out of the place. Gen. Holmes has ordered government property to be removed from the river & all negro[es] to be taken out of the country & they have been sending them several days to Texas. The Yankees is still advancing on us. . . . The citizens are expecting gun boats at this place in less time than thirty-six hours. If they should come I do not know what would become of us sick. They would take all of us prisoners I expect what could not get away. . . . Your loving son,
>
> T. J. Rounsaville[40]

The actual facts concerning the Yankees and their movements were quite at variance with Rounsaville's letter and General Holmes' assumptions. Maj. Gen. William T. Sherman later wrote, "On the 13th we reembarked; the whole expedition returned out of the river by the direct route down the Arkansas during a heavy snow-storm, and rendezvoused in the Mississippi, at Napoleon, at the mouth of the Arkansas. Here General McClernand told me he had received a letter from General Grant at Memphis, who disapproved of our movement[s]."[41] Grant later expressed his unqualified approval after receiving a more complete report.

Capt. John T. Stark of Burkeville, Newton County, Texas, commanded Company H of the 13th Texas during the confusion following the attack on Arkansas Post. Although his company was at less than twenty-five percent strength, the men were eager to fight any Union force that dared force its way up the Arkansas River. He wrote his wife a few days later.

In camp 7 miles below Pine Bluff Ark Jan 20th 1863
Dear Martha

I have received no letter from you now since the one dated 19th Dec it does seem like a long time but it has been a busy time with us and I never want to see such another time. in the first place we started from Little Rock to Relieve Arkansas Post but like every thing Genl Holmes does we got there too late or rather we got in about 20 miles of there and found we were too late. then learning that the Feds were advancing up the River we threw up a breast work and prepared to receive them. I tell you it made me feel bad to walk around he lines and think how many a poor fellow would bite the dust or rather the swamp mud but all my feeling[s] on the subject were thrown away, for the enemy from some cause backed out and we then left too and came back up the River 18 miles to our present camp. but of all cold frozen times that ever I saw it was the coldest it first rained then sleeted and then snowed the snow was about ten inches deep and lay on the ground four or five days all this time we were expecting to be attacked every hour . . . fatigue parties by the hundreds at work on the breast work and every thing as lively as possible Generals, Colonels and the Governor of Arkansas riding up and down the lines. I shall never feel more certain that we were going to have a fight even if I hear the fireing commence.[42]

The men knew the place as "Camp Freeze Out." Their discomfort was amplified by orders at two in the morning to move the stiff, frozen tents to a landing on the river for transport by the riverboats to a new camp. After a miserable night sleeping in the open with only their blankets, they departed the hastily built defensive positions when it became clear that the Federal forces were not attacking. Captain Stark described the march back to Pine Bluff:[43]

But of all muddy roads I ever saw I think the one we traveled over yesterday was the muddest. the snow has melted through the combined influence of the sun and the rain and the road lying right along the river all the time with hundreds of wagons Artillery wagons and Cavalry passing all the time made it [illegible] as a river bottom road can get to be. I made about [illegible] miles yesterday carrying my arms, overcoat, and blankets, for the wagons were so heavy loaded we had to carry nearly all our baggage and slept in a corncrib without any supper and came to camp in time to cook my dinner. We certainly have the poorest management that ever was seen all this time we have been marching and countermarching up and down the River the steamboats are passing us as if to tantalize our Misery. [I]f Holmes had put the troops on board the boats they could have relieved the Post and given the Yankees another lesson. [B]ut instead of that after we started we lay one day at Little Rock then came on at easy stages of about 12 miles a day to Pine Bluff then we lay up another day and then went on at the same easy gate until we met the news of the fall of the Post but I must close for the present. We will all fight our battles over again when we get home.[44]

The day after Captain Stark wrote his letter, the Union forces arrived at the landing at Milliken's Bend, Louisiana, on the west bank of the Mississippi River north of Vicksburg.[45] Similar failures by Confederate commanders to collect timely and accurate intelligence regarding enemy movements would doom many of their efforts throughout the Vicksburg Campaign. After arriving near Pine Bluff, the 13th Texas Cavalry and the remainder of Walker's Division were ordered to establish winter quarters at Camp Mills, four miles northwest of the city on the hills overlooking the Arkansas River.[46]

News from Texas was encouraging. General Magruder had attacked and defeated Union naval and ground forces and expelled them from Galveston on New Years Day of 1863. Brig. Gen. William "Dirty Shirt" Scurry led his infantry across the disused railroad bridge that linked the island with the mainland and surprised three companies of Massachusetts infantry and 150 sailors and marines on Kuhn's wharf at the port of Galveston. Coordinated with Scurry's attack, two riverboats "armored" with cotton bales and filled with sharpshooters from the 5th and 7th Texas Cavalry attacked the Federal fleet anchored in the bay. One Union warship was captured after a battle that heavily damaged both Confederate vessels. Union Commander William Renshaw, whose ship had run aground, was killed when an explosive charge detonated prematurely. The liberation of Galveston did much to lift the morale of the Texans wintering in Arkansas.

1. Sherwood F. Spivey to Martha Spivey, Oct. 18, 1862, H. B. Simpson Research Center, Hill College.

2. Blessington, *Campaigns of Walker's Texas Division*, 42.

3. Ibid., 42.

4. Ibid., 44.

5. Pvt. Sherwood Franklin Spivey was one of those who "deserted" from Capt. Hiram Brown's Company F to Company D, 22nd Texas Infantry. Hewett, *Texas Confederate Soldiers*, I: 498. Sherwood F. Spivey to Martha Spivey, Oct. 18, 1862.

6. CSR, M323, roll 75, Shadrach Collins. Dr. Collins was relieved November 13, 1862.

7. Blessington, *Campaigns of Walker's Texas Division*, 44.

8. Jeffrey S. Sartin, "Infectious Diseases During the Civil War: The Triumph of the 'Third Army'," *Clinical Infectious Diseases* 16 (April 1993): 581.

9. A. J. Bollett, "To Care for Him That Has Borne the Battle: A Medical History of the Civil War," *Resident and Staff Physician* 36 (1991): 107.

10. Pvt. Sherwood F. Spivey to Martha Spivey, Oct. 18, 1862, H. B. Simpson Research Center, Hill College.

11. CSR, M323, roll 76, Creed M. Collins. Lt. Collins died in Searcy Valley, Arkansas.

12. *Jasper (Texas) Newsboy*, May 17, 1911.

13. CSR. Pay records indicate "C. H. Jones, A.A.Q.M." conducted the October 1862 muster and pay call.

14. The terms used are euphemisms for slaves. The printed forms list female slaves as "laundresses" and male slaves as "servants." CSR, M323, roll 77, Charles H. Jones.

15. CSR, M323, rolls 75-80. These totals include soldiers who died of disease or were discharged for disability.

16. Blessington, *Campaigns of Walker's Texas Division*, 44.

17. CSR. Requisitions for firewood exist in the personal papers of seven company commanders or acting commanders.

18. *Galveston Tri-Weekly News*, Dec. 3, 1862. As a result of the Union occupation of Galveston this newspaper was being published in Houston, Texas.

19. John T. Stark to Martha Stark, Aug. 9, 1862, H. B. Simpson Research Center, Hill College.

20. Marshall, *Jasper Journal*, 24.

21. CSR, M323, roll 76, Andrew W. Collier, personal papers, inventory of personal effects. Collier evidently had symptoms of both typhoid fever and pneumonia; multiple infections were not uncommon.

22. CSR, M323, roll 78, William H. McWilliams Jr. personal papers, inventory of personal effects.

23. Richard Taylor, *Destruction and Reconstruction* (New York: Longmans, Green, & Company, 1955), 19.

24. Sartin, "Infectious Diseases During the Civil War," 582.

25. Thomas W. Cutrer, ed., "'Bully for Flournoy's Regiment, We are some Punkins, You'll Bet': The Civil War Letters of Virgil Sullivan Rabb, Captain, Company 'I,' Sixteenth Texas Infantry, C.S.A.," *Military History of the Southwest* 19 (Fall 1989): 172.

26. See, for instance, E. C. Marchant, ed., *Xenophon: Scripta Minora, Constitution of the Lacedaemonians* (Cambridge, MA: Harvard University Press, 1984), 144–45.

27. John Elsberg, *American Military History*, 236–37.

28. CSR, M323, rolls 75–80. Regimental musters for November and December and the company muster for December 31, 1862 list twenty-five dead in November and over four hundred hospitalized at various times during those months. At least thirty soldiers were detailed as nurses several of whom died at Camp Nelson.

29. Diary of Milton Pinckney Gaines, Jun. 11, 1862 –May 25, 1865. Papers of Charles H. Ham, Anderson County, Texas.

30. CSR, M323, roll 75, John J. Burroughs, muster rolls and personal papers.

31. Blessington, *Campaigns of Walker's Texas Division*, 61–63.

32. Ibid, 64.

33. Special Order 264, Adjutant and Inspector General's Office, implemented by Special Order 121, Trans-Mississippi Department, Maj. Gen. T. H. Holmes.

34. John C. Porter, "Early Days of Pittsburg, Texas, 1859-1874," 10-11, 18th Texas Infantry file, H. B. Simpson Research Center, Hill College.

35. Blessington, *Campaigns of Walker's Texas Division*, 66–67.

36. Ibid., 68.

37. William T. Sherman, *Memoirs of General William T. Sherman, by Himself* (New York: Appleton, 1875), 1: 324–25.

38. Sherman, *Memoirs*, 1: 325.

39. O. R., XVII, pt. 1, 754-57; Blessington, *Campaigns of Walker's Division*, 69–70.

40. Thomas J. Rounsaville to his mother and sisters, Jan. 15, 1863. USAMHI, papers of James B. Rounsaville.

41. Sherman, *Memoirs*, 1: 330–31.

42. Captain John T. Stark to Martha Stark, Jan. 20, 1863, H. B. Simpson Research Center, Hill College.

43. Blessington, *Campaigns of Walker's Division*, 66–75.

44. Stark, Jan. 20, 1863, Hill College.

45. Sherman, *Memoirs*, 1: 330–331.

46. Blessington, *Campaigns of Walker's Texas Division*, 75.

Chapter 5

The Vicksburg Campaign

"The damned old Arkansas never did have anything in it."
—Col. John H. Burnett[1]

Once settled at Camp Mills, General Walker ordered that each company in the division could grant leave to two soldiers. Captains were authorized to grant the fortunate soldiers leave for forty-five days on Wednesday, February 4. Many others were granted sixty days sick leave by medical authorities in January and February 1863. Some improvements were noted, the first being the weather, which became clear and warmer. Newer tents, blankets, and shoes were issued from the depot at Little Rock. The roads passing through Camp Mills became so muddy and degraded by heavy traffic that they were a constant problem for teamsters bringing supplies to the regiments. A better site for the camp was identified four miles northwest of Pine Bluff and the division relocated from Camp Mills to Camp Wright on February 9, 1863. Many of the extreme physical adversities they had experienced over the past four months seemed to be behind them. The camp's fields were described by Blessington as, "covered over with white tents, arranged with street-like precision, with regiments or battalions on parade or review, with martial music echoing along the riverbank, from splendid bands . . .

add to this the Arkansas River, flowing on in majestic grandeur . . . such was our encampment."[2]

As the memory of major adversities faded, mundane matters began to cause dissatisfaction. It is impossible to decide if the rowdiness of the 13th Texas Cavalry's Houston County Company C resulted from bad food or from the impending expiration of many soldiers' one-year enlistment contract. Both had been the topic of loud complaints for some time. About sundown on Friday, February 20, 1863, the company quartermaster sergeant, mess orderlies, and detail soldiers of Company C went to draw rations from the commissary. The beef they received was literally blue with putrescence. Lt. Thomas Rounsaville remarked, "It was so poor that we could not eat it."[3] Although the quantity was not large, it stank, and one soldier suggested it should be buried. Quickly the idea of a ceremonial funeral spread, and a number of torches were lit. The company was soon formed as a guard of honor for the departed. Drums and mess pans were beaten at a slow tempo as the company crossed the creek and buried the beef at the edge of the forest.

By that time nearly every idle soldier in the regiment would likely have gathered around out of curiosity. Not satisfied with a quiet interment, Company C solemnly presented arms, "fired several platoons over it," and set up head and footboards in lieu of a monument. They now had the attention of everyone in camp. Still carrying their torches, they "then marched up to Colonel Burnett's headquarters for a speech." Burnett, recognizing the brand-burning "honor guard" as his own Houston County soldiers, emerged with a combination of good humor and seriousness, and stood on a stump. He said he did not think any less of them for carrying torches through the camp, but their threats to stack arms and go home could not be carried out with their honor intact. In senatorial style, an appropriate classical exhortation would have been in order. Perhaps it was that of the women of Sparta to their departing soldiers, to "return with your shield or on it." The demands for pork were especially loud, but Burnett was forced to admit that none could be procured. He concluded, "the damned old

Arkansas never did have anything in it from the start." At this point the colonel was loudly cheered and the rowdy spirits returned peacefully to their company areas.[4] When confronted with such behavior, some commanders, perhaps less certain of their men's loyalty, reacted with arrests and punishments.[5]

Colonel Burnett quickly confirmed the temporary staff appointments made by Lt. Col. Anderson F. Crawford when he returned from Houston County in January. Sgt. Maj. Riley J. Blair of Houston County was commissioned a captain as the quartermaster officer, replacing acting quartermaster 1st Lt. Charles H. Jones of Company K. Pvt. James Brown Rounsaville of Crockett was promoted to sergeant major. Lt. John L. Cornish joined the regiment as assistant surgeon following his transfer from Company G of Randal's 28th Texas Cavalry. The position of surgeon was held for Dr. Thomas H. Hollis, formerly of the 27th Texas Cavalry, who had been temporarily transferred to command the Rock Hotel hospital at Little Rock. Because of these duties, Captain Hollis was unable to join the regiment until the late summer of 1863. Capt. J. Pat Henry of Company I, Orange County, was selected as the regimental adjutant. He had served with Burnett and Crawford earlier as the enrolling clerk of the Texas Senate during the Eighth Legislature. Henry relieved Lt. William F. Seale of Company G, who had served as acting adjutant during December 1862. James H. Finch, also of Company I, replaced Lt. Wilson E. Hail as the commissary officer. All of the new staff officers were appointed by the end of February 1863.[6]

The regiment's company officers were more likely to complain about the state of their health and the management of the war than terms of enlistment or the duration of their service. None seem to have aspired to positions on the staff. Capt. John T. Stark of Company H wrote, "It has been a long time now since I received one of your ever welcome letters and I feel very low spirited on the account of that and many other things. one thing is that I am not very well myself. I have a smart touch of the Jaundice, and I reckon it makes a man feel about as trifling and no account as any thing can. There has been a great many cases of it in our camp. in fact you can hardly see a man but what is more or less touched with it." Commenting on the fall of Arkansas Post, he reflected, "So many Texians have fallen into the hands of the enemy and we not there to help all through the imbecility or incompetency of <u>Granny</u> <u>Holmes</u> as he is now by common consent called—we suffered a great deal during the time we were down on the River and two of our men belonging to the Regiment were actually frozen to death, one of them a Lieutenant Gaston[,] one of the finest looking men in the Regiment. Our men are generally becoming very low spirited and desertions are frequent six men are said to have left last night. I am sorry and I hope we will escape that disgrace." Referring to the sick recovering at Little Rock, who had still not rejoined the company, he wrote, "Maybe they will get here as soon as they are needed, though I wanted them mighty bad when we had our breastworks thrown up and was expecting a fight every hour. We only had 25 in all to go into the fight with but I think they would have counted. The boys seemed as lively as usual, rather elated than otherwise at the prospect of giving the enemy a drubbing."[7]

Following the ritual funeral for the decayed beef, Lt. Thomas J. Rounsaville told his mother and sisters, "We have a great deal of dissatisfaction through out our regiment simply because our time is about to expire, & no prospect of going home very soon just raving and pitching about it & swore they will not stand it. They say they will go home or die, it is nearly a unanimous thing through out the Regiment, the majority of our company is in favor of it, but I am opposed to any such & I am confident I do want to go home as bad as any man aliving, but I do not want to go that way. I went into this thing honorable & I want to go out of it the same way."[8] Rounsaville went on to say that in his opinion, army supplies were nearly exhausted, and that he doubted the war could last beyond the fall. The fact that a "three year or duration of the war" enlistment had been affirmed by their participation in the May 1862 reorganization of the regiment had still not been clearly communicated to the enlisted soldiers of the 13th Texas Cavalry.

While opportunities for entertainment and social interaction were probably quite limited, soldiers occasionally took meals at the hotels or boarding houses of Pine Bluff. Thomas Rounsaville told his niece, "Jimmie and I taken a fine dinner in town together the day we came out. We had a great deal of fun looking at the Yankee prisoners in the [jail in the] Court House." On March 17 soldiers of the 16th Texas Infantry presented a show entitled the "Lone Star Minstrels" in the same courthouse in Pine Bluff, which featured comedy and dancing, and the full cast were "all blacked like Negroes." The entertainment filled the house with ladies and soldiers and produced more than $400 for their regimental hospital. However, few enlisted soldiers of the 13th Texas Cavalry were able to secure the required pass to town to take advantage of these limited attractions.[9]

Thomas Rounsaville's brother James, now the regimental sergeant major, wrote home concerning the ultimate punishment for desertion, described at the time as "death by musketry." The frequency of the offense that spring in the Texas Division compelled Major General Walker to make examples of a few deserters. Sergeant Major Rounsaville described the victims and their circumstances. "I witnessed on the 13th of [March] . . . two soldiers executed for desertion. They both resided in the City of Houston, & one of them with a wife and three little children to moan his loss, also one was executed yesterday for same offence, a young man some 20 years old, he had been sick for three weeks I hear not been out of bed, but was taken out to be shot, he looked very thin and meager, was an object of pitty, but was not cheated out of many days life." He added that at that time, "There are also some fifteen or sixteen others, to be executed soon for similar offence, there is little chance for a deserter to excape death, as nothing but the most extenuating circumstance will induce the General to exercise his clemency in such cases."[10]

About March 21, 1863, Lt. William M. Walton, a military aide to the Governor of Texas, arrived at Camp Wright from Austin with a message from the Texas legislature for the soldiers of the Texas regiments.

Regimental adjutants read the resolution at evening formation the next day. Some Texas counties had already passed resolutions providing for the soldiers' families and authorizing the purchase of provisions and supplies at county expense.[11]

> Section 1. Be it **Resolved** by the Legislature of the State of Texas, That the people of Texas, acknowledging with heartfelt gratitude the favor of God in the brilliant achievements of our Confederate armies, do, hereby, formally and sincerely, tender to the Officers and Privates in the Military service of the Country, from the State of Texas, the thanks and praises they have so justly merited, by their self-sacrificing devotion to their country, and their many deeds of valor upon every battle-field of the Confederacy.
>
> In the name of a gallant State and a gallant people we thank you for your gallant deeds.
>
> You have won for yourselves imperishable renown. You have won for your State the highest honors.
>
> Section 2. **Resolved,** That while our brave troops are battling so gloriously for the dearest interests of our people, we recognize it as a sacred obligation to provide for their comfort, and to support and cherish their families at home.
>
> Section 3. **Resolved,** That the faith of the State of Texas, is hereby pledged to our soldiers in the field, that their families shall be nourished and supported during the war.
>
> Section 4. **Resolved,** That the Governor be instructed to have a copy of this Resolution transmitted to every Texas Regiment now in the service, with the request that it may be read out to every Company.
>
> C. W. Buckley
> Speaker of the House of Representatives

Jno. M. Crockett
President of the Senate
Approved Feby 21, 1863
F. R. Lubbock[12]

Problems and protests, primarily related to the terms of enlistment, the quality and quantity of rations, and homesickness, persisted in some companies through the spring of 1863. Pvt. Milton P. Gaines of Company D, Anderson County, recorded on April 8 that, "Our Company [was] put under guard [for sixteen days] for refusing to do duty."[13] Because of this punishment, the 13th Texas Cavalry may have been among the last units of the division to leave Camp Wright. The specific cause of the soldiers' refusal to perform duty in this case is unknown, but was likely related to the twelve-month enlistments. One week later, their commander, Capt. James Steel Hanks of Company D, tendered his resignation on April 14, 1863, saying:

> He would most respectfully state that he entered the service for twelve months when he was nearly 53 years of age and has been in service nearly 14 months, that his only son was killed at the Battle of Richmond, Virginia at the age of 17 years, except one about ten years old, that his wife has been in bad health ever since the month of September last, so that she has not been able to look for business, that he has between 25 and 30 negroes and no overseer that can be procured to look for them and taking his age into consideration, how returning he can do more for the benefit of the Southern Confederacy at home than in the service.[14]

Well past the age for infantry service, and perhaps indirectly taking responsibility for his company's misconduct, Hanks stated that any one of his three young lieutenants was well suited to command. 1st Lt. John C. Oldham, aged thirty-five years, took command and was promoted to captain June 10, 1863.[15] He commanded the company for the remainder of the war.

In early March of that year, Lt. Gen. Edmund Kirby Smith arrived west of the Mississippi River, relieving General Holmes of command of the Trans-Mississippi Department. Smith, a graduate of the U. S. Military Academy, a Mexican War veteran, and a highly successful brigade commander in the east, had been selected by President Davis to bring improved coordination and leadership to the districts of the west. Smith established his headquarters at Shreveport, Louisiana, and commanded the department for the duration of the war.[16]

Walker received orders to move his division south to Louisiana in late April. Maj. Gen. Richard Taylor, coordinating an undermanned defense of the state against superior Union forces, later wrote, "At Alexandria a communication from General Kirby Smith informed me that Major-General Walker, with a division of infantry and three batteries, four thousand strong, was on the march from Arkansas . . . I was directed to employ Walker's force in some attempt to relieve Vicksburg, now invested by General Grant, who had crossed the Mississippi below [that city] on the 1st of May."[17]

The lead elements of Walker's Division departed Camp Wright on April 24, 1863. Private Gaines reported that his company followed on the twenty-sixth. After a few days on the road, Sgt. Maj. James B. Rounsaville wrote, confirming the date of departure, "I hastily write you a few lines to let you know that we are on a hurried march to Alexandria, Louisiana, that is all of our division, as the Feds are approaching Monroe and that place both by land and water. The health of our Corps is fine and in good spirits, but you may guess our progress is slow, as the roads are almost impassable. We have been four days marching [only] fifteen miles and had to throw away a great deal of plunder, but I have not lost any myself, as yet."[18] He went on to say that all of the "fifteen or sixteen" deserters, even those who had been captured and forcibly returned, had been restored to duty. Although the men still faced a possible court martial, the need for every able-bodied soldier compelled the division commander to order their release.

During the first four days, they passed slowly through Monticello, Lacey, Fountain Hill, and Hamburg, Arkansas. On May 1, 1863, the division crossed the state line and camped on a prairie three miles inside Louisiana. The next few days were made difficult by the increasing heat and the lack of clean drinking water. By May 5, they reached the confluence of Bayou Bartholomew and the Ouachita River. Here they boarded about thirteen riverboats of various types for the trip to Trenton, near Monroe, Louisiana, a distance of thirty-six miles. Camp was made two miles from Trenton. They remained there for three days, perhaps waiting for information regarding enemy movements.[19]

The division was ordered to Alexandria, so on May 9, the troops boarded on the riverboats for a trip of nearly one hundred miles. They were almost to Harrisonburg when a courier from Taylor hailed the lead boat. He reported that Federal gunboats had left the Alexandria area, intending to attack Fort Beauregard, a few miles from Harrisonburg. After receiving assurances from the garrison commander, Lt. Col. George W. Logan, that he did not require any assistance, General Walker ordered the boats to reverse course.[20] Pvt. Milton Gaines of Company D recorded, "Went down the river seventy-one miles and back that night, [but the way was] obstricted by Federals."[21] They tied up at the docks of Monroe at 3:00 that morning. The soldiers stayed on board until morning, sleeping on cotton bales or piles of sacking. A wasted trip was certainly less a burden when it could be made on a riverboat rather than afoot.

Camp was made the next morning four miles west of Trenton. Couriers continued to ride between the Confederate commanders keeping them abreast of enemy actions. It was soon evident that the Federal attack on Fort Beauregard had failed. The Union commander, General Banks, began a withdrawal from Alexandria to support General Grant's campaign against Vicksburg with a coordinated attack on Port Hudson. Some in Walker's Division believed their arrival had

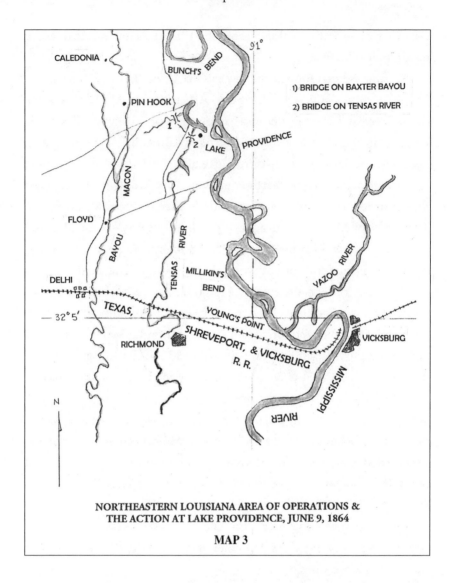

1) BRIDGE ON BAXTER BAYOU

2) BRIDGE ON TENSAS RIVER

NORTHEASTERN LOUISIANA AREA OF OPERATIONS &
THE ACTION AT LAKE PROVIDENCE, JUNE 9, 1864

MAP 3

precipitated Banks' eastward movements toward the Mississippi. Another enemy force was reported moving toward Monroe, but before the division's supply wagons arrived at Trenton, it was reported to have turned and begun moving east. While the threat against Alexandria was still real, the Texans began a march toward Campti on the sixteenth. The town was on the Red River a short distance north of Natchitoches. Their route took them through Vernon and the villages of Woodardville and Sparta. On May 22, they arrived at Black Lake, about two miles northwest of Campti.[22]

They remained camped near Black Lake, waiting for riverboats to help them overtake the Federal forces. Boats arrived on the morning of May 26, but were unable to gain on the enemy, who steamed toward the Mississippi at full speed. A campsite near the rapids on the Red River was chosen, two miles upriver from Alexandria, and the division rested there until Thursday, May 28.

General Walker had been ordered to move his troops from their camps near Pine Bluff, Arkansas, to northern Louisiana as part of an effort to relieve Union pressure upon Vicksburg and Port Hudson on the Mississippi. A plan to sever enemy lines of communication and supply on the west bank of the Mississippi River was developed by Kirby Smith. The action against Federal forces at the logistical support base near Lake Providence was part of the implementation of that plan by Richard Taylor.[23] Although Taylor strongly believed the best course of action would have been to attack New Orleans, he quickly fell in with the department commander's plan. Taylor's implementation of Smith's plan included a series of attacks on bases at Perkins' Landing, Young's Point, Milliken's Bend, and Lake Providence. Forces available for Confederate operations included Walker's Texas Division and partisan cavalry units commanded by Brig. Gen. Paul O. Hebert, which were operating in northeastern Louisiana. General Taylor made it clear that the attacks were crucial to the continued viability of the Confederate cause and "constantly expressed the utmost anxiety to relieve Vicksburg."[24] The abortive Union expedition up the Red River to Alexandria ordered by Maj. Gen. Nathaniel P. Banks ended in mid-May 1863, allowing Taylor to turn his attention to Grant's supply lines.

The selection of the Union garrison at Lake Providence as a target was steeped in political considerations. Lake Providence was part of a chain of Union supply depots and was also one of several training bases for newly organized African American regiments. The 8th Louisiana Infantry Regiment (African Descent), primarily recruited from slaves in occupied eastern Louisiana, was being drilled at Lake Providence.[25] This was perceived in the South as Federal support for a slave rebellion. In addition, some local plantation owners had sworn loyalty to the Union government and were trading cotton and agricultural produce for cash and the protection of Yankee military forces. Brig. Gen. Paul O. Hebert, commander of Confederate forces in north Louisiana, had been harassing Union troops at Lake Providence since early May 1863, but lacked sufficient strength to stage a serious attack.[26] Joseph Blessington recalled that Hebert "endeavored to obtain a brigade of [Walker's] division, to assist him in driving back, or rather to capture, a brigade of the enemy that was encamped on the banks of the Mississippi River, making raids all over the country."[27] As a part of the assault on Grant's supply lines, Major General Taylor assigned Hebert the task of destroying the garrison at Lake Providence. Since such a limited operation would not require a brigade, Taylor detached Burnett's 13th Texas from Walker's Division to augment his force.

Col. Frank A. Bartlett, a thirty-three-year-old New Orleans newspaper editor and former Louisiana militia officer, was selected by Hebert to command the operation.[28] Bartlett had originally been assigned commander of the Confederate garrison at Monroe, Louisiana, by General Taylor but was relieved and named to command all Confederate forces on Bayou Macon in northeastern Louisiana in late April 1863 when Hebert assumed command of the district of northern Louisiana.[29] Writing after the war, Napier Bartlett (probably not a relative of Frank Bartlett) recalled the situation

> On the [1st] May, 1862, Col. Frank Bartlett received information from Capt. Corbin, who commanded the pickets at Caledonia, (near the Arkansas line on Bayou Macon, and six miles from Bunch's Bend on the Mississippi River) that the enemy had surprised his guard and crossed Bayou Macon in force at Williams' plantation. Collecting every available man who could be spared from guarding the railroad crossing at Delhi and the

Court House at Floyd, Col. Bartlett, at once marched to meet the enemy. His force when united to Corbin's numbered only 85 men, while that of the enemy was two regiments of cavalry numbering in the aggregate, about 500 men.[30]

Bartlett crossed Bayou Macon on the second of May near Ashton, Louisiana, and abducted fifteen or twenty slaves from plantations of Union sympathizers. Concentrating his cavalry near Caledonia at a brick kiln and some abandoned slave cabins, Maj. Richard L. Capers' 13th Louisiana Battalion Partisan Rangers was soon confronted by a force of 400 mounted and dismounted Union infantry, commanded by Maj. William Y. Roberts of the 1st Kansas Mounted Infantry.[31] The Confederate cavalry withdrew toward the village of Pin Hook, a distance of nine miles, where Union accounts reported, "They took refuge in log-houses, from which they could not be dislodged without artillery, which we did not have."[32] In his account written twelve years after the conflict, Napier Bartlett recalled, "From that day he acted upon the offensive, and some detachment of the force under his command inflicted loss and annoyance upon the enemy on the Mississippi River, capturing prisoners, supplies, and war material."[33] Based on this raid, Colonel Bartlett had a clear idea of the Federal strength of the Lake Providence garrison. After the Union forces departed, he withdrew his troops west of Bayou Macon. They camped near Delhi, Louisiana, near the tracks of the Texas, Shreveport & Vicksburg Railroad, forty miles east of Monroe, and waited for reinforcements.

The 13th Texas Cavalry arrived in camp with the remainder of Walker's Texas Division at the Red River rapids just north of Alexandria on May 28, 1863. Reduced by exposure and epidemics of malaria, pneumonia, and typhoid fever, the regiment had fewer than 600 soldiers remaining when it arrived at Alexandria.[34] Lt. Col. Anderson F. Crawford of Jasper, Texas, was in temporary command of the 13th Texas at the time. Colonel Burnett had become ill on the march, and had left the regiment and gone to Shreveport.[35] They had been unsuccessfully chasing the withdrawing Union forces for a week. One soldier wrote on May 23 the regiment "left camp [near Grand Ecore] on a steam boat for Snaggy Point four miles below Alexandria, Louisiana, to Marksville and Boyough Deylaise [Bayou de Glaize], May 28 and then back to the steam boats at Snaggy Point; then to Alexandria."[36] They had only one day to rest in camp before being ordered to march six miles east toward Little River, where they cooked rations for four days. The next morning the soldiers left everything but one change of clothes and a blanket with the regiment's supply wagons.[37] The division then marched fourteen miles to meet transports at the landing on Little River.

After boarding, guards were posted on the upper decks of each steamboat to watch for enemy activity. As darkness fell, they steamed the length of Catahoula Lake into Little River, turning south on Black River and reaching the partially destroyed village of Trinity near midnight. Here the 13th Texas Cavalry disembarked briefly for a muster formation in near total darkness and boarded a transport that carried them north on the Ouachita River, while "the rest of the Division went up the Tensaw [Tensas] toward Vicksburg."[38] The regiment arrived in Monroe, Louisiana, and marched from the river landing to the railroad station, where the Texans loaded onto freight cars at 10:00 PM on June 1. The ride on the poorly maintained railroad was evidently a jolting and unpleasant experience. Cpl. Bluford Cameron of the 18th Texas Infantry described it a few weeks later as "rough sailing on the cars."[39] Financial and labor constraints made it nearly impossible for railroads in the South to maintain roadbeds and equipment during the war. Late that night the train came to a stop in Delhi, where the soldiers slept near the warehouses until dawn. That morning Capt. John T. Stark of Company H commented that they "were placed under command of Col Bartlett one of Genl Hebert's pets."[40] Joined by several companies of the 13th Louisiana Battalion Partisan Rangers and an artillery detachment with a six-pounder cannon, they marched eight miles to the north on the road along the west bank of Bayou Macon.[41] Their mission from Major General Taylor was to destroy the camps of instruction for African

American troops at Lake Providence and the Federal plantations south toward Milliken's Bend.[42]

The next day as the regiment continued northward, the sounds of heavy bombardment could be heard across the flat floodplain of the Mississippi from the direction of Vicksburg. Arriving at Floyd in Carroll Parish early on June 5, Colonel Bartlett ordered a bridge over the Bayou Macon rebuilt, but for some reason, once the work was completed, he decided not to cross there. This elicited some comment on the quality of Bartlett's leadership by at least one of the Texans. Perhaps due to fear of detection by Union scouts, the Confederates left Floyd at 9:00 PM on the night of June 6 and marched seven miles farther north on the west bank of the bayou. Pvt. Henry Ralph of Company G wrote, "we Leave here . . . for Lake Providence in serch of negroes & feds[.] If I Live & am favored By divine Providence I shall in a few days see the Mississippi— the father of waters . . . the feds claim all the country from here to the Mississippi[,] they have plantations worked by our slaves [and] have several negroes regiments drilling at Lake Providence."[43]

The Texans' route through the heavy timber and dense canebrakes along the bayou was "dark and dismal, and as desolate and dreary as the imagination could picture." After a few hours of rest, they were up at dawn and "marched hard all day long" on the seventh. The next day, a sergeant and fifty of the Texans were detailed to build a floating log bridge over Bayou Macon near Caledonia. The bayou was described as "a deep, dirty, sluggish stream, stocked with a variety of fish and alligators."[44] The remainder of the men rested and prepared to attack Lake Providence in the morning. Following Confederate attacks at Perkins' Landing on May 31 and Milliken's Bend and the aborted advance toward Young's Point on June 7 it should have been apparent that the garrison would be on a high state of alert.[45]

Capt. John Stark recalled, "We crossed on the bridge about 7 in the forenoon with our Regt [,] 300 Cavalry and one 6 pounder field piece [,] loaded our muskets for the first time and pushed for Lake Providence."[46] After a march of several miles, the column turned south at Bunch's Bend and skirted along the western banks of the lake. There they encountered two companies of the 1st Kansas Mounted Infantry on picket duty. Following a brief skirmish, the Union forces abandoned a column of nine supply wagons and began a hasty retreat toward Baxter Bayou. With Lt. John McNeil's squadron of Major Caper's cavalry battalion in close pursuit, the Federals tried to turn and fight every one hundred yards, but each stand became a rout. At Baxter Bayou, "where they had cut down and set fire to the bridge, our boys carried it by storm, although it was in a blaze and sunk, at its middle, below the surface of the water." After taking casualties, the Federals gave up an effort to defend the bridge and continued withdrawing toward the post.[47]

One mile west of the camps at Lake Providence, the harassed Union troops reached the bridge on the Tensas River. They immediately began throwing the bridge's loose planking into the river. The Confederate cavalry could have pressed their advantage and secured the eastern bank, but instead, Stark wrote, "Col Bartlett ordered the Cavalry to hold up & wait for the infantry and the cannon. The Feds succeeded in tearing up the bridge."[48] Bartlett then ordered Lieutenant Colonel Crawford to send the 13th Texas' skirmishers forward. Capt. John T. Smith's Company B, of Houston County, armed with Enfield rifles, took positions behind trees along the river and began to engage the Federals at a range of about four hundred yards. The artillery section was directed to place their gun near the river. After the artillery fired five rounds toward the Union positions at long range, enemy sharpshooters took advantage of the Confederates' lack of cover and wounded two of the artillerymen, forcing them to temporarily abandon the gun.

Crawford ordered the remainder of the 13th Texas forward in a column facing the bridge. Captain Stark recalled that although exposed to direct fire from the Federals, now numbering nearly 400, and reinforced by light artillery, they "behaved . . . as cool as veterans laughing and joking with one another about the singing balls that were passing over and around them." The Texans, led by Lieutenant Colonel

Crawford and Major Beaty, deployed along the wooded banks of the river and got under cover. They laid down a fair volume of fire, but since three-quarters of them were armed with shotguns, it had little effect on the men of the 1st Kansas and 16th Wisconsin, who maintained their position at a distance of several hundred yards. A Confederate observer estimated "the loss of the enemy must have been considerable as their ambulance wagon came out three times before dark."

The engagement lasted over an hour. An attempt to rebuild the bridge by the Confederates was abandoned because of the high volume of enemy fire. As darkness fell and the accuracy of Yankee sharpshooters was reduced, Colonel Bartlett gave the order to withdraw. Men from Company B, 13th Texas, and a few Louisiana cavalrymen were left behind in the underbrush to cover the retreat. Thirty-year-old Pvt. King D. Shiflett, of Houston County, was probably suffering from malaria or intermittent fever and was too sick to be moved. Thirty-one-year-old Sgt. Carlisle McClung, of Angelina County, Company F, died of his wounds before the regiment withdrew. He was the first combat casualty of the 13th Texas Cavalry. Pvt. Frances M. Welch of Company F and 2nd Lieutenant John J. Burroughs of Company K, who was a physician, remained with Shiflett after the regiment withdrew.[49]

Union Brig. Gen. H. T. Reid, the garrison commander, ordered his white soldiers to retire, and drew up the 8th Louisiana Volunteers (African Descent) up in a line of battle on the river's east bank. The General reported, "They fired four volleys into the rebels, which cleaned them out, and greatly encouraged the darkies."[50] Despite the fact that his forces outnumbered the Union defenders, Col. Frank Bartlett made no effort to cross the Tensas farther south to flank the Federals. The Texans retreated until about midnight, stopping briefly to burn a gin house belonging to a Yankee sympathizer and a quantity of his baled cotton at Spencer's plantation, seven miles from Lake Providence. Pvt. Milton P. Gaines of Company D recalled that later, he "crawled into a house, full of furniture" and "slept on the furniture cramped up."[51] The next morning they withdrew toward Bayou Macon at Floyd in a driving rainstorm that lasted until late afternoon. Pvt. Henry Ralph of Company G complained of marching "all day through the rain & mud."[52] Milton Gaines reported eating honey, probably from the supplies taken from the captured Union supply wagons. Captain Stark wrote, "at this season of the year [the plantations, which are] generally covered with the growing crops are lying idle[;] the negroes either run to Texas or to the enemy. . . . The enemy burns awhile[,] then some of the planters take oath of allegiance then our men burn them out and the plunderers and robbers end by sweeping what is left [,] and the country once in the highest state of cultivation and pride of the South is nothing but a desert."[53]

The action at Lake Providence was the 13th Texas Cavalry's first combat experience. The soldiers could be justifiably proud of the physical courage they displayed, but they were clearly disappointed for being ordered to retreat without making any serious attempt to cross the river and close with the enemy. The distant thunder of the guns at Vicksburg was a constant reminder of their failed mission. After seeing the results of the almost total social and physical destruction of the plantation country, their resolve to defend their homes was stiffened. Captain Stark probably expressed the feelings of many of the regiment's soldiers when he wrote, "Thus far our loved State has been saved from the horrors of this desolation . . . long may it remain so."[54]

The campaign to relieve Vicksburg had nearly disabled the Texas Division. Major General Walker reported to the department commander from Delhi on July 3 that, "At no time since my arrival in this region has my force amounted to more that 4,700 effective men, and such has been the deleterious effect of the climate and bad weather, that in two weeks' time in the three brigades I had barely 2,500 men fit for duty."[55] Within a few weeks of the retreat from Lake Providence, the 13th Texas Cavalry lost five company commanders through resignations for physical disability.[56] This group, comprising half of the subordinate commanders in the regiment, included two former members of the Texas House of Representatives, a former county sheriff, a delegate to the Texas secession convention, and a veteran who had served in the Texas War of Independence, the frontier service, and the Mexican War.

The effects of malaria, typhoid fever, and other insect and waterborne diseases continued to degrade the ability of Walker's soldiers for several months. Again, as at Camp Nelson, the "third enemy," disease, had proved a more formidable opponent than Union soldiers. Colonel Burnett was sufficiently recovered to meet his regiment when they returned to camp near Delhi. There they were rejoined by the division, and returned by rail to Monroe.

Col. Frank A. Bartlett resigned his commission the next year, on September 22, because of physical disability.[57] After a protracted struggle, and facing the prospect of mass starvation, the besieged city of Vicksburg surrendered to General Grant on July 4, 1863. It was a defeat that may have doomed all later military efforts of the Confederacy.

1. Thomas J. Rounsaville to his mother and sisters, Feb. 23, 1863, USAMHI, James B. Rounsaville Papers.

2. Blessington, *Campaigns of Walker's Texas Division,* 76; CSR. Eleven soldiers were noted as still on leave as of Feb. 28, 1863. Camp Wright was divided into a number of other named camps; the 13th Texas Cavalry was located at Camp Bee, probably named for Brig. Gen. Barnard E. Bee, a Confederate brigade commander at the battle of First Manassas.

3. Thomas J. Rounsaville to his mother and sisters, Feb. 23, 1863, USAMHI, James B. Rounsaville Papers.

4. Ibid.

5. Johansson, *Peculiar Honor,* 86. A similar performance led to arrests in the 17th Texas Infantry in January 1864.

6. CSR, Riley J. Blair, John L. Cornish, James H. Finch, J. Pat Henry, Thomas H. Hollis, Wilson E.Hail, and William F. Seale; *Members of the Texas Legislature,* 37; Thomas J. Rounsaville to his mother and sisters, Feb. 23, 1863, USAMHI, James Rounsaville Papers; Hewett, *Texas Confederate Soldiers,* 1: 110, 248.

7. Capt. John T. Stark to Martha Stark, Jan. 25, 1863. H. B. Simpson History Complex, Hill College; "Eighth Census of the United States, Population Schedule," 1860, M653, 1306, Tyler County, Texas, household 395. The two soldiers who died of exposure were 1st Lt. George A. Gaston of Company D and Pvt. Joseph Mitchell of Company K, formerly a hired hand on Levi Moody's farm in Tyler County, Texas.

8. Thomas J. Rounsaville to his mother and sisters, Feb. 23, 1863, USAMHI, James B. Rounsaville Papers.

9. Thomas J. Rounsaville to Mattie Bond, Feb. 8, 1863, James B. Rounsaville Papers; Cutrer, "Bully for Flournoy's Regiment," 174–75.

10. James B. Rounsaville to his mother and sisters, Mar. 22, 1863, James B. Rounsaville Papers.

11. Wheat, *Sketches of Tyler County History*, 182.

12. James M. Day, *Senate Journal of the Ninth Legislature, First Called Session of the State of Texas,February 2, 1863 – March 7, 1863* (Austin, TX: Texas State Library, 1963), 190–91. Burnett's Cavalry is listed on the document's distribution.

13. Diary of Milton P. Gaines, Charles H. Ham Papers, Anderson County, Texas.

14. CSR, M323, roll 77, Capt. James S. Hanks to General Samuel Cooper, Adjutant and Inspector General, April 14, 1863, personal papers.

15. CSR, M323, roll 78, John C. Oldham, personal papers. Lt. Oldham succeeded 1st Lt. George A. Gaston, who had died of exposure in January 1863.

16. Robert L. Kerby, *Kirby Smith's Confederacy: The Trans-Mississippi South, 1863–1865* (New York: Columbia University Press, 1972; reprint, Tuscaloosa: University of Alabama Press, 1991), 51–53.

17. Taylor, *Destruction and Reconstruction*, 164.

18. James Rounsaville to his mother and sisters, Apr. 29, 1863, James B. Rounsaville Papers.

19. Blessington, *Campaigns of Walker's Texas Division*, 79; Diary of Milton P. Gaines, May 9, 1863, Charles H. Ham Papers, Anderson County, Texas.

20. Blessington, 81.

21. Diary of Milton P. Gaines, May 9, 1863.

22. Blessington, *Campaigns of Walker's Texas Division*, 83.

23. Maj. Gen. Richard Taylor was the Confederate commander of the District of West Louisiana. The only son of General and former President Zachary Taylor, he was a graduate of Yale University and not a professional soldier. His striking successes under Maj. Gen. Thomas J. "Stonewall" Jackson during the Valley Campaign in 1862, initially as commander of the 9th Louisiana Infantry, led to his promotion to major general. Prior to the war he was a sugar planter and had served in the Louisiana State Senate. T. Michael Parrish, *Richard Taylor: Soldier Prince of Dixie* (Chapel Hill: University of North Carolina Press, 1992). See also Taylor, *Destruction and Reconstruction*.

24. Maj. Gen. John G. Walker to Lieut. Gen. E. Kirby Smith, July 3, 1863, O.R., ser. I, 36 pt. 3, 915.

25. O.R., ser. I, 24, pt. 2, 446-50; John D. Winters, *The Civil War in Louisiana* (Baton Rouge: Louisiana State University Press, 1963), 199–201.

26. Brig. Gen. Paul Octave Hebert graduated first in his West Point class of 1840, was a veteran of the Mexican War, a former governor of Louisiana, and had succeeded Maj. Gen. Earl Van Dorn as commander of the Confederate District of Texas. Hebert was relieved in Texas by Maj. Gen. John B. Magruder in late 1862 and was given the command of north Louisiana. Davis, *The Confederate General*, 84-85; Brigadier General H. T. Reid to Major General U. S. Grant, May 12, 1863, O.R., ser. I, 24, pt. 3, 302–3.

27. Blessington, *Campaigns of Walker's Texas Division*, 80.

28. "Eighth Census of the United States, Population Schedule," 1860, Microfilm M653-419, New Orleans, Ward 6, 124. Frank A. Bartlett is listed as a newspaper editor, thirty-one years old, born in Georgia.

29. Louisiana State Archives, Beauregard Battalion and Regiment of Louisiana Militia, microfilm L69, 320, roll 368; Personal correspondence, Ray Bartlett. The unit is known in Union accounts as the 13th Louisiana Cavalry Battalion.

30. Napier Bartlett, *Military Record of Louisiana* (1875. repr., Baton Rouge, LA: Louisiana State University Press, 1964), 34–35. Union accounts report the combined Federal strength at 400.

31. Winters, *The Civil War in Louisiana*, 198.

32. Brig. Gen. H. T. Reid to Maj. Gen. U. S. Grant, May 12, 1863, in O.R., ser. I, 24, pt. 3, 301-303. Union forces included 300 soldiers from the 1st Kansas Mounted Infantry and 100 from the 16th Wisconsin Infantry. Union losses were one killed, one accidentally drowned, nine slightly wounded, and three taken prisoner. Confederate losses by Union accounts were four killed.

33. Bartlett, *Military Record of Louisiana*, 35.

34. CSR, M323, reels 75-80. The 13th Texas Cavalry's assigned strength fell from 842 on May 23, 1862, to 613 on Feb. 28, 1863. The regiment left Pine Bluff, Arkansas, for Louisiana on Apr. 26, 1863.

35. CSR, M323-75, John H. Burnett was diagnosed with "gastro enteritis of five months' duration" by Surgeon Thomas H. Hollis Nov. 11, 1863. Records indicate Burnett remained in Shreveport at least until Jun. 9, 1863.

36. Diary of Pvt. Milton P. Gaines, entries for May 23 and 28, 1863, Charles H. Ham Papers, Anderson County, Texas.

37. Ibid., May 29 and 30, 1863; Blessington, *Campaigns of Walker's Texas Division*, 85.

38. Diary of Milton P. Gaines, May 31, 1863.

39. Diary of Bluford Cameron, E. C. Barker Library, University of Texas, Austin.

40. Capt. John T. Stark to Martha Stark, Jun. 14, 1863, H. B. Simpson Research Center, Hill College.

41. Diary of Milton P. Gaines, Jun. 2, 1863, Charles Ham Papers; Winters, *The Civil War in Louisiana*, 201–2. The Confederate force totaled 900 men. Several companies of the 13th Louisiana Battalion Partisan Rangers may have been on duty elsewhere.

42. Winters, *The Civil War in Louisiana*, 202.

43. Carson, *From the Desk of Henry Ralph*, 86.

44. Diary of Milton P. Gaines, Jun. 3–8, 1863, Charles Ham Papers; John T. Stark to Martha Stark, Jun. 14, 1863, H. B. Simpson Research Center, Hill College; Blessington, *Campaigns of Walker's Texas Division*, 86, 93; Report of Brig. Gen. H. T. Reid, Jun. 10, 1863, O.R., ser. I, 24, pt. 2: 449-450.

45. Blessington, *Campaigns of Walker's Texas Division*, 87, 95–109.

46. John T. Stark to Martha Stark, Jun. 14, 1863, H. B. Simpson Research Center, Hill College.

47. Ibid.; Bartlett, *Military Record of Louisiana*, 35; Brig. Gen. Elias S. Dennis to Lt. Col. John A. Rawlins, Jun. 13, 1863, O.R., ser. I, 24, pt. 2, 448-50. Captain Stark believed the 1st

Kansas had one killed and one wounded at the Bayou Baxter bridge. He estimated their strength at forty.

48. John T. Stark to Martha Stark, Jun. 14, 1863, H. B. Simpson Research Center, Hill College.

49. CSR, M323 rolls 75-80, Lieutenant Burroughs and Privates King Shiflett and Francis M. Welch were taken prisoner by Union forces at Lake Providence. As late as Feb. 29, 1864, Shiflett is listed as "sick at Lake Providence since Jun. 9, 1863." Private Welch died at Fort Delaware of scurvy a few days after the war's end. Lieutenant Burroughs and Private Shiflett survived their imprisonment.

50. Brigadier General Reid to Major General McPherson, Jun. 10, 1863, in O.R., ser. I, 24, pt. 2: 450. Colonel Hiram Scofield, a white officer, commanded the 8th Louisiana Volunteers. General Reid says he received information about the Confederate operation from a "rebel deserter." This characterization of one of the prisoners of war is likely a bit of Yankee hyperbole.

51. Diary of Milton P. Gaines, Jun. 10, 1863, Charles Ham Papers.

52. Carson, *From the Desk of Henry Ralph*, 89.

53. John T. Stark to Martha Stark, Jun. 14, 1863, H. B. Simpson Research Center, Hill College.

54. Ibid.

55. Maj. Gen. John G. Walker to Lt. Gen. E. Kirby Smith, Jul. 3, 1863, O.R., ser. I, 36, pt. 3: 915–16. In reference to the possible relief of Vicksburg, Walker said, "I consider it absolutely certain, unless the enemy are blind and stupid, that no part of my command would escape capture or destruction if such an attempt should be made."

56. CSR, M323, 75-80, Captains Jerome N. Black, John T. Smith, George English, Hiram Brown, and John T. Bean. They commanded companies A, B, C, F, and K, respectively.

57. Personal communication, Ray Bartlett; Louisiana State Library, Beauregard Battalion and Regiment, L69, 320, microfilm roll 368; Emma G. Bartlett, "Widow's Application for Pension," May 27, 1915. After his death, his widow was denied a pension, since he had never held a Confederate commission, but only one in the Louisiana militia. Franklin A. "Frank" Bartlett died in New Orleans May 26, 1891, and is buried in Metairie Cemetery.

Chapter 6

Texans in the Bayou Country

"I do long to be at home. My very soul is sick
of all this noise and turmoil."
—Capt. John T. Stark, Company H, 13th Texas Cavalry[1]

A week after the 13th Texas arrived at Delhi, the rest of the division joined the East Texans. They soon learned that General McCulloch's brigade had enjoyed momentary success in battle at Milliken's Bend, nearly destroying a major Federal supply storage depot. Finally, though, they had been repulsed by a Union counterattack. Their own brigade had fared no better in its Young's Point mission than had the 13th Texas at Lake Providence. With Burnett's regiment detached, General Hawes was at a numerical disadvantage from the beginning. The twenty-eight-hour operation began with a long night march and continued with difficulties finding the bridges on the route and intense heat. The soldiers, weakened by disease and bad water, were in no condition to attack when they reached their objective. Cpl. Bluford A. Cameron of Company B, 18th Texas Infantry, described the battle. "We marched on the Young's Point, distance about 12 mi[les] where we found the enemy encamped. As we advanced we drove the pickets. We had a very hot time. Some men fainted and a great many others came near being exhausted. Our Brigade took Fed prisoners, 4 negroes, 4 mules, 1 horse and killed 2 men. Got one horse killed and one man wounded in the hand. We went retreated in order as their camps were protected by their gunboats. We retreated about 5 mi[les] across Willow Bayou and stopped."[2] Major General Walker was ambivalent in his official report on the matter. "I am convinced that from what I know of the state of exhaustion resulting from excessive heat and fatigue, that General Hawes' men were incapable of the physical exertion necessary to carry a fortified position defended on the flanks by gun-boats. How far these considerations justify a failure to obey an unconditional and imperative order, I am not prepared to say."[3] Gen. James Hawes' days as one of Walker's brigade commanders were probably numbered at that point.

Walker's Division remained camped near the railroad terminal at Delhi where it rested until the morning of June 22, 1863. The Confederate forces in northeastern Louisiana engaged in a number of actions in the following weeks all designed to deny Federal forces access to cotton and other agricultural produce. Records cast some light on the activities of the 13th Texas Cavalry during that time. General Walker wrote,

> I am now engaged in burning all the cotton I can reach, from Lake Providence to the lower end of Concordia Parish, and shall endeavor to leave no spoil for the enemy. I have also instructed the cavalry to destroy all subsistence and forage on abandoned plantations, that, from its proximity to the river, may give the enemy facilities for invasion. When this destruction is effected, I shall withdraw the greater portion of my force towards the Washita [Ouachita] River, to some more healthy locality. The ravages of disease have fearfully weakened my force, and I consider it essential to its future usefulness that it should be removed from here as early as practicable.[4]

The division attacked lines of communication, burned cotton warehouses, and destroyed Union plantations worked by freed slaves as far north as Lake Providence and as far south as Simmesport. Toward the close of these operations, Sgt. Maj. James Rounsaville wrote, "our division started to make another raid into the [Mississippi] Swamp on the 7th inst. . . .but they turned back."[5]

The troops returned to Delhi after receiving news that Vicksburg had surrendered on July 4, 1863. There were many rumors of a betrayal and the soldiers became quite agitated. On July 7, Walker ordered them out on the military highway for a twelve-mile march toward Monticello, Louisiana, just to give them an opportunity to cool off. They returned to Delhi the next day, and on the morning of July 11, the division boarded the train for the forty-mile journey to Monroe. Joseph Blessington recalled, "On our arrival we marched through the principal streets of the town, to see and be seen by the ladies. After our promenading we encamped about a half a mile south of the town, on the banks of the Washita [Ouachita] River."[6] James Rounsaville had been sent to Monroe by train on July 7 by the assistant regimental surgeon because of chronic chills, fever, and diarrhea. On July 9 he wrote,

> I can buy a plug of tobacco in this place for one dollar in greenback (Fed money) and have to pay four dollars for the same article in Confederate. This is indeed discouraging. I have been out to the convalescent camp, it being the place I was sent to, but I will not remain there, as it is so very loathsome. I will take the cars in the morning and rejoin my command if they do not come this way, or board at the hotel or some private house, that is if I do not get off in the morning. I am improving, but my bowels have been disordered for the last four months and the doctor says it's likely to run into something chronic, but I think not.[7]

The fall of the Confederate strongholds at Vicksburg on July 4 and Port Hudson on July 8 had dramatic results in the vast territory known as the Trans-Mississippi Confederacy. For the next two years Lt. Gen. Edmund Kirby Smith commanded this empire from his headquarters on the Red River in Shreveport, Louisiana. Communication with the government at Richmond was slow and troublesome. Although Union forces were unable to intercept the majority of Confederate couriers and soldiers determined to cross the Mississippi, the traffic was slowed. The extreme risk and difficulty of moving bulky ordnance and supplies across the river diverted much of the increased production of military depots in Texas and northwestern Louisiana to the army of the Trans-Mississippi. While the soldiers continued to joke and complain about the quality and quantity of rations and supplies, the levels of shortages experienced in the first years of the war were not repeated.[8]

Late in July the division was ordered to return to Alexandria. A five-day road march brought them to Campti on July 27, 1863, where steamboats from Shreveport took them on to Alexandria. The 13th Texas Cavalry remained camped near Pineville on the east bank of the Red River opposite Alexandria until August 10, when it moved to Camp Green, a site in the piney woods near Cheneyville, twenty miles farther south. On Friday, August 7, Lt. Charles H. Jones of Company K finally had an officer's uniform tailored. Records indicate that the decision by officers of the 13th Texas Cavalry to wear a uniform was probably not voluntary, or merely due to the availability of material in Alexandria. Their superiors may have exerted some pressure. Lt. Col. Arthur J. Fremantle, a British observer, noted in May 1863 that the entire division was "dressed in ragged civilian clothing."[9] Jones signed for twelve yards of Confederate gray cloth for himself and the two other lieutenants in the company, some gold flax thread, and six spools of other thread, probably cotton. His total cost from the regimental quartermaster was $55.22.[10] Similar receipts are found in the personal papers of virtually every officer in the regiment. These uniforms would have been tailored at additional expense in Alexandria, Cheneyville, or Marksville.

Remaining at Camp Green as the summer passed, some soldiers benefited from the healthier climate and recovered from the fevers and disabilities contracted in the swamps of eastern Louisiana. Many others did not. Capt. John T. Bean of Company K resigned his commission due to chronic hepatitis and migraine and was replaced by 1st Lt. Charles

H. Jones. In Company F of Angelina County, Lt. Samuel B. Thomas took command, replacing Capt. Hiram Brown, who, at fifty-four, was disabled by "old age." Both of the commanders of the Houston County companies had been disabled. Capt. George English of Company C, also fifty-four, turned over his unit to his nephew, Lt. Crockett J. English. 1st Lt. Joshua B. Young relieved Capt. John T. Smith of Company B. Capt. Elias T. Seale of Jasper County, who had been on medical leave since early 1863, resigned and was replaced by 1st Lt. Thomas F. Truett. While a few of these personnel changes did not become official until November 1863, most actually took place in July and August at Camp Green.[11]

A rigorous program of officer examinations required by the government in Richmond gradually began to be implemented that summer. Capt. Thomas F. Truett later wrote, "I was promoted to Captain of Co G, 13th Regt. T. C. and assigned to duty as such subject to the approval of examining board . . . until the 5th day of November 1863 when I was ordered before the Board of Examiners and having passed a satisfactory examination my promotion was ratified."[12] Capt. John T. Stark of Company H had mentioned the tests as early as August 1862, writing his wife, "We are all studying our infantry tactics hard and trying to qualify ourselves for our new position. It has been said that Gen. Hindman who commands at Little Rock has appointed a board of military Officers who examine all the officers of the Volunteer Regts. and those who are not able to pass are reduced to the ranks whether true or not some of our Officers are a great deal more industrious then they have ever been before. It will thus be of great benefit to us."[13] The earliest record of an infantry examination in the 13th Texas Cavalry comes from the file of Lt. Thomas J. Rounsaville of Company C, who was "assigned to duty as Sen'r 2nd Lt. by the examining board to take rank from August 7, 1863."[14]

In practice, the tests were a tool administered by the senior officers of each regiment and used primarily to establish eligibility for promotion. There is no evidence of testing to allow retention of an officer's current rank. In Randal's 28th Texas Cavalry, Capt. Theophilus Perry mentioned in a letter to his wife, "Lt. Wagnon has been examined for first Lt. and rejected. Lt. Fitzpatrick was also rejected for 2nd Lt. They have to hold their old position."[15] Historian M. Jane Johansson states, "in the 28th Texas, perhaps as in other units, officers were given preparation time."[16] As John T. Stark mentioned in his letter, the tests did have a very beneficial effect by forcing officers to master basic tactical skills and tasks that improved a unit's viability and performance in combat.

While at Camp Green, General Walker authorized thirty-eight-day furloughs for three or four soldiers from each company. In actual practice these often were extended by circumstances beyond the soldiers' control to around sixty days. Pvt. Milton P. Gaines of Company D probably had a typical experience while on furlough. He left his unit on August 9, taking nine days to walk the two hundred miles to his home in Anderson County, Texas. Arriving home, he found that his wife Mary was very ill. After she recovered, he left Mound Prairie by stagecoach on September 14. Following a brief rest stop in Tyler, the stagecoach continued all night. Early on the morning of September 16 the coach turned over, but the passengers righted it and they arrived in Marshall, Texas, later that day. The next stage of the journey from Marshall to Shreveport was by a combination of freight cars on the railroad and a stagecoach for the final leg of the trip to Shreveport. Gaines reported to Department Headquarters on September 17, 1863, and was assigned post duty until September 25, when he was released to report to his regiment. After walking and looking for his unit for seventeen days, he finally rejoined the company on October 12, 1863, having overstayed his furlough by twenty-six days.[17]

The 13th Texas left Camp Green on September 25, 1863.[18] The regiment was assigned a patrol area southeast of Alexandria. The route of march took it through Cheneyville, Evergreen, Goudeau, and Big Cane. After arriving and setting up a camp about five miles northwest of Big Cane village on September 27, a patrol routine was established. This routine moved the 13th Texas every few days from the Big Cane camp to another camp north of Evergreen on the Mansura road. This duty continued until October 13, when the Texans marched to Moreauville. On October 17 Blessington reported, "Shortly after our arrival in camp, the 13th Dismounted Cavalry, commanded by Colonel Burnett, was ordered on picket below the town of Opelousas." Colonel Flournoy's 16th Texas Infantry relieved them on October 21.[19] On October 23 and 24 the regiment had picket duty in the area south of the Red River. After being relieved, the men returned to the area of Cheneyville and the Bayou Boeuf, where they made camp and stayed until November 7. On November 2, the division witnessed the execution of a deserter, Private J. J. Boman of the 28th Texas, Company K, who had been apprehended while trying to reach enemy lines.[20]

According to a report by the regimental surgeon, Dr. Thomas Hollis, Colonel Burnett suffered from "gastro-enteritis" from early May 1863 until November 1863, when he was forced to submit a request for reassignment to garrison duty. He declined the option of resignation, since he felt he could still be of service to the Confederacy. Burnett returned home to Crockett in November 1863 after handing command of the 13th Texas to Lt. Col. Anderson F. Crawford. The soldiers were already accustomed to having Crawford as their field commander and probably assumed that Burnett would return when he recovered. Maj. Gen. John Magruder, commander of the District of Texas, assigned Colonel Burnett as the "commander of the garrison at Crockett," despite the fact that there was no "garrison" in Houston County.[21]

On November 8 the regiment was ordered to relieve other units of Walker's Division nearer the Mississippi River. Before they broke camp, a column of nearly one thousand defeated Yankee prisoners from General Franklin's expeditionary force passed through their camp on the way to Shreveport.[22] On the third day, the 13th Texas reached Simmesport camped briefly, and "built a pontoon bridge," which the Texans used to cross the Atchafalaya River on November 12. Most of the division lost patience with the efforts to build the pontoon bridge and ferried across on flatboats.[23] A short march brought them to the Mississippi, where they visited the division's artillery batteries stationed on the river and were picketed southeast of Simmesport. The artillery was intended to harass Federal shipping; one Union transport was hit and reported sunk about four miles south of the batteries on the eighteenth. Only one Federal transport, the *Black Hawk*, suffered any major damage. It was hit on November 21, caught fire, and was totally burned as it floated downriver.[24] The guard duty on the Mississippi River continued until the end of November. The 13th Texas occupied the patrol area just south of Red River landing on November 20. Union forces retaliated for the attack on their transports by sending five gunboats to shell the Confederate positions. While most of the soldiers stayed under cover on the west side of the levees, two men from General Mouton's Louisiana division were killed by naval gunfire. One was among a group playing cards "near the top of the levee."[25]

The 13th Texas pickets were spread along the river for nearly three miles. On November 29, Pvt. Milton Gaines recorded, "I stood guard that night on the West bank of the river, 30 minutes at a time. It was bitter cold weather. The [Union] gun boats on the East side of the river would ring their bells every 30 minutes." Although the Confederates were using the Federal gunboat's bells to signal their guard changes, it could not be safely assumed that the Yankees were becoming friendly or familiar. The next day, Capt. John C. Oldham and Pvt. Mack A. Fitzgerald of Company D were standing on the top of the levee when the gunboat fired on them. Pvt. Milton Gaines wrote that one solid ball cut in half a nearby tree "two or three feet through. The other was Canestor [*sic*] shots about the size of green walnuts scattered among our company."[26] Fortunately, the fire injured no one. The weather remained very rainy and cold, and the rivers continued to rise. It was reported, "Some of the men of Scurry's brigade stole hogs. This act angered Scurry who ordered a hog skinned and the skin placed around one of the thieves. The culprit was then marched through the brigade accompanied by laughing, hog calls, and various remarks."[27]

Major General Walker was ordered to destroy the Union garrison at Plaquemine, a town on the west bank of the Mississippi south of Baton Rouge. On December 1 the Texans made a twenty-five-mile march down the river. The next day's travel brought them to the old battleground at Fordoche. After following the river another sixteen miles, they made camp and rested one day before marching back to the north.[28] Walker believed that the mission had been compromised, and that Union forces at Plaquemine were aware of his intentions. A second consideration was the rapid rise of the rivers, which threatened the pontoon bridges on the Atchafalaya, the division's only route to the west.[29]

It would seem that Union forces had abandoned the western bank during this time, since neither Captain Stark nor Private Gaines recorded a single skirmish or captured Yankee throughout the regiment's movement down the Mississippi. In a letter to his daughter, Capt. Elijah Petty reported, "I do reckon that Walkers Division has traveled more and fought less than any troops in the Confederacy."[30] As December continued predictably cold and wet, they returned to the area north of Simmesport, recrossing the Atchafalaya on the pontoon bridge on December 10. The next day, the 13th Texas made camp on the west bank of the Atchafalaya at Morgan's Ferry, remaining until December 15, when the East Texans moved to a camp on Bayou DeGlaize, three miles west of Simmesport. One day after Christmas, they returned to Simmesport on their way to winter quarters near Marksville, twenty-four miles to the west, where they camped one mile south of Fort De Russy and the Red River on the evening of December 27, 1863.

In the fall and early winter of 1863, there was a great enthusiasm for religious revivals throughout the division. Among the most popular revivalists was a former company commander of Randal's 28th Texas Cavalry, the Rev. Martin V. Smith.[31] Understandably, commanders appreciated any influence that curtailed profanity, gambling, liquor, the pursuit of low women, and the inevitable effect such vices had on morale and discipline. In January 1864, Lt. Col. Anderson F. Crawford was able to recruit the 13th Texas Cavalry's second chaplain, a position that had been vacant since October 1862. He wrote Gen. Samuel Cooper, respectfully nominating "Rev. Richard F. Fancher, a citizen of Newton County, Texas as Chaplain of the Regiment, to take rank from the 10th (inst.) Mr. Fancher was born in the State of Tennessee is forty nine years of age, is an intelligent & exemplary Minister of the Baptist Church. His character is irreproachable and I think him eminently qualified for the position of Chaplain."[32] Rev. Fancher was probably already well known to the soldiers of Newton and Jasper Counties. Typical of East Texas, many soldiers had no use for preachers and would go to great lengths to avoid them. None of the extant letters or diaries of the 13th Texas makes any reference to religion, revivals, or the Rev. Fancher.

Winter quarters near Marksville at Camp Rogers were scenic with huge magnolias and fig trees, as well as "the largest Aligators [sic]" that Milton Gaines had seen. Gaines and his squad built a fireplace with a chimney of green branches and clay between two of his company's wall tents. Adding to their comfort, Spanish moss from the trees was used to stuff mattresses. The cold wet weather temporarily came to an end, and on January 24, 1864, the regiment participated in a four-hour division review with weather "almost like Summer time."[33]

Unlike Generals McCulloch and Scurry, who severely punished "hog thieves," Brigadier General Hawes encouraged his East Texans to scour the Red River valley for the sleek porkers, fattened by autumn's acorns. On January 28 Private Gaines "was detailed and sent down Red River to hunt hogs and kill for Brigade. Killed some 28 hogs." Another expedition was sent out on February 23 under the command of Lt. Matthew McAlister of Company H, Newton County, Texas. Given the level of experience the soldiers from the Sabine and Neches River valleys had hunting hogs, it can be assumed to have been equally successful. Questions of earmarks, brands, and ownership were probably not issues addressed by the mission's directives.[34] There is no record of any soldiers of the 13th Texas being caught while stealing hogs.

The choice of the Marksville area for Walker's Division winter quarters was driven by one of Gen. Edmund Kirby Smith's pet projects, rebuilding the fortifications on the Red River known as Fort De Russy. In spite of valid objections by both Gen. Richard Taylor and General Walker concerning the site's viability in the event of an infantry attack, work on the defensive positions was among the highest priorities in the Trans-Mississippi Department. Throughout the winter months, a small army of slaves levied from plantations from as far north as Shreveport augmented by soldiers from every unit in the area, labored on the earthworks, cleared forests, and emplaced artillery pieces to guard the river from Yankee gunboats. Each regiment in Walker's Division was directed to detach a company to serve at Fort De Russy.

In a sequence of events that cannot be adequately explained, Lieutenant Colonel Crawford relieved Capt. James Eastland of his command of Company E, replaced him with Sgt. Maj. James B. Rounsaville of Houston County, who was eventually promoted to Captain, and detached Company E to Fort De Russy on December 3, 1863.[35] The company, the smallest in the regiment, could only boast an assigned strength of thirty-four men as of the February 1864 muster, ten of whom were on either furlough or medical leave. The "company" had one first lieutenant, one sergeant, and one corporal. Augmented by other soldiers detailed from the 13th Texas and other regiments of Walker's Division, they were assigned to dig "rifle pits" outside the defensive earthworks of Fort De Russy. Shortages of tools, the heavy red clay subsoil, and frequent sub-freezing temperatures slowed these efforts, and made progress very difficult.

To augment the defenses of Fort De Russy, a "raft" of pilings, timbers, and floating logs was constructed downriver. Working on the unstable timbers, often in very cold weather, was particularly dangerous. Pvt. William Y. Glover of Company A, about nineteen years old, lost his footing and drowned on January 22.[36] On February 11, 1864, Pvt. Milton Gaines noted in his diary, "went down to work on the raft. We are throwing timber and cutting trees into the river to keep the Gun Boats from coming up the river. I caught a fine fish."[37] The 13th Texas took a break from its labors on February 12 to participate in a drill competition

The Battle of Fort De Russy, Marksville, Louisiana

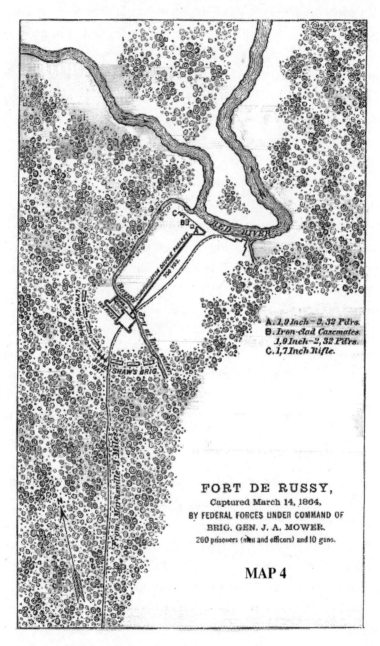

FORT DE RUSSY,
Captured March 14, 1864,
BY FEDERAL FORCES UNDER COMMAND OF
BRIG. GEN. J. A. MOWER.
260 prisoners (men and officers) and 10 guns.

MAP 4

Source: *Official Records*, ser. 1, 34, pt. 1, 224.

for all the regiments in the division. After elimination rounds, the final contestants were the 8th Texas of Hawes' brigade and the 11th Texas of Randal's brigade. General Walker finally awarded the banner to Col. Overton Young's 8th Texas Infantry.[38] Returning to work on the raft for another eight days, the 13th Texas was relieved on February 20 and returned to Camp Rogers.[39]

During the drill competition, the soldiers of the 13th Texas discovered that they had a new brigade commander. At his request, Brig. Gen. James M. Hawes had been reassigned as commander of the fortifications and garrison at Galveston, Texas. Brig. Gen. Thomas N. Waul, who had been promoted after his heroic actions as the regimental commander of Waul's Texas Legion during the defense of Vicksburg, replaced him.[40]

Throughout the war, Walker's Division experienced many problems and failures to gather timely intelligence because of a lack of cavalry scouts. During his initial organization of the division, Brig. Gen. Henry E. McCulloch had formed a cavalry squadron by reassigning Capt. Alsdorf Faulkner's Company G of the 15th Texas Cavalry to the division headquarters.[41] In the fall and winter of 1863–4, Major General Walker began to increase the strength of Faulkner's cavalry by detailing some of the best horsemen from his infantry regiments. By February 24, 1864, eleven soldiers and one lieutenant had been detached from the 13th Texas to serve with Faulkner. These men were selected from nearly every company, and at an average age of twenty-eight, can be assumed to have been among the most experienced.[42] As the early phase of the Red River campaign began, Walker's Division also was augmented by the 2nd Louisiana Cavalry, at least one company of which was working closely with Captain Faulkner.[43] This force, although quite small, would prove its value as threats of a Union invasion and the need for reconnaissance grew.

In early March 1864, there was growing dissatisfaction through the division when the soldiers learned of rumors that some high officials in the Trans-Mississippi Department had been conducting a clandestine cotton trade with Union forces in southeastern Louisiana. In the

13th Texas, Private Gaines recorded that on March 6, "About 100 men refuse to do duty from our Regiment on account of free trade with the Federalist Government." The next day, two of the ringleaders were sent to Marksville in handcuffs.[44] After months of hard campaigning in the swamps of east Louisiana to deny cotton to the Yankees, it is easy to see why the rumored trade was obnoxious to the soldiers of the division.

The mutiny seems to have originated in the 28th Texas Cavalry and in Gould's 6th Texas Battalion. On March 4–5, "approximately half of the 28th . . . refused to do duty." In order to isolate the disruptive soldiers, the unit was moved seven miles southwest of Marksville near Pearl Lake.[45] The 13th Texas evidently recovered from its excitement and returned to its routine duties. Private Gaines reported that he helped a detail from his company dig a new well on March 8.[46] Almost at the same time that the mutinies were taking place, the adjutant of the 12th Texas Infantry, also of Waul's brigade, wrote his wife, "Red River is rising rapidly. The raft which we have been so long constructing below Fort De Russy has been swept away by the first freshet, and no obstruction now interposes between the fort and the mouth of the river."[47] The peaceful routines of life in winter quarters were about to be shattered by the largest invasion force that had ever threatened Louisiana and Texas.

1. John T. Stark to Martha Stark, June 14, 1863, H. B. Simpson Research Center, Hill College.

2. Diary of Bluford A. Cameron, Jun. 7, 1863, E. C. Barker Library.

3. Blessington, *Campaigns of Walker's Texas Division*, 122.

4. Ibid., 126.

5. James B. Rounsaville to his family, Jul. 9, 1863, James Rounsaville Papers.

6. Blessington, *Campaigns of Walker's Texas Division*, 118.

7. James B. Rounsaville to his family, Jul. 9, 1863.

8. Kerby, *Kirby Smith's Confederacy*, 1–2.

9. Lord, *The Fremantle Diary*, 69.

10. CSR, M323, roll 77, Charles H. Jones.

11. CSR, M323, rolls 75–80, John Bean, Hiram Brown, George English, John Smith, and Elias Seale.

12. CSR, M323 roll 80, Capt. Thomas F. Truett to Brigadier Gen. W. R. Boggs, July 24, 1864, personal papers.

13. John T. Stark to Martha Stark, Aug. 9, 1862, H. B. Simpson Research Center, Hill College.

14. CSR, M323 roll 79, Thomas J. Rounsaville, note on muster of Feb. 29, 1864.

15. Johansson, *Widows by the Thousand*, 174.

16. Johansson, *Peculiar Honor*, 85–86.

17. Diary of Milton P. Gaines, Aug. 9 –Oct. 12, 1863, Charles H. Ham Papers, Anderson County, Texas.

18. CSR, M323, rolls 77, 79. When the 13th Texas departed, two soldiers, Wm. H. Jones of Company C and Eli Pace of Company G, were noted as "left sick at McNutt Hill," or "sick at Camp McNutt's Hill."

19. Blessington, *Campaigns of Walker's Texas Division*, 134–45.

20. Johansson, *Peculiar Honor*, 84; Diary of Milton P. Gaines, Nov. 2, 1863.

21. Col. John H. Burnett to Gen. E. Kirby Smith, Nov. 15, 1863, with endorsements by Dr. Thomas Hollis, Brig. Gen. James Morrison Hawes, and Maj. Gen. Richard Taylor, CSR, M323, roll 75, personal papers.

22. Diary of Milton P. Gaines, Nov. 8, 1863, Charles Ham Papers, Anderson County, Texas.

23. Diary of John T. Stark, Nov. 10–12, 1863, H. B. Simpson Research Center, Hill College; Diary of Milton P. Gaines, Nov. 10–12, 1863; Johansson, *Peculiar Honor*, 84.

24. Blessington, *Campaigns of Walker's Texas Division*, 153, 155.

25. Norman D. Brown, *Journey to Pleasant Hill: The Civil War Letters of Captain Elijah P. Petty, Walker's Texas Division, C.S.A.* (San Antonio, TX: University of Texas Institute of Texan Cultures, 1982), 280–82.

26. Diary of Milton P. Gaines, Nov. 29–30, 1863, Charles H. Ham Papers, Anderson County, Texas.

27. Johansson, *Peculiar Honor*, 85.

28. Diary of John T. Stark, Dec. 1–5, 1863, H. B. Simpson Research Center, Hill College.

29. John G. Walker, "The War of Secession West of the Mississippi River during the Years 1863-4-& 5," 40, Myron G. Gwinner Collection, USAMHI, Carlisle Barracks, PA.

30. Capt. Elijah Petty to his daughter, Dec. 3, 1863, Brown, *Journey to Pleasant Hill*, 283.

31. Johansson, *Peculiar Honor*, 76–77. Concerning these trends, historian M. Jane Johansson concluded, "Most of the men came from east Texas, an area heavily influenced by Protestant denominations that relied on revivals as a tool for reaching sinners. Defeats on the battlefield, and the corresponding demoralization, led to a belief in many that God would not allow a Southern triumph until the South did penance."

32. CSR, M323 roll 76, R. F. Fancher, personal papers. Rev. Fancher's son James had joined the 13th Texas in March 1862, but had been discharged in May because he was underage.

33. Diary of Milton P. Gaines, Jan. 22, 1864, Charles H. Ham Papers, Anderson County, Texas.

34. Diary of Milton P. Gaines, Jan. 28, 1864; CSR, M323, roll 78, Lieutenant Matthew McAlister, muster of Feb. 29, 1864. The muster notes that McAlister was "detailed to hunt hogs by Genl. Hawes."

35. CSR, M323 roll 79, James B. Rounsaville, promoted to "Sr. Lieutenant 1.31.64," and to captain in early March 1864. This was highly irregular, and at variance with Gen. S. Cooper's General Order No. 65, dated Sep. 9, 1862, which stated, "Promotion of company officers, as such, in the Provisional Army, take place in the respective companies in which the officers are serving, and not through the line of the Regiment or Battalion: that is, on the vacancy of the Captain, the First Lieutenant of the company will succeed; and the second of the same company will be entitled to succeed to the vacancy created by the promotion of the First Lieutenant." This order had been published in the *Arkansas State Gazette*, Oct. 11, 1862, and had probably been provided to the 13th Texas about the same time.

36. CSR, M323 roll 77, William Y. Glover, noted on muster of Feb. 29, 1864. Company A is noted on this muster as "stationed on the lower Red River."

37. Diary of Milton P. Gaines, Feb. 11, 1864, Charles H. Ham Papers, Anderson County, Texas.

38. Blessington, *Campaigns of Walker's Texas Division*, 164.

39. Diary of Milton P. Gaines, Feb. 20, 1864.

40. Tyler, *The New Handbook of Texas*, 3: 509, 6: 852. Waul had been promoted to brigadier general Sept. 18, 1863, shortly after being paroled at Vicksburg.

41. Blessington, *Campaigns of Walker's Texas Division*, 67; Hewett, *Confederate Soldiers from the State of Texas*, 1: 165.

42. CSR, M323, rolls 75–80. The soldiers are noted on the muster of Feb. 29, 1864, as detailed "to Capt. Faulkner's cavalry," or "detailed as cavalry scout."

43. Maj. Gen. John G. Walker to Maj. Gen. Richard Taylor, Mar. 19, 1864, O.R., ser. I, 34, pt. I: 599-600.

44. Diary of Milton P. Gaines, Mar. 6–7, 1864, Charles H. Ham Papers, Anderson County, Texas.

45. Johansson, *Peculiar Honor*, 88.

46. Diary of Milton P. Gaines, Mar. 8, 1864.

47. Volney Ellis to Mary Ellis, Mar. 4, 1864, Thomas W. Cutrer (ed.), "'An Experience in Soldier's Life,' the Civil War Letters of Volney Ellis, Adjutant, Twelfth Texas Infantry, Walker's Texas Division, C.S.A.," *Military History of the Southwest* 22 (Fall 1992): 149. It is worth noting that the 12th Texas (also known as the 8th Texas Infantry) was the unit commanded by Col. Overton Young, the original first brigade commander. It is clear from reading Captain Ellis' letters that this unit's officers, perhaps because of Colonel Young's relationship with Brig. Gen. Thomas N. Waul as the senior regimental officer, were much better informed than the officers of the 13th Texas.

Colonel John Howell Burnett, ca. 1898
(courtesy Texas State Library and Archives Commission)

Colonel Anderson Floyd Crawford, 1858
(courtesy Texas State Library and Archives Commission)

Captain William Blewett, Company H, 1851
(courtesy Mrs. Manie Blewett Whitmeyer)

Private Milton Pinckney Gaines, Company D, 1862
(courtesy Charles H. Ham)

Captain John Thomas Stark, Company H
(courtesy Floyd Boyett)

Captain James
Steele Hanks,
Company D, 1867
(courtesy Michelle
Ule)

Captain John Thomas
Bean, Company K, ca. 1854
(courtesy Mrs. Jackie Barnes)

Chapter 7

Long Road to Mansfield

"Aim low boys, and trust in God."
—Maj. Gen. John G. Walker[1]

The stillness of Camp Rogers, and indeed of all of Avoyelles Parish, was shattered on Sunday, March 13, 1864. The enemy had landed, and was on the march from Simmesport. As the division wagon trains were loaded and moved toward Cheneyville, the 13th Texas and Waul's first brigade quickly marched to reinforce the bridges on the primary avenue of approach.[2] General Scurry's third brigade was stationed the farthest forward, near Yellow Bayou, four miles west of Simmesport. After determining the overwhelming strength of the invasion force, Scurry withdrew to the long bridge on Bout de Bayou, ten miles east of Marksville on the Simmesport road. The 13th Texas and the other regiments of Waul's first brigade marched as far as Scurry's position, but were ordered four miles back and placed in reserve between Scurry's brigade and Randal's second brigade, which was guarding the bridge on Bayou de Lac, eight miles from Bout de Bayou. An unusually dry winter had turned the swamps, normally a natural barrier to Union movements, into solid ground, converting a maze of natural defensive wetlands into a broad field of battle, surrounded by major watercourses; the only exit for Walker's Division was the bridge on Bayou de Lac.[3]

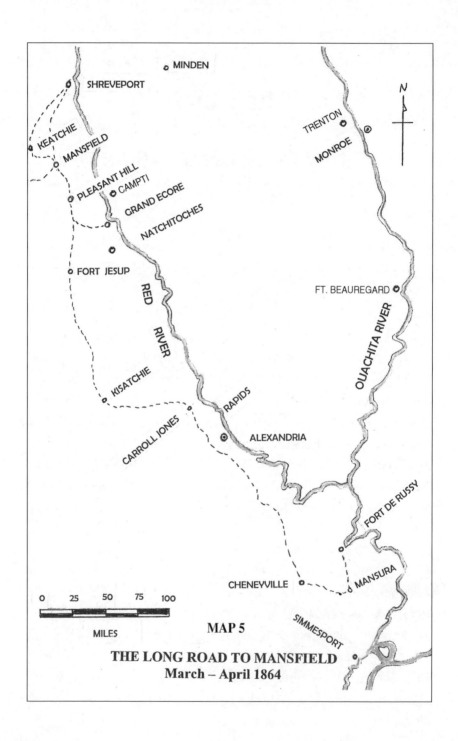

MAP 5

THE LONG ROAD TO MANSFIELD
March – April 1864

As Walker's reserve, the 13th Texas and the rest of Waul's brigade did nothing on Monday, March 14, until they were ordered to march to the bridge on Bayou de Lac, where they arrived before four that afternoon. The sound of skirmishing gunfire could be heard in the distance.[4] Thus began the series of epic marches that characterized the division whose rapid movements had earned it the nickname "Walker's Greyhounds" during the previous year.

Once the division was out of immediate danger, Captain Faulkner's cavalry and a company of the 2nd Louisiana Cavalry joined General Walker. Walker sent them to reconnoiter the area around Marksville and Mansura to gather intelligence on Union forces and movements. Walker quickly learned that the enemy force was commanded by Maj. Gen. Andrew Jackson Smith, and amounted to 15,000 infantry, with a large contingent of artillery. The force arrived in Marksville at 3:00 PM, "and a column of about 4,000 men pushed directly through to Fort De Russy, while the greater portion of the command halted in the immediate vicinity of the village."[5] Three hundred and fifty Confederate defenders at Fort De Russy faced an attacking force of more that ten times their number. Generals Walker and Taylor had both pointed out to Lt. Gen. Kirby Smith that a force of enemy infantry had a telling advantage if it took the high ground to the south of the fort's walled enclosures. That high ground was immediately occupied by Union troops as soon as the column emerged from the Marksville road. They soon formed a line of battle and began a determined artillery barrage on the upper fortifications.

Seven hundred yards away from the fort, down a narrow, muddy, claustrophobic passage with sheer, twenty-foot, timber-reinforced walls, lay the Confederate artillery batteries on the Red River. These batteries, shielded by twelve inches of timber and heavy railroad plate-iron, were as invulnerable as any gunboat that could possibly navigate the river. Capt. A. L. Adams' Company D, 28th Texas Cavalry, and Capt. James B. Rounsaville's Company E, 13th Texas Cavalry, were stationed in the water battery. Although their combined strength was less than sixty soldiers, their mission was to support Capt. T. H. Hutton's Crescent Artillery, Company A, that manned the guns. On demand, the Texans were to run the length of the nearly half-mile-long communication trench to the magazine and return with bags or kegs of powder and heavy solid or explosive projectiles. These exertions, however, soon proved unnecessary.[6]

Union Capt. James M. Cockefair of the 3rd Indiana Artillery Battery completed laying his guns 300 yards southwest of the upper works of Fort De Russy at about 4:15 PM. He estimated the range to the "outermost works of the fort," or the water battery, to be 800 yards to the north. After one or two rounds, his gun crews corrected their range to about 1,000 yards and quickly began placing fire on the river batteries. The fire from an unexpected and unprotected direction caused intense confusion among the defenders. The Louisiana artillerymen looked for direction from Captain Hutton, but he was no longer there.[7] Quickly they trained the one remaining mobile gun in the battery on the enemy. After firing one round, the Confederates were driven over the front parapet and down the slope toward the river by incoming fire from the Yankees as flying shrapnel and large fragments of hard red clay scattered through the position. The 3rd Indiana Artillery continued its fire for nearly two hours until 6:00 PM. If only one gun in three had targeted the fortifications on the river, 100 rounds struck the position.[8]

After a time, the Louisiana artillerymen dispensed with all military impedimenta and slipped away in the direction of their homes. Captain King and Lieutenant Brooks, with nine men, were determined to reinforce the "upper works," and disappeared down the communication trench in the direction of the main fortifications.[9] Captain Rounsaville of Company E had probably been called to a meeting with garrison commander Lt. Col. William Byrd and the other company commanders when the bombardment began.[10] Artillery continued to strike the water battery. Captain Adams, 1st Lt. Elbert E. Jennings of Company E, and twenty-one of their men took cover behind the parapet on the bank of the Red River as darkness began to fall.

After hearing loud cheering, one of the Texans on the river saw the Union colors flying above the bastion. Knowing that hesitation would lead to their capture, Captain Adams ordered the Texans to collect their arms and equipment and led them quickly through the river bottoms to the west as night fell. General Walker reported, "it is unnecessary to look to other causes than the overwhelming superiority of the enemy's force; but even with this disadvantage Fort De Russy might have been held for some days, perhaps, without relief from the outside, but for the vicious system of engineering adopted and the wretched judgment displayed in the selection of the position."[11]

Union forces at Fort De Russy captured five soldiers of Company E, 13th Texas, all of whom were probably sick in the garrison dispensary at the time. Later records indicate that all five were admitted to St. Louis U. S. Army General Hospital in New Orleans within a few weeks of their arrival, with such complaints as intermittent fever, chronic pneumonia, and typhoid fever. One Company E soldier, twenty-four-year-old Pvt. John W. Mitchell, was hospitalized with "congestion of the brain," probably meningitis, and died there on May 24, 1864. The other four soldiers were exchanged at Red River Landing on the Mississippi River on July 22, 1864, and returned to their unit.[12]

On the night of March 14, four hours after the fall of Fort De Russy, the division was ordered to fall back ten miles toward Cheneyville, passing their wagons and ambulances about 10:00 AM the next morning. The men marched four miles to Cheneyville and turned north for twenty-four miles farther before camping and cooking rations. This was followed by a night march of five miles to Beaver Creek, where they rested until 4:30 AM on the morning of March 16. Their fifty-three-mile march in three days placed them a few miles west of Alexandria. Capt. Volney Ellis of the 12th Texas Infantry, also of Waul's brigade, later wrote to his wife, "It became a race for life or death, the enemy pressing our rear and the fleet moving up the river to cut off our escape, but true to our reputation for marching, we beat the race, gunboats and all, and are safe from capture at least. . . . It is truly remarkable what a man can stand!"[13] The diarists of the 13th Texas, Capt. John T. Stark of Company H and Pvt. Milton P. Gaines of Company D, were notably spare in their entries during this forced march. Stark sketched a few laconic daily comments about his unit's location and miles marched; Gaines remained silent until he finally "washed and cleaned up" two weeks later.[14] Accustomed to reporting rumors and bits of distant news, the soldiers of Walker's Division and the 13th Texas may have slowly begun to realize that they were now at the center of the most important Civil War campaign west of the Mississippi.

Union Maj. Gen. Nathaniel P. Banks' invasion force numbered over 40,000 soldiers and sailors. It was, however, not clearly focused on its military mission. Banks' orders to destroy the industrial base of the Trans-Mississippi Confederacy had been confused by his political and presidential aspirations and constant pressure from Yankee mill owners and cotton brokers starved for raw material. Added to these distractions was the corps of infantry attached from General Sherman's forces. Commanded by Maj. Gen. Andrew Jackson Smith, this corps adopted a scorched-earth policy no matter what orders it received, thus destroying the good will of any potential Union sympathizers Banks may have hoped to influence politically.[15]

Waul's brigade, including the 13th Texas, was still well ahead of Banks' main invasion force as it marched northwest parallel to the Red River. Union gunboats and troop transports on the river were already ranging north of Alexandria looting and loading cotton bales from riverside warehouses. The goals of the invasion force were to destroy the industrial capacity of East Texas and northwestern Louisiana, to capture the Confederate headquarters of Shreveport, and to supply the mills of the northeastern United States with huge quantities of cotton.[16] General Banks knew that speed was essential in such an operation. With this in mind, his ground forces moved away from the Red River valley west of Alexandria to take advantage of what were believed to be better roads leading to Natchitoches, Mansfield, and Shreveport. In doing so, he gave up the critical advantage of supporting naval gunfire for his operations. That later proved to be a fatal error.

The 13th Texas was roused at 4:30 AM on March 16 to begin a thirty-one-mile forced march toward Kisatchie. The men passed through many large plantations as well as miles of old pine forest. In his journal, Capt. John Stark marked their progress by recalling the names of the planters. On March 17 they camped on the land of Carroll Jones, where General Taylor had earlier positioned a large cache of supplies and rations, and rested there until March 21. Jones, a wealthy African American planter, was a novelty to the Texans, since there were few free African Americans in Texas. Stark referred to him as "Carroll Jones, F.M.C.," for "free man of color." Captain Ellis of the 16th Texas wrote, "We have been having some of the most disagreeable weather I have ever experienced at this season, exceedingly cold and wet." March 20–21 were particularly miserable, with a constant heavy, cold rain mixed with hail and sleet.[17]

On the morning of March 20 a large Union reconnaissance force commanded by Brig. Gen. Joseph A. Mower left Alexandria for Natchitoches. Late that evening the Federals arrived near Henderson Hill, where the 2nd Louisiana Cavalry and Capt. William Edgar's 1st Texas Field Battery of Scurry's Brigade were camped. Mower's troops lit a number of campfires, giving the Confederates the impression that they were settling in for the night. At the same time, a large Union force began a difficult trek through the freezing mud and deep swamps to flank the rebels and attack their camp from the rear. Due to the treachery of a local civilian, the Yankees had obtained the challenge and password used by the Confederate pickets. After capturing the dispirited sentries, Mower's force quickly surrounded and captured the 200 or so cavalrymen and Edgar's artillery crews. Among the men of the 2nd Louisiana Cavalry were some of Capt. Alsdorf Faulkner's Texans. Pvt. David C. Ragan, aged thirty-two, of Company B, 13th Texas, was listed among those taken prisoner.[18] One Union soldier wrote that like a treed raccoon the Rebels soon "saw the point and came down as gracefully as possible."[19]

Capt. John T. Stark wrote, "Left Carroll Jones at daylight—Skirmish with Feds on 20th, Feds surprise 2nd La. Cavalry and Edgar's Battery and take them—reached camp on Kisatchie [Bayou] same evening—marching 25 miles." The camp at Kisatchie Bayou was deep in the pine woods near the bridge, one mile north of the village of the same name. The 13th Texas was sent north ten miles on March 23 for advance picket duty to relieve another dismounted unit, the 24th Texas Cavalry. Their tour on guard was uneventful, but tension mounted as more reports of enemy movements were received.[20]

After three days camped on the plantation of Mrs. Rosaline Kyle, the division moved north toward Fort Jesup on the old San Antonio Road. The fort, first established and commanded by Lt. Col. (later President) Zachary Taylor, in 1822, had been abandoned in 1846 as the frontier moved far into central and west Texas. The 13th Texas passed Fort Jesup on March 31 during a march of seventeen miles. On April 1 another twenty-six miles brought them to the village of Pleasant Hill, where Pvt. Milton Gaines recalled that "he washed and cleaned up."[21] Captain Stark recorded that they marched four miles the next day to the junction of the Natchitoches road, where the 13th Texas remained until it was nearly dark. Suddenly gunfire was heard in the distance and the men were ordered, "double quick back to Pleasant Hill and three miles [south on the] Ft. Jessup [sic] road. . . slept on arms to 5 o'clock."

As dawn broke on the third the entire division was ordered to form a line of battle. Waul's brigade was near the right of the line facing south. The open fields of a large plantation and the cavalry were to their front. A section of artillery was in position near a cotton gin building far to their left. When it became clear that there was no enemy threat, Walker's Division and the other units there were ordered back to Pleasant Hill. After passing through Pleasant Hill and joining more of General Taylor's forces, the Texans continued another eight miles up the Shreveport road toward Mansfield.[22]

The evening of April 4 found the 13th Texas camped on Bayou Fodoche, six miles north of Mansfield and a few miles south of the hamlet of Keatchie. The entire division rested there for three days, if waiting for an enemy force could be called resting. Rumors were that the Yankee army filled the Shreveport road from Alexandria to north of Natchitoches. The soldiers were facing the first certain battle after two years of drill and road marches. It was difficult to know how to deal with the combination of tension and inactivity. Extra attention was paid to rifles, powder, shot, and things as insignificant as shoelaces. On the evening of the seventh, four days' rations were issued. That had seldom happened since the preparations for the assault at Lake Providence. On a positive note, everyone in the regiment knew the men they would stand with when battle began. Everyone knew that their dedication to the Southern ideal was about to be tested, and that their friends and neighbors would see how they acted under fire. The level of excitement and anticipation could probably never be repeated.

Lt. Thomas Rounsaville wrote his mother and sisters that day as well.

> I would suppose that you have heard that the enemy is in possession of Alexandria and at this time also Fort Derry [De Russy] which was surrounded, [only] a few days ago they came here with such an overwhelming force . . . we were compelled to fall back as far as Mansfield, where we are at the present time seven miles north of Mansfield on the Shreveport road leading to Keatchie. In regard to the movement of the enemy, we learn today that they are falling back to Alexandria and furthermore I heard that the river is falling & that ten gunboats and forty-two transports were above the fall & could not get back because the water fell. This is glorious news, though I cannot credit this report. . . . excuse this short letter for I will be with you soon.[23]

Throughout the retreat to Mansfield, General Kirby Smith had recommended that Taylor exercise caution because of the weakness of his forces. He advised that like Lieutenant General Pemberton at Vicksburg, Taylor should withdraw within the fortifications of Shreveport and await reinforcements, or, as an alternative, move his forces into Texas, from where he could resist the Union attack. Taylor probably correctly concluded that a withdrawal to Shreveport would result in the desertion of the troops recently called from Texas, and that movement into Texas would put him in a position from which "we could give no more aid to our brethren on the east of the Mississippi than from the [Hawaiian] islands."[24] The only real option, in Taylor's estimation, was to give battle south of Mansfield.

At first light on April 8, 1864, Walker's Division and the 13th Texas left their camp and marched through Mansfield. Brass bands played "Dixie," ladies scattered flowers in the road and exhorted them to destroy the invaders. On that warm April morning, Lieutenant Colonel Crawford's 13th Texas was among the largest regiments in the division, with over 500 soldiers.[25] The 28th Texas had fewer than 440 and the 11th Texas about 422.[26] The Texans marched to a large farm three miles south of Mansfield near a road junction known as Sabine Crossroads. Taking a position just south of the Shreveport road, they watched as the cavalry engaged the enemy in the open fields and a procession of supply wagons and wounded passed north along the road a short distance away. In the early afternoon, a staff officer came along the line to reposition the units. The 26th Texas Cavalry rode forward a short distance to screen the movement. Randal's brigade moved north of the road to reinforce Brig. Gen. Camille Armand Jules Marie, Prince de Polignac's brigade. The units executed the movement with precision and moved the line until Waul's brigade replaced Randal's just south of the Shreveport road. Capt. John T. Stark described the line of battle. "[To] our right . . . infantry, artillery, and cavalry as far as I can see. The sun [is] shining brightly over all. All of God's creatures seem to be rejoicing in the beautiful spring day except man, and he only is bent on destroying his kind."

General Taylor allowed Brig. Gen. Alexander Mouton's division to make the initial attack. Charging quickly across the bare fields, the

Confederates suffered staggering casualties. Virtually every mounted officer was killed or wounded. General Mouton was killed. Artillery cut wide swaths through the advancing Louisianans, but without hesitation, they closed with four Union regiments and quickly drove them from their positions with heavy losses. About 5:00 PM the sounds of battle to the front of the 13th Texas began to diminish. Moments later a courier passed by shouting that to the left an artillery battery and one thousand prisoners had been captured.[27]

At 5:30 PM Waul and Scurry's brigades were ordered forward. They soon crossed the fence before them and after passing through a belt of trees, emerged in an open field. The volume of fire rapidly increased. Captain Stark recalled, "A poor dead soldier here and there and a few dead horses showed us where the cavalry had been skirmishing." The 13th Texas moved up Honeycutt Hill, whooping and cheering one another on. As they came to the crest of the hill, General Walker rode by, saying, "Aim low boys, and trust in God!" Yelling wildly, they gained

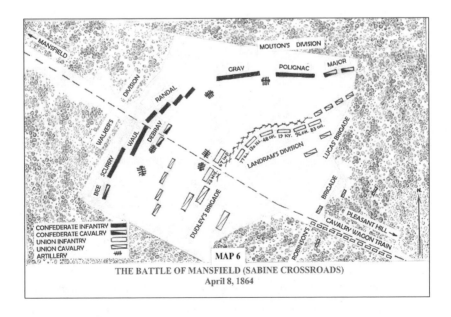

MAP 6

THE BATTLE OF MANSFIELD (SABINE CROSSROADS)
April 8, 1864

the hilltop and ran toward the enemy positions. "Here one . . . wounded Texan raised on his elbow and waving his hat over his head said, 'crowd them boys, crowd them,' and well was he obeyed." At that time the 13th Texas came under fire from both enemy artillery from the 6th Missouri Battery and small arms fire from the 23rd Wisconsin Infantry. Casualties began to fall in the ranks. They paused to fire a volley and cheered wildly as each rank fired. Captain Stark said the Union troops' "fire was warm but soon slackened as they fell back with a wild whoop. We again sprang forward." Their comrades from Scurry's brigade closed ranks with them on the right as the line surged forward down the road. The Texans were slowed briefly as Federal reinforcements formed a battle line in the forest to the left and right of the road, which was blocked with supply and ammunition wagons and ambulances. Walker's Division soon broke that line, throwing the Yankee troops into a complete panic. For the next two miles, the enemy before them seldom slowed down enough to return fire.[28]

As the Confederates approached the enemy camp near Pleasant Grove, the road was blocked with supply and commissary wagons, artillery, and ammunition caissons. The Confederates continued cheering and firing into the confused enemy. The enemy returned fire sporadically but was primarily concerned with escape. That pattern was repeated for nearly four miles toward Pleasant Hill. The enemy retreated until they were bunched up by the troops ahead or by mired wagons or artillery. They would then make a brief stand and fire a volley to slow the Confederate advance. But in the case of Walker's Texas Division, the Federals were receiving two years' worth of pent-up hostility. The 13th Texas was prepared to chase them to the mouth of the Mississippi if necessary.

Captain Stark described the struggle in his journal.

> The enemy made another stand and the firing became heavy for a few minutes. Our advance was checked but as the men came up they deployed to either flank and the enemy again fell back.

Now came the final struggle [as] the enemy, now reinforced by a whole army corps . . . disputed every inch of ground. Darkness was coming on. We had now drove the enemy about four miles and had good cause to be weary, but there was no hesitation. [With] the Thirteenth on the extreme left and again we moved on at a charging pace, on through the brush and fallen timber we drove under one continual roll of musketry and the engagement became general all along the line, peel after peel resounded from our side. The enemies fire was one continued roar, it was now too dark to distinguish friend from foe, but at short distance and our boys fell back."[29]

As darkness became nearly total, an officer, unidentified in the confusion, exhorted the Texans to one more attack, which they attempted. Soon repulsed by an almost solid wall of gunfire along the entire line, they withdrew to the creek at the foot of the hill. No more could be done.

As the soldiers of the 13th Texas leaned exhausted on their rifles, there began an endless procession of captured wagons, equipment, prisoners, and commissary stores through the lines. They guarded the front line centered on the road that night. When the sky began to show a pale light, two brigades of Sterling Price's Missouri division passed through their lines to resume the pursuit of the hastily retreating Union forces. This gave the soldiers of the 13th Texas a chance to build a few campfires, eat, and make necessary repairs to equipment. The captured wagons passing during the night yielded ammunition, rifles, and rations. A letter written a few days later by Sgt. George B. Layton of Newton to Mrs. William Blewett, widow of the original commander of Company H, reported that the enemy that day "broke, leaving a good many cannon wagons and a little of every thing else that you could mention except hard money." Pvt. Milton Gaines of Company D recalled that the Confederate forces "captured 1,000 Feds, 200 wagons, and some Artillery."[30]

That night the regiments of Walker's Division made an effort to muster and determine the number of casualties, but darkness, scattered units, and the need to prepare for a continuation of the struggle the next day would have rendered the count highly inaccurate. Extant casualty reports for Waul's brigade combine those of April 8 and 9.[31] While agreement on the number of casualties was elusive, all seem to have realized that the Confederate forces had achieved a stunning but incomplete victory that day.

1. Diary of John T. Stark, April 8, 1864, H. B. Simpson Research Center, Hill College.

2. Diary of John T. Stark, Mar. 13, 1864.

3. Maj. Gen. John G. Walker to Maj. Gen. Richard Taylor, Mar. 19, 1864, O.R., ser. I, 34, pt. 1: 598. The Union force was estimated at 15,000 to 17,000 infantry, 300 cavalry, and thirty to forty pieces of artillery.

4. Diary of John T. Stark, Mar. 14, 1864, H. B. Simpson Research Center, Hill College.

5. Maj. Gen. John G. Walker to Maj. Gen. Richard Taylor, Mar. 19, 1864, O.R., ser. 1, 34:1, 599-600.

6. Ibid.; Johansson, *Peculiar Honor*, 94.

7. O.R., ser. I, 34: 1, 601.

8. Capt. James M. Cockefair to Brig. Gen. Richard Arnold, Chief of Artillery, Apr. 18, 1864, O.R., ser. I, 34:1, 371.

9. Hewett, *Texas Confederate Soldiers*, 2: 503. This may have been Capt. E. T. King of King's Louisiana Artillery, also known as the St. Martin Rangers. 1st Lt. J. R. K. Brooks was from the 19th Texas Infantry, Company H. Major General Walker noted their heroism in his report.

10. Lt. Col. William Byrd had been detached from the 14th Texas Infantry to command Fort De Russy; Thomas Rounsaville to his mother and sisters, Apr. 7, 1864. James Rounsaville Papers. Capt. James B. Rounsaville escaped and reported to Maj. Gen. Richard Taylor near Alexandria several days later.

11. Walker to Taylor, Mar. 19, 1864.

12. CSR, M323, rolls 77-79. The soldiers taken prisoner at Fort De Russy were Privates Elisha Gosnell, John W. Piearcy, Thomas P. Mathews, Littleton B. McBride, and John W. Mitchell. Gosnell, Mathews, and Mitchell were original members of the unit; Piearcy and McBride enlisted in April 1863.

13. Volney Ellis to Mary Ellis, Mar. 18, 1864, Cutrer, "An Experience in Soldier's Life," 151.

14. Diary of John T. Stark, H. B. Simpson Research Center, Hill College; Diary of Milton P. Gaines, Charles H. Ham Papers, Anderson County, Texas.

15. Ludwell H. Johnson, *The Red River Campaign; Politics and Cotton in the Civil War* (Baltimore, MD: Johns Hopkins Press, 1958), 223.

16. Ibid., 41–48.

17. Diary of John T. Stark, Mar. 17 – 21, 1864, H. B. Simpson Research Center, Hill College; Capt.Volney Ellis to Mary Ellis, Mar. 20, 1864, Cutrer, "An Experience in Soldier's Life," 152.

18. CSR, M323, roll 79, David C. Ragan. Private Ragan was listed as captured Mar. 21, 1864, at Natchitoches, Louisiana, and transferred to the Federal Military Prison at New Orleans on Mar. 26, 1864. He appears to have died in prison, since he was not exchanged with the other soldiers of Walker's Division.

19. William R. Brooksher, *War Along the Bayous: The 1864 Red River Campaign in Louisiana* (Washington and London: Brassey's, 1998), 54–56. The Confederates were suffering from exposure and near exhaustion. Union accounts reported that the mules were still harnessed to the gun caissons and the cavalrymen's horses were still saddled. Most of the men were huddled around smoky fires of pine knots, the only fuel that would burn in the cold rain.

20. Diary of John T. Stark, Mar. 23, 1864, H. B. Simpson Research Center, Hill College.

21. Diary of Milton P. Gaines, Apr. 1, 1864, Charles Ham Papers, Anderson County, Texas.

22. Diary of John T. Stark, Mar. 26–Apr. 3, 1864, H. B. Simpson Research Center, Hill College; Brooksher, *War Along the Bayous*, 59–61. In addition to Walker's Division, Polignac's Brigade, Gray's Brigade, Terrell's Texas Cavalry, Vincent's Brigade, Bagby's Brigade, and Lane's Brigade reinforced Taylor's force.

23. Thomas J. Rounsaville to his mother and sisters, Apr. 7, 1864, Papers of James B. Rounsaville. Lt. Thomas Rounsaville was critically wounded during one of the battles that followed in the next two days; his brother James found him a private home nearby in which to recover, and his sister Narcissa came from Houston County to Keatchie to care for him until he died in late April.

24. Taylor, *Destruction and Reconstruction*, 190–91.

25. CSR, M323, rolls 75–80. The regiment's assigned strength as of Feb. 29, 1864, was 565. It can be assumed that at least ten percent of the soldiers were absent on furlough or on convalescent leave.

26. Johansson, *Peculiar Honor*, 103.

27. Diary of John T. Stark, Apr. 8, 1864, H. B. Simpson Research Center, Hill College; Johansson, *Peculiar Honor*, 103–4; Brooksher, *War Along the Bayous*, 95–7.

28. Diary of John T. Stark, Apr. 8, 1864; G. B. Layton to Nancy Blewett, Apr. 18, 1864, H. B. Simpson Research Center, Hill College; Johansson, *Peculiar Honor*, 104–5; O.R., ser. I, 34, pt. 1, 169, 228, 564; Diary of Milton P. Gaines, Apr. 8, 1864, Charles Ham Papers, Anderson County.

29. Diary of John T. Stark, Apr. 8, 1864. H. B. Simpson Research Center, Hill College.

30. G. B. Layton to Nancy Blewett, Apr. 18, 1864, H. B. Simpson Research Center, Hill College; Diary of Milton P. Gaines, Apr. 8, 1864, Charles Ham Papers, Anderson County.

31. *Galveston (Tex.) Weekly News*, Apr. 20, 1864.

Chapter 8

The Battle of Pleasant Hill

"His loss is lamented by the Regiment
more than any man that has fallen."
—Capt. James B. Rounsaville, Company E,
13th Texas Cavalry.[1]

The losses to the 13th Texas had been significant at Mansfield. If the experiences of the other regiments in Walker's Division were any indication, the 13th lost at least three killed, ten wounded, and two missing.[2] Of those killed, it was known that Pvt. James B. Carleton of Company H and Lieutenant Runnels, whose company was not reported, died in battle at Mansfield on April 8.[3] Initial reports listed as many as forty-six men missing, since most of the wounded were evacuated away from the regiment to field hospitals in Mansfield.[4] Few soldiers of the 13th Texas would have had more than a fitful nap on their weapons that night, knowing they were guarding the Shreveport road from thirsty Yankees soldiers just a few yards away from the position on Chapman's Bayou. First light at Pleasant Grove revealed a more hopeful reality. Union troops had not altogether lost their enthusiasm for flight the previous evening, and had silently slipped away from their defensive positions in the darkness, after capturing a few Confederates who made it clear that they intended to continue the battle. There was little time for reflection in the morning as General Taylor ordered his forces forward to pursue, and hopefully destroy, Banks' army.[5]

General Banks had ordered his troops back to a position held by Union Maj. Gen. Andrew Jackson "Whiskey" Smith, who commanded the 16th Army Corps near the village of Pleasant Hill. By Saturday morning when the 13th Texas was ordered to move out, it was obvious that the enemy had slipped away during the night. Walker's Division moved onto the Pleasant Hill road an hour after sunrise and began marching south. The roadsides were littered with enemy dead and wounded, as well as partially burned wagons, and damaged, lost, or discarded equipment. As the early morning warmed, high columns of gray vultures and turkey buzzards circled in the sky above the battlefield south of Mansfield. The Texans were elated after their victory. Casualties had been relatively light, and most of the men with minor wounds were still with the regiment.[6] There probably were many comments about the lack of intestinal fortitude on the part of the "Feds." Sergeant Layton of Company H related in a letter, "When our men charged, yelling like Indians, [the Yankees] could not stand it. They only fired three or four rounds and broke."[7]

General Taylor's infantry reached the area of Pleasant Hill and began moving into positions at 3:00 PM. Churchill's Arkansans took the ground on the right and moved southwest of the village, hoping to flank the Federals. Taylor granted them the honor of opening the battle. Walker's Texans took their position in the center behind a skirt of heavy timber to the west of the road to Mansfield. The brigades retained the order of the previous day, with Randal on the left, Waul in the center, and Scurry on the right. The far left of the line was occupied by the remnants of Mouton's division, now commanded by Brigadier General Polignac, and acting as Taylor's reserve. They were screened by two regiments of Gen. Tom Green's Texas cavalry commanded by Brig. Gen. Hamilton P. Bee and the dismounted cavalry of Brig. Gen. James P. Major.[8]

The enemy facing Walker's Texas Division was the 2nd Brigade, 3rd Division, of Smith's 16th Army Corps commanded by Col. William

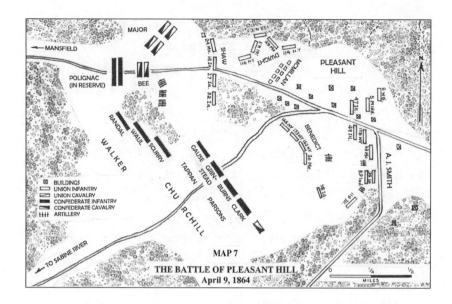

MAP 7
THE BATTLE OF PLEASANT HILL
April 9, 1864

T. Shaw. His forces consisted of the 24th Missouri, 14th Iowa, 27th Iowa, and 32nd Iowa infantry regiments. It was clear that Shaw's brigade was numerically inferior to Walker's Division. However, Shaw's Union infantry had not fought at Mansfield and had seen no major engagements after the fall of Fort De Russy in March. In addition to being fresh, well fed, and rested, Shaw's brigade had spent nearly six hours fortifying its positions. Brig. Gen. Hamilton P. Bee of Tom Green's Texas cavalry later described "the superb line of battle . . . with its serried lines compact and entrenched." This was very much at variance with General Taylor's assumption that the Union line was "a mere feint to cover the retreat of their wagon train."[9] Colonel Shaw's greatest concern was not the disparity in numbers, but the gap in the Union line to his left. Brig. Gen. Charles P. Stone, Banks' Chief of Staff, assured him that the situation would be corrected, but as the afternoon progressed, no Federal unit was within a quarter-mile of Shaw's left.[10]

The 13th Texas approached Pleasant Hill at 3:00 PM, and the enemy was prepared for it. Dug in behind heavily constructed barriers of logs and rail fences, the Union forces gave no sign that any further withdrawal was planned. General Taylor ordered that all the troops be given two hours rest. Brig. Gen. Thomas J. Churchill's Missouri and Arkansas divisions had marched forty miles in thirty-six hours, and the remainder of the infantry had marched twenty miles to Pleasant Hill after the hard fought battle the day before.[11] As they rested and waited for the artillery to move into position, the men of the 13th Texas lounged or stood leaning on their rifles, many chewing tobacco and spitting into the pine straw. The thoughts of some would have been occupied by General Taylor's orders "to rely on the bayonet, as we [have] neither ammunition nor time to waste."[12]

A ravine blocked by a heavy stand of old trees and fallen timber stood between the Texans and the Union line, making observation of the preparations impossible. Capt. Joshua B. Young's Company B, from Houston County, went forward with other skirmishers of Waul's brigade to scout the enemy and screen the regiment's position. Shadows grew longer. It was nearly 5:00 PM when the first Confederate batteries began shelling the enemy line. The sounds of Churchill's attack on Federal positions to the right triggered the attack. Captain Stark recalled in his journal that they were soon ordered forward. "Our batteries were now pouring in a deadly and continuous fire upon the foe. After passing through a heavy skirt of timber our brigade emerged on a rising ground to the right of one of the batteries and without pausing pushed on to attack the enemy."[13] The brigades marched in a column through the dense tangle of brush and fallen trees. As the Texans cleared these obstacles, their skirmishers passed through them, withdrawing hastily to the rear, after unsuccessfully probing the entrenched Federal lines. Stark commented dryly, "our sharp shooters instead of drawing [the enemy] fire retired by the right flank."[14]

Capt. Horace Haldeman's 4th Texas field battery fired on the Union line from the border of an "old field . . . dotted over with small pines."[15] This field sloped gently downhill toward the base of the small plateau on top of which the village stood. The regiments quickly reformed their line of battle and marched across the field. As the 13th Texas drew closer to the enemy line, the Union forces suddenly fired a continuous volley. The leading Confederate companies melted away as the dead and wounded fell. Col. John Scott, commanding the 32nd Iowa, reported, "the fire of my command was reserved until the enemy was within easy range, and when opened was so destructive that [the Rebels] faltered."[16] The supporting Confederate units moved forward and took cover in depressions and behind the brush and timber at the edge of the field, and were soon placing accurate fire on any exposed enemy with devastating effects. The Federals continued to stand and fire volleys, but the volume of smoke and the superior cover and concealment of the Southern troops made such fire less effective. Fighting at close quarters with shotguns loaded with buckshot gave the Texans some advantage. Randal's brigade, attacking the 27th Iowa to the left, was hard pressed, and appealed for help, which Waul's brigade was in no position to provide.[17]

Continuing their attack on the 32nd Iowa, the 13th Texas fought at less than ten paces from the enemy in the dense thickets as the Federals slowly gave ground. Sgt. Maj. B. C. Crawford, the regimental commander's nephew, fell mortally wounded.[18] Miraculously, Pvt. Ransom P. Hoarde, the 13th Texas' color bearer, survived the battle unscathed.[19] Colonel Shaw reported the 32nd Iowa "had fallen back, so as to enable the enemy to pass in rear of my left."[20] Light was waning but the fighting on that front continued for over an hour and a half. Large numbers of Union troops surrendered and passed through the line to the rear. Fire still came from Shaw's other units which had fallen back into the timber and been resupplied with ammunition. Colonel Scott was now isolated, "without orders, and virtually in the hands of the enemy, had he dared to close in and overwhelm us with his masses now around us. This was my position until after sunset, by which time the enemy had left my front, passing now by my right to the rear, where the fight was still raging."[21]

Bypassing the mutilated 32nd Iowa, Lieutenant Colonel Crawford, regimental commander of the 13th Texas, then ordered a charge, which led to the loss of his second horse that day. Blessington recalled, "General Walker perceiving the critical position of Scurry's brigade, almost surrounded by four times their number, immediately ordered the brigades of Waul and Randal to charge the enemy at the point of the bayonet, as the only possible means of saving Scurry's brigade from destruction."[22] After scattering or capturing the many Union defenders, the regiment sprinted through the timberline into a second open field, only to be fired on by soldiers of Randal or Scurry's brigade who had flanked the Federals and attacked them from behind. The 13th Texas returned the fire before it realized that they were friendly troops. This confusion among the brigades was largely due to the wounding of General Walker, who was compelled to withdraw from the field. As smoke cleared in the dim twilight, the mistake was realized and a ceasefire called.[23] It was probably during this last engagement that the 13th lost its only known prisoner of war to the Federals. Pvt. James A. Birdwell of Newton County, Company H, was captured.[24]

Darkness in the brush and timber became almost complete and fighting diminished to occasional poorly directed shots. Moving back out of the woods, the 13th Texas was recalled and withdrawn from the field of battle. The enemy had been driven from the broad hilltop, leaving "piles of . . . [their] dead [to] attest the correctness of our aim, and the obstinacy of the conflict."[25] Other units would hold the ground, evacuate the casualties, and bury the dead. The adjutant of Young's 12th Texas wrote, "Night again closed the conflict, and the young moon looked down on many a bloody corpse which the rising sun had found buoyant with life and hope, now cold and stark in death."[26]

Refuting later Union contentions that Confederate forces retreated following the battle, Brig. Gen. Hamilton P. Bee recalled drinking coffee at his campfire about 800 yards from the village of Pleasant Hill at 9:00 PM that night with General E. Kirby Smith and Maj. Gen. Richard Taylor. Taylor then ordered Bee to "return to the battlefield, picket up to the enemy's lines, and give him the earliest report of their movements in the morning." Bee noted that after some Federal movement by wagons to recover the wounded, by midnight "all was quiet."[27] Pvt. Milton P. Gaines of Company D recorded that the 13th Texas "fell back to the mill about seven miles [for water]. A ball cut my hat brim. . . Missed my forehead about two inches in front."[28]

As the 13th Texas slowly marched toward Mansfield and its campsite at Carroll's Mill, the many gaps in their ranks became painfully obvious. Company C of Houston County had lost both junior lieutenants. Company D of Anderson County lost ten soldiers, including First Sgt. Romulus Masters. Company E of Henderson County, with barely thirty men remaining after its defense of Fort De Russy, had four wounded. Captain Stark's Newton County Company H had one dead and seven wounded. First Sergeant Henderson Brack, an avid fiddler, was wounded in both his shoulder and leg, and later lost his right arm to amputation. The emotional numbness caused by the loss of fifty-seven comrades in two days was increased by physical exhaustion, dehydration, and the damp cold of an early spring night. Captain Stark stated without hesitation, "Victory crowned our worries. The foe, after burning his stores, was in full retreat, pursued by our cavalry under Gen. Green."

After an elated General Banks observed the Southerners leaving the field that evening, he rode to General A. J. Smith and shook his hand, saying, "God bless you General, you have saved the army." General Smith, who had little use or respect for Banks, reportedly responded, "By God, I know it, sir."[29]

From the Texans' perspective, the Yankees had mounted an invasion aimed at Texas, failed, lost huge quantities of supplies, and run like rabbits. Letters from soldiers of the 13th Texas put the casualties at five to one. The current estimates are closer to three to two, but if the victors are allowed to write the histories, one should gracefully accept the former estimate in spirit, if not as fact. Incomplete records from Walker's Division document 83 killed, 435 wounded, and 157 missing. The relatively light casualties in the 13th Texas and two major victories in two days had had a profound impact on the confidence, spirit, and morale of the regiment. Letters home listed captured equipment and supplies. "The fruits of our victory were found to be twenty-one pieces of artillery, 250 wagons and ambulances, [and] 6,000 [stands] of small arms of the best quality."[30]

In discussions with his commanders following the battle, Banks was initially inclined to continue his march on Shreveport. Support for this plan quickly dissolved as Maj. Gen. William B. Franklin, Brig. Gen. William Dwight, and Maj. Gen. William H. Emory pointed out other courses of action. In particular, Franklin had "no stomach for another pitched battle under Banks's generalship." He commented, "I was certain that an operation depending on plenty of troops, rather than skill in handling them, was the only one which would have probability of success in his hands."[31] It was finally decided that nothing short of a retreat to Grand Ecore would satisfy the requirements to reconstitute and resupply the Union army. Gen. Richard Taylor reported, "The morning of the 10th found us in possession of Pleasant Hill, the enemy retreating secretly in the night, leaving his dead unburied and some 400 wounded in our hands. [Brigadier General] Bee took up the pursuit and held it for 20 miles without receiving a shot, capturing prisoners and finding at every step the same evidence of rout as had marked the pursuit of the previous day."[32]

TABLE 5
CASUALTIES IN WALKER'S DIVISION—APRIL 8–9, 1864

	Killed	Wounded	Missing	Total
Waul's Brigade				
12th Texas Infantry (1)	7	41	3	51
18th Texas Infantry	6	47	7	60
22nd Texas Infantry	7	50	5	62
13th Texas Cavalry	10	41	6	57
Totals (2)	30	179	21	230
Randal's Brigade (3)				
28th Texas Cavalry	13	61	2	76
11th Texas Infantry	5	24	2	31
14th Texas Infantry	6	44	2	52
Gould's Battalion (4)	7	23	6	36
Totals	31	152	12	195

	Killed	Wounded	Missing	Total
Scurry's Brigade (5)				
16th Texas Infantry	6	53	64	123
17th Texas Infantry	16	35	60	111
19th Texas Infantry		16		16
16th Texas Cavalry		(Data Missing)		
Totals	22	104	124	250
Division Totals	83	435	157	675

(1) Often referred to as Col. Overton Young's 8th Texas Infantry in period reports. In a letter to his wife, Apr. 11, 1864, Young's adjutant, Capt. Volney Ellis reported 6 killed, 40 wounded, and 5 missing.

(2) *Galveston Weekly News,* Apr. 27, 1864, and May 11, 1864. The newspaper reports twenty-five dead in Waul's brigade, but lists thirty in casualty lists.

(3) Jane H. Johansson and David H. Johansson, "Two 'Lost' Battle Reports," *Military History of the West* 23 (Fall 1993): 169–80.

(4) Also known as the 6th Texas Cavalry Battalion.

(5) Alwyn Barr, "Texan Losses in the Red River Campaign, 1864," *Texas Military History* 3 (Summer 1963): 103–10.

Despite rejoicing in western Louisiana and Texas as news of the two battles dominated letters and editorials, the veterans of the operations would later find that their victories had little or no long term effect beyond prolonging the war by a number of months. As President Jefferson Davis's most recent biographer wrote, "This military success had limited impact, for the Trans-Mississippi remained strategically isolated and could not fundamentally affect events east of the great river."[33] Strategic considerations aside, the Confederate Congress passed a laudatory message of congratulation to the veterans of Mansfield and Pleasant Hill in a Joint Resolution on June 10, 1864.[34] The soldiers were also pleased to later learn that as a result of their victories, President Davis promoted Richard Taylor to the rank of lieutenant general on July 18, 1864. Taylor was, at that time, the only Confederate officer promoted to that rank who was not a graduate of West Point.[35]

1. Letter, May 14, 1864, Captain James B. Rounsaville to his family, USAMHI.

2. Johansson, *Peculiar Honor,* "Tables 4 & 5," 105, 109. Casualties for Randal's brigade were divided thirty percent at Mansfield on Apr. 8, 1864, and seventy percent at Pleasant Hill on Apr. 9, 1864.

3. Diary of John T. Stark, Apr. 16, 1864, H. B. Simpson Research Center, Hill College. No Lieutenant Runnels appears in any roster of the 13th Texas. The name could have been an East Texas vernacular corruption of Thomas Rounsaville's; he was severely wounded at Mansfield.

4. Ibid. Initial reports repeated by Capt. Stark in his diary listed two killed, eleven wounded, and forty-six missing.

5. Brooksher, *War Along the Bayous,* 109.

6. Due to the soldiers' fear or mistrust of army surgeons, minor gunshot wounds reported in initial casualty lists later appeared when soldiers were hospitalized with abscesses and infections. Pvt. James M. Rees of Company G, listed among the wounded, was admitted to the hospital in Shreveport Apr. 16, 1864.

7. George B. Layton to Nancy Blewett, Apr. 18, 1864, H. B. Simpson Research Center, Hill College; Diary of John T. Stark, Apr. 16, 1864, H. B. Simpson Research Center; Capt. V. Ellis to Mary Ellis, Apr. 11, 1864, Cutrer, "An Experience in Soldier's Life," 154.

8. Johnson, *Red River Campaign,* 154–55; Brooksher, *War Along the Bayous,* 113; Johansson, *Peculiar Honor,* 106; Diary of John Stark, Apr. 9, 1864, H. B. Simpson Research Center, Hill College.

9. Hamilton P. Bee, "Battle of Pleasant Hill—An Error Corrected," *Southern Historical Society Papers* 8 (April 1880): 184.

10. Colonel W. T. Shaw to Captain J. B. Sample, Asst. Adj. Gen., Apr. 15, 1864, O.R., ser. 1, Vol. 34, pt. 1, 354–357; Johansson, *Peculiar Honor,* 108; Brooksher, *War Along the Bayous,* 111, 113. Union forces available to Banks are estimated at 12,193 and Confederate forces at 12,500.

11. Maj. Gen. R. Taylor to Gen. E. Kirby Smith, Apr. 18, 1864, O.R., ser. 1, 34, pt. 1, 566.

12. Ibid., 567. General Taylor commented, "These orders were well carried out, as many ghastly wounds among the Federals testify."

13. Diary of John T. Stark, Apr. 9, 1864, H. B. Simpson Research Center, Hill College.

14. Ibid.

15. Colonel Shaw to Captain Sample, Apr. 15, 1864, O.R., ser. 1, 34, pt. 1, 354.

16. Col. John Scott to Col. William T. Shaw, Apr. 12, 1864, O.R., ser. 1, 34, pt. 1, 366.

17. Diary of John T. Stark, Apr. 9, 1864, H. B. Simpson Research Center, Hill College.

18. CSR, M323, roll 76, Sgt. Maj. B. C. Crawford; *Galveston Tri-Weekly News,* Apr. 27, 1864.

19. Ibid., roll 77, Ransom P. Hoarde. Private Hoarde of Company G was appointed color bearer Dec. 10, 1863.

20. Colonel Shaw to Captain Sample, O.R., ser. 1, 34, pt. 1, 355.

21. Colonel Scott to Colonel Shaw, Apr. 12, 1864, O.R., ser. 1, 34, pt. 1, 366, 313. The 32nd Iowa suffered nearly fifty percent casualties, having thirty-five killed, 115 wounded, and sixty captured or missing.

22. Blessington, *Campaigns of Walker's Texas Division*, 196.

23. Johansson, *Peculiar Honor,* 108; Diary of John T. Stark, Apr. 9, 1864, H. B. Simpson Research Center, Hill College.

24. CSR, M323, roll 75, James A. Birdwell. He was later exchanged by General Taylor at Blair's Landing on Apr. 20, 1864.

25. Blessington, 197.

26. Capt. Volney Ellis to Mary Ellis, Apr. 11, 1864, Cutrer, "An Experience in Soldiers' Life," 155.

27. Bee, "Battle of Pleasant Hill," 185.

28. Diary of Milton P. Gaines, Apr. 9, 1864, Charles Ham Papers, Anderson County; Brooksher, *War Along the Bayous*, 85. This was Carroll's Mill on Ten Mile Bayou, where Brigadier General Major had harassed Banks' forces on Apr. 7, 1864.

29. Brooksher, *War Along the Bayous*, 135.

30. Diary of John T. Stark, Apr. 9, 1864, H. B. Simpson Research Center, Hill College.

31. U. S. Congress, Joint Committee on the Conduct of the War, *Red River Expedition, Report of the Joint Committee on the Conduct of the War* (1866; reprint, Millwood, NY: Kraus Reprint Co., 1977), 35.

32. Maj. Gen. Richard Taylor to Gen. E. Kirby Smith, Apr. 18, 1864, O.R., ser. 1, 34, pt. 1, 569.

33. Cooper, *Jefferson Davis, American*, 475.

34. Joint Resolution of the Congress of the Confederate States, June 10, 1864, O.R., ser. I, 34, pt. 1, 597.

35. T. Michael Parrish, *Richard Taylor: Soldier Prince of Dixie* (Chapel Hill, NC: University of North Carolina Press, 1992), 405–6.

Chapter 9

A Battle at Jenkins' Ferry

"Now what few citizens are left sit and look on coldly while our army march through and not a single smile to cheer us, or a single kerchief waving good will to us and our cause." —Capt. John T. Stark, Company H[1]

After a few hours' sleep, on the night of April 10, 1864, the Texans moved four miles farther north and camped near a creek. One of the six soldiers listed as missing in action, Pvt. Thomas Cliburne of Company K, rejoined them.[2] That evening word came that Union gunboats and troop transports were steaming up the Red River toward Shreveport. To counter this threat, the division began moving north in the morning. A series of short marches brought it to Shreveport on April 15. The gunboats were having a very difficult time with constant Rebel harassment and low water and had reversed course. A new challenge to Walker's Division appeared: a Union force under Maj. Gen. Frederick Steele forced its way south to occupy Camden, Arkansas.[3] The Federals' original intention had been to join General Banks in Shreveport but this plan had clearly failed. Confederate cavalry commanded by General Sterling Price harassed Steele, but without infantry, Price could not compel Steele to withdraw.[4]

It was inevitable that after two particularly bloody battles some desertions would follow. Before the 13th Texas began the march to

Shreveport on April 12, Aaron and George Fagan, two brothers in Company K, disappeared. When they did not catch up with the unit the next day, their commander, Capt. Charles H. Jones probably wrote a letter to Tyler County Sheriff Lemuel A. Cook. About two weeks later the wayward privates were apprehended hiding at the farm of Phillip Williams, a neighbor of their father. The young soldiers were held in the county jail at Woodville, until called for by the military authorities. Phillip Williams was arraigned in the District Court of Tyler County on May 6, 1864, for harboring "deserters from the Army of the Confederate States of America." District Judge Henry C. Pedigo freed Williams that same day after he posted a $4,000 bond.[5]

At the headquarters of the Trans-Mississippi Department in Shreveport, Anderson Crawford's promotion to colonel was being processed. While the 13th Texas was in winter quarters at Marksville, Lieutenant Colonel Crawford had written General Walker, making it clear that Col. John H. Burnett remained physically incapable of field duty and would not return to the regiment. Crawford requested that in the light of this fact, as well as the Department's approval and transfer of Colonel Burnett to post or garrison duty in Texas, the position of regimental commander should be declared vacant and promotions authorized.[6] To hold the "office of Colonel of this Regiment" was clearly a point of honor to Crawford. In conclusion, he stated, "I do this not only in justice to myself, but also to the faithful & gallant officers, whom I have the honor to command." Brig. Gen. James M. Hawes fully supported Crawford's request and added, "Col. Burnett is a very delicate man, & will probably never be able to do duty in the field. He is wealthy & in no way dependent on his Commission for a support." Generals Walker and Taylor agreed with both Crawford and Hawes, and forwarded the letter to Department headquarters. General Taylor added, "I have no doubt from my Knowledge of Col. Burnett, that he will resign if his health does not permit him to do duty with his Regiment." In referring Crawford's letter to Colonel Burnett for comment, General Kirby Smith's adjutant added, "The assignment to Post duty does not vacate the Regimental Commission."[7] This put Colonel Burnett in the difficult position of terminating his service to the Confederacy as an officer or blocking the promotion of his friend Anderson Crawford.

General Steele's Federal army occupied Camden, Arkansas, after being harassed by Price's cavalry nearly all the way from Arkadelphia. Steele's failure to establish dependable supply lines from Little Rock had left his troops half starved. A large foraging party was sent to gather food and fodder west of Camden. It was quite successful in pillaging the countryside and was about to return to Camden with many wagonloads of provisions when Price's cavalry ambushed it on April 18 at Poison Springs. The action ended with the loss of all of the supplies, as well as over two hundred Union soldiers killed, a large number being from the 1st Kansas Colored Infantry. Another effort to resupply Steele's forces by wagon train from Little Rock reached Camden, but it was ambushed on its return and was nearly destroyed by Confederate forces April 23 near Mark's Mills. These failures, together with news that General Banks was retreating toward Alexandria, left Steele few options other than to withdraw to Little Rock.[8]

This, however, did not convince General Kirby Smith that Shreveport was secure. At Mansfield four days after the victory at Pleasant Hill, Kirby Smith rejected Taylor's proposal that a feint toward Arkansas would convince Steele to retreat. It was Smith's plan to strip Taylor of both Walker and Churchill's infantry and to lead them personally into Arkansas to confront Steele. Following the war, Walker was highly critical of Kirby Smith's decision. Richard Taylor believed Smith was betraying the defenseless people of Louisiana and squandering an opportunity to utterly destroy Banks and his army. This began a feud between the two generals that eventually led to Taylor being relieved of duty.[9]

Walker's Division passed through Shreveport and marched east toward Minden and the military road to Camden, Arkansas. By April 17 it reached the bridge at Bayou Dorcheat on the Minden road and turned north. Before crossing into Arkansas, the units were allowed to camp along Walnut Creek and rest. On April 20, Pvt. Milton P. Gaines boxed up his winter clothing, "one coat, one blanket, and two Linsey shirts," and sent it home to Anderson County with Cpl. David B. Evans, who was released on a delayed furlough.[10] Their first payday in six months was conducted on April 21, 1864. It was then discovered by the privates that their monthly pay had been increased from $11 to slightly over $13. This was during a period when inflation was rampant. Earlier, another Texan, Pvt. James Watson, had written home from east of the great river, "Everything is [priced] out of all reason except Confederate money. It is tolerably low down."[11] For the next two days they were allowed to "lay by" as Capt. John Stark described any pause in the march. Gen. Edmund Kirby Smith had joined the divisions of Churchill and Walker on the twentieth and had taken personal charge of the expedition. To reward the regiments of Walker's Division, General Smith allowed them to blazon "Mansfield" and "Pleasant Hill" on their regimental colors.[12] Resuming the trek north at 6:30 AM on April 24, the division passed into Arkansas at noon.

After news reached Crockett of the two victories at Mansfield and Pleasant Hill, John H. Burnett realized that blocking Crawford's promotion could not be justified. He resigned his commission on April 22, 1864.[13] A few weeks later, Anderson F. Crawford was promoted to colonel of the 13th Texas. This enabled Charles R. Beaty of Jasper to be promoted to lieutenant colonel. Elias T. Seale of Company G was later selected as major of the regiment, leading to the promotion of his brother 1st Lt. William F. Seale to captain of "Crawford's Rebels." Pvt. Henry Ralph of Company G replaced the fallen B. C. Crawford as sergeant major.[14] For the duration of the war, nearly every field and staff position in the regiment would be held by men from Jasper County.[15]

In three days "Walker's greyhounds" marched slightly more than fifty miles, reaching the camp of Brig. Gen. Sterling Price's Confederate cavalry near Woodlawn on April 26.[16] Union forces had been preparing fortifications around Camden, but General Steele was not prepared for the large reinforcements the Southern army had quickly drawn from Louisiana. On April 27 the 13th Texas was within three miles of Camden. Stark commented, "Gen. Steele evacuated that place this morning at daylight, leaving his sick behind."[17] Pvt. R. S. Wilson of the 14th Texas Infantry, Randal's brigade, wrote, "[We] arrived within ten miles of Camden before the Federals knew we had left Shreveport; and some of the Federals we captured contended that we marched one hundred and ten miles in one night."[18] The next day the division marched through Camden at 10:00 AM and received a tumultuous reception from the townspeople. Children crowded schoolroom windows and waved. Men and ladies lined the main street cheering. The 13th Texas marched proudly, in spite of its ragged clothing and dirty bandages. Being cheered as liberators was an altogether new experience. The more mature members of the company may have tempered their feelings with the knowledge there was a very large unbeaten enemy on the road just ahead. After Mansfield and Pleasant Hill, it was widely agreed that retreating armies were every bit as deadly as attacking ones.

After they arrived at the open fields beyond town, a short halt was allowed to cook two days' rations for the anticipated pursuit and attack.[19] The supply trains would be left behind to follow later. In the early afternoon the division crossed the Ouachita River northeast of town on a pontoon bridge as the horses were ferried across in boats. The scene along the road was one of utter devastation. Heaps of blankets, clothing, and food burned or smoldered in piles of ash. Half-burned wagons, bed frames, and looted furniture often blocked the way. In an effort to speed their retreat, the enemy had abandoned everything that slowed their progress. Civilians had picked through some of the unburned supplies and broken open boxes and trunks, scattering the contents in the road. The occasional sack of coffee, flour, or sugar was quickly secured by the soldiers and distributed at rest halts. The march continued until dark when pickets were posted and blankets were thrown down for a few hours of sleep. Commanders met briefly around campfires to discuss plans for the morning.

Orders to march came at 2:00 AM April 29. The soldiers of the 13th Texas scratched, stretched, and made half-audible comments about military leadership in general. Blankets were soon rolled and tied to knapsacks. There were many searches for equipment mislaid in the dark. Sleepless pickets rejoined the unit. A few moments later they filed onto the northbound Princeton road. Roll was quickly called and reported. Moments later the entire division was on the march. At dawn it halted briefly to breakfast on captured Yankee hardtack and beef or salt pork cooked the day before. Other delicacies that found their way from Union supply and commissary wagons into the men's knapsacks at Mansfield were canned herring, lobster, and oysters. At 4:00 PM it passed through Princeton, learning that they were about eight hours behind the enemy column. Again the Texans found that the "citizens hail us as their deliverers from tyranny." Once north of the town, gunfire could be heard in the distance. After marching a total of twenty-two miles, the division bivouacked near the village of Pince.[20]

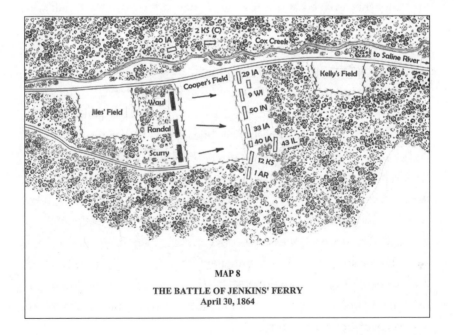

MAP 8

THE BATTLE OF JENKINS' FERRY
April 30, 1864

In the early morning of April 30, Walker's Division was ordered to continue its march toward the ferry landing on the Saline River where the Federals were attempting to cross. Light rain fell from an overcast sky. Kirby Smith had already committed the Confederate troops who arrived first. Churchill's Arkansans and Parsons' Missouri contingent had begun to engage the enemy at 8:00 AM. The Union forces were barricaded behind log emplacements in the woods on the south side of the road. On their right was the barrier of Cox Creek, to the left a flooded swampy area. The only way to approach the enemy was across an open field in a direct frontal assault. A steady rain had been falling, and the field began to turn to mud. Skirmishing between the lines was sporadic for nearly half an hour after Waul's brigade and the 13th Texas arrived at 10:30 AM using the main road from Camden. Randal's and Scurry's brigades were ordered to follow a road to the right of Cooper's field believing that it would allow them to flank the Federals. The road proved to be little more than a bog as the men sank in mud over their ankles.[21] The order to advance was then given, and heavy exchanges of fire became general along the line. The 13th Texas was assigned the extreme left of the line between the ferry road and the muddy banks of Cox Creek. In spite of intense enemy fire, it moved into a position near a bend in the creek commanding a good field of fire.[22] They began to engage the Union troops effectively but were not allowed to continue for long.

Captain Stark reported that Col. Richard B. Hubbard and the 22nd Texas Infantry, in an attempt to flank the enemy on the left, had moved into a position forward of the 13th Texas, which was compelled to cease fire. Hubbard's troops were in an open area and soon took heavy fire from the Union positions. As it fell back into the timber, the 13th Texas was forced back to its original location away from the front line. General Price then moved his division to the left of the line but was halted by the creek and boggy ground. The battle, which had slackened when Walker's troops pulled back, now increased in intensity and Southern casualties mounted. Price's soldiers were slowly withdrawing toward the protection of the timber. Stark commented, "all this time [Steele's army] were engaged in crossing the Saline on a pontoon bridge and burning and destroying part of their train and baggage. It was now 3 o'clock in the P.M. and [we] were wearied men who had nothing to eat since the day before. Besides marching and fighting all day in the rain and mud."[23] Their brigade commander, Brig. Gen. Thomas N. Waul had been wounded, but remained with his soldiers until the units withdrew. Waul later reported to General Walker, "When we consider the heavy marching and exposure of the men to the rain and mud for days preceding the fight, the rapidity of the day's march, and the disadvantage of the position that seemed without remedy, their conduct was worthy of all praise."[24] Slowly, the 13th Texas moved away from the battlefield to find a higher site without the mud and slick clay of the river bottom fields. Here it rested, the companies building fires to dry clothing and dispel the cold chill that follows exertion.

Unlike after earlier battles, there was no feeling of victory or exhilaration. They had marched over five hundred miles and fought three major battles in less than two months. Their casualties at Jenkins' Ferry had been light. The 13th Texas had only eleven wounded and one soldier on guard duty killed, probably by a sharpshooter. Other units in the Confederate force had not been so fortunate. Both of the other brigades in the division had lost their commanders. William R. Scurry and Horace Randal died within two days of the battle. A depressing column of ambulance wagons drawn by mules or oxen passed through the lines evacuating the wounded to a hastily organized field hospital near Tulip, Arkansas. Many would not survive the ten-mile journey.

As shadows grew long, the last of the dead and wounded were removed from the cratered mud and shattered timber of the battlefield. Men in twos and threes moved slowly across the trampled field, returning to their unit's positions and searching for their dead and missing. Union orderlies also searched for their wounded. They had already filled three houses and a stable near the ferry landing as a temporary hospital. On the road to the ferry, hundreds of Southern soldiers were looting the enemy supply wagons and commissaries as they burned, prying open chests and boxes and scattering the contents. As darkness fell, details buried the dead by the light of the burning Union supplies. Across the river, General Steele's crippled army limped slowly northward toward Little Rock. The soldiers of the 13th Texas ate whatever remained of their rations and slept where they were. Lieutenant Colonel Crawford, the adjutant, Captain Pat Henry, and Chaplain Fancher visited each company commander and spoke with the officers and men huddled around the campfires.

TABLE 6
CASUALTIES AT JENKINS' FERRY, APRIL 30, 1864

	Killed	Wounded	Missing	Total
Waul's Brigade (1)				
12th Texas Infantry	8	68	0	76
18th Texas Infantry		(Data Missing)		
22nd Texas Infantry	5	19	0	24
13th Texas Cavalry (2)	1	11	0	12
Totals	14	98	0	112

(1) Alwyn Barr, "Texan Losses in the Red River Campaign, 1864," *Texas Military History* 3 (Summer 1963): 103–10.

(2) Journal of Capt. John T. Stark, Commander, Company H, 13th Texas Cavalry, April 30, 1864. H. B. Simpson Research Center, Hill College, Hillsboro, Texas.

On May 1, 1864, the division left the area of Jenkins' Ferry and marched ten miles to camp near the field hospital at Tulip. It rested there the next day so the lightly wounded could be treated and their wounds cleaned and freshly bandaged. The 13th Texas held a muster formation and pay call. Its supply train had caught up with the division, and hot rations were prepared. At the regimental staff meeting, the commanders learned that the division had been ordered back to Camden, Arkansas, and that they were to move out at first light. They retraced their route through Princeton. After three days and fifty miles, they crossed a pontoon bridge on the Ouachita River, passing through

Camden on May 6, and camped a few miles south of the city. Two days' rest was granted while General Walker waited for orders from department headquarters in Shreveport. A mounted courier soon arrived. General Taylor was determined to intercept Union forces under General Banks before his naval and ground forces could reach the safety of the Mississippi River. Walker's Division was to proceed immediately to Alexandria to rejoin Taylor's army. It left Camden on May 9, 1864.[25]

While camped eight miles outside Camden, Capt. James Rounsaville received word that his brother Thomas, who had been wounded at Mansfield, was growing worse. He got a short leave of absence, and in spite of his own illness, walked back to Minden, Louisiana, intending to catch a stage to Mansfield. There, to his "utter astonishment," he met Dr. Hollis, the regimental surgeon, who told him that Thomas was dead. Their sister, Narcissa, had come from Texas to care for Thomas and had left only a few days before to return home. Learning this, Rounsaville turned and began the long walk back to his unit in Camden. He met his regiment marching south a short time later. A few days later he wrote his family in Crockett, "He was beloved and respected by all who knew him, not only as a soldier and officer but as a man brave and worthy & his loss is lamented by the Regiment more than any man that has fallen . . . I did not have the most distant thought when I left him that he would die nor neither did he for we were in great hopes, but in this we were sadly, sadly disappointed."[26]

Their marches averaged nearly twenty miles a day over rutted muddy roads. For the next ten days their route took them through Mt. Holly and Emerson in Arkansas. Shortly after crossing the Louisiana state line, they went beyond Haynesville on May 1 and quickly passed Homer and Mount Lebanon. At that point, Captain Stark estimated they had marched 652 miles since leaving Camp Rogers in March. On May 14 the regiment was twelve miles east of Grand Ecore on the Red River and about sixty miles southeast of Shreveport. The same day James Rounsaville wrote, "I learn that old Banks has left Alexandria and gone by way of Opelousas, he burnt up Alexandria and all his boats before leaving. Our army is following him, taking a great many prisoners."[27] On the morning of May 20, the 13th Texas arrived at Calhoun's Landing, where it boarded the steamer *New Champion No. 3* for the remainder of the trip to Alexandria.[28]

After miles of bad road, the soldiers found that lounging on the deck of a riverboat watching the changing vistas of the shoreline was a real boost to morale. Officers adjourned to the crowded salon for drinks or conversation. The barroom scene changed continuously as junior officers and company commanders came and went. An old black man played a lively medley of popular and patriotic songs on an upright piano, very much out of tune from the humidity. Later, Colonel Crawford and his staff arrived, a clear sign to junior officers that the salon was suffering from overcrowding. They politely excused themselves and spent the remainder of the trip leaning on the railings of the upper deck enjoying the scenery. The steamer tied up at the east landing above Alexandria Falls shortly after 4:00 PM. The 13th Texas disembarked and marched two miles to a camp near Pineville. The remainder of the division was shuttled south from Calhoun's Landing on May 21–22.[29]

A subtle change was taking place in the early summer of 1864. The soldiers of the 13th Texas privately acknowledged that the battle at Jenkins' Ferry had been a bloody failure in spite of General Kirby Smith's unsupportable assertion that it had been the culmination of a string of victories.[30] Unlike Mansfield and Pleasant Hill, it did not reverse an enemy advance; it only sacrificed lives to hasten a retreat that was already in progress. The men's dedication to the Southern cause was still intense and their loyalty to the unit and their commanders was unshaken. They still felt that they were right. But could even a just cause prevail against the superior numbers and seemingly inexhaustible supplies that the Union commanded? No argument was persuasive enough to get that unspoken thought out of their heads.

If activity was a cure for negative thoughts, they should soon have been cured. The units were moved to nearby Camp Raines for a week. On June 5, 1864, the order came to march east toward Ladoes Ferry, twenty-two miles east of Pineville. After camping near the landing for six days, they were ordered another twenty miles east to Little River. There was no enemy activity, and most of the country was deserted. On June 17 the troops learned that General Walker had been promoted to command the District of Western Louisiana, replacing General Taylor, who had been reassigned by President Davis as commander of the Department of Alabama, Mississippi, and East Louisiana. General Wilburn King temporarily became acting division commander. The soldiers had an abiding trust and respect for Walker, and his loss was a real blow to the division. The 13th Texas spent the next several weeks foraging, camping, and patrolling in an area south along Little River and west toward Black River. In mid-July, it was camped on Holloway's Prairie west of Catahoula Lake.[31] Companies D and E were detached by General King and put aboard the steamer *Frolic* to serve as guards and as deck hands. Pvt. Milton Gaines had just been released from a five day detail near Alexandria where, "[We] help[ed] to gather and hall [*sic*] shucks and shell corn for to make meal. [I] shucked and shelled corn all day and part of the night on Sunday. [On June 21 I was] released from the mill." After four uneventful days steaming as far north as Harrisonburg on the Ouachita River, the Texans spent nearly six days loading and unloading 4,000 bushels of corn for Walker's army. They returned to the 13th Texas near Holloway's Prairie on July 22.[32]

On July 23 the division was ordered toward Trinity to the southeast. The summer had been dry, and Catahoula Lake was now largely a prairie of hard cracked mud. Their route took them along the eastern shore. On July 25 the division camped two miles south of Trinity on the banks of the Black River. After resting on July 26, a march of eleven miles brought it to a small lake on the Black River at Bird Creek, about four miles from Harrisonburg. It was at this camp that the soldiers of the 13th Texas learned of plans to move Walker's and Polignac's divisions across the Mississippi River to form a new command in eastern Louisiana commanded by General Richard Taylor. To many Texans, the idea of abandoning the defense of their own area of operations and moving into defeated country already dominated by the enemy was the last straw. Commanders were unable to prevent the orders from becoming a matter of democratic discussion. Desertions became common in some units, but it is impossible to know if this problem had a serious impact on the 13th Texas, since there are no muster records from that period. An estimate supported by contemporary sources cites two hundred desertions in Waul's brigade by August 24, or what may have been fifty in each of the four regiments.[33] Many commanders were on leave or home recruiting and seeking conscripts at the time the problem arose. Major Robert Gould reported that other than himself, only one major was present in Maclay's (formerly Randal's) brigade.[34]

Another controversy that arose during this period led to the resignation of Capt. Thomas Truett as commander of Company G. Truett had been promoted in March 1863 when Capt. Elias T. Seale resigned due to medical disability. In the summer of 1864 Seale had recovered and petitioned the headquarters of the department to reinstate his commission, which was approved and published in Special Order 181. Truett, who had led the company in all four of its combat engagements, was unwilling to be reduced in rank to serve under Seale and submitted his resignation on July 24, 1864. The officers in the chain of command seem to have been sympathetic to the unfortunate results of Seale's reinstatement, and Truett's resignation was accepted August 12. The incident may be an example of local politics, since Colonel Crawford, Lt. Col. Charles R. Beaty, and Captain Seale were all members of Jasper County's social elite, while Truett originated in that class known in the South as "plain folk."[35]

Capt. John T. Stark does not record the causes or effects of these problems in his journal. He made no entry between July 29 and August 12, 1864. He did record that the unit was "placed in arrest for a raid" on August 13. General King had resumed control of the division by dispersing the units along Black River, where there were enemy patrols. King had received orders from General Walker "to prevent all intercourse with the enemy at Natchez, or elsewhere, for the purpose of trade, or upon any pretext whatever. You will warn persons who are or have been in the habit of visiting places occupied by the enemy, that such visits will be treated as cause of arrest, and the confiscation of any goods that they may introduce within our lines."[36]

Being "placed in arrest" meant that no one left the unit for any reason. All leaves and passes were cancelled. It did not mean officers could not continue their practice of calling on the local gentry. Captain Stark noted they "camped near Mrs. Wade's, recd. invite to come to see her." Private Gaines was evidently not concerned about the possible redeployment across the Mississippi. He made almost daily entries during late July and early August but related only two notable events. On August 8, while "In camp six miles east [of] Harrisburg [*sic*] on the Washatau [*sic*] River. Drilled four hours per day. We did some cannon-ery 136 rounds that night." Other than the artillery practice, Gaines also must have thought the acquisition of a quantity of liquor significant, and on August 22 made the cryptic entry, "Benn Tippens stayed all night with me."[37]

Dissatisfaction flared again when it was revealed that Maj. Gen. John H. Forney had been selected to command Walker's Division. The Texans thought him to be too strict a disciplinarian for their taste. Forney had the good judgment to delay his assumption of command until the news was received that the plan to move the division across the river had been cancelled. He arrived with his staff, most of whom were not Texans, but from his native state of Alabama, and took command on September 3.[38]

On August 26 the division was ordered to Boeuf Prairie. At noon the Texans crossed the Ouachita River at Harrisonburg and continued north. The town had been almost entirely destroyed by the enemy and few homes were still occupied. They were directed to turn east toward the Tensas River on August 27. After resting the next day, the division again turned north toward Monroe. A march of twenty miles brought them to Boeuf Prairie on August 31. That evening a muster formation was conducted and the troops were paid. In addition to pay, the quartermaster issued the men four ounces of hardtack and three-quarters of a pound of flour.[39] Another rest was authorized on September 1, 1864. Moving out on September 2, they crossed Boeuf River and continued northwest toward the Ouachita, which they reached that evening. The next two days the division moved thirty-three miles north along the Ouachita. Marching on the sandy roads was exhausting. Blessington remarked that the men "were physically worn out, and much reduced in flesh." The afternoon of September 4 they camped. A sandy beach provided a much-needed opportunity to bathe and wash clothing.[40] General Forney's assumption of command on September 4 must have been a quiet affair involving only the division headquarters. Captain Stark did not mention any formation or unusual formalities.

The division continued the march toward Monroe. On September 6 the Texans crossed the Ouachita on a pontoon bridge at Trenton and camped four miles from town at Bluff Springs. The site was scenic and signs of the war were few. The division enjoyed the quiet routine of camp life for a week. On Monday everyone was issued twenty rounds of ammunition. Officers conducted a round of inspections with their sergeants. Weapons were satisfactory, but clothing and shoes were marginal at best. There was little chance of getting anything replaced from the depleted regimental supply stores, so the Texans patched and made repairs with rawhide or twine. Salt pork, sugar and syrup, and white flour were now only a memory, replaced by stringy beef and cornmeal. The beef, from Texas longhorn cattle, was said to be so lean that it would not leave a mark inside the barrel it occupied.[41]

The 13th Texas broke camp and was on the march again at 4:30 AM on September 14, 1864. The regiment passed through Monroe and crossed the Ouachita at Trenton, then turned on the road to Bastrop, Louisiana. Captain Stark noted with some disappointment, "the difference is very plain now [from] the first time we were ever in these towns. Then it was all smiles and cheers from the ladies and huzzas from the men. Now what few citizens are left sit and look on coldly while our army march[es] through and not a single smile to cheer us or a single kerchief waving good will to us and our cause."[42] Three years of sacrifice, shortages, and casualties were slowly destroying popular support for the war.

As they approached the Minden road, ill soldiers were loaded on ambulance wagons bound for the hospital at Shreveport. Suffering from fevers, diarrhea, and dysentery, they could no longer keep up with their units. Many would spend a week or ten days in the hospital and then be transferred to the convalescent camp at Greenwood, Louisiana. The division now moved by forced marches between twenty to twenty-five miles a day. Swiftly passing Bastrop and the state line, they reached Berlin and Hamburg, Arkansas, on the September 17. Water was scarce, and the men were compelled to use the farmers' wells, often over strong protests.[43] The dry late summer roads yielded clouds of choking dust, which coated everything and created an illusion of uniformity.

After camping near Lacey on September 19, the division arrived in the suburbs of Monticello the next day. There the Texans joined General Price and the remainder of the Confederate forces in Arkansas. Their commander, General Forney, ordered a division review on the twenty-first in preparation for the arrival of General Magruder, commander of the District of Arkansas. Captain Rounsaville wrote on September 25, "General Forney has taken command of us, though we greatly miss General Walker, he has issued many [new] orders & reiterated old ones in proportion, which has proved obnoxious to some & herculean to perform. The soldiers who left on account or through fears of having to cross the Mississippi River have nearly all returned. A great many of them have been respited & put to duty in their companies, while the remainder is put in the guardhouse."[44] The next three days were spent on work details clearing brush, erecting tents, and turning the forest clearings into a model military camp. The soldiers of the 13th Texas dug their "best clothes" out of the bottoms of their knapsacks and hung them on tent ropes to dispel the odor of mildew. On the morning of September 26, 1864, the entire army began leaving camp at nine o'clock bound for a parade ground north of Monticello.

The inspection of the army was to be the last gathering of the forces of the Trans-Mississippi Department of the war. Divisions from Arkansas, Louisiana, Missouri, and Texas were assembled. The commanders and staff wore their best dress uniforms. Colonel Crawford and the officers of the 13th Texas wore their gold sashes and cavalry sabers, ignoring the fact they were standing in front of an infantry unit. General "Prince John" Magruder, hero of the battles of Galveston and Malvern Hill, and commander of the Department of Arkansas, arrived with an entourage of civilians and ladies in carriages. The formalities included an open ranks inspection, as well as close order drill and a grand pass in review. As General Magruder passed the lines, the massed regimental bands played "Dixie," now considered to be the national anthem of the Confederacy. In his comments, the general praised Forney's Division and suggested it would soon play an important role in his coming struggle to expel General Steele and the Union forces from the state. The units returned to camp that afternoon and resumed their usual routines, unaware of the significance of the day.[45] Pvt. Milton Gaines was evidently not impressed. He noted in his diary that "Old General Magrader" reviewed twenty-five regiments and thirty batteries of artillery that day.[46]

As September drew to a close, the weather turned cooler and rainy. On the morning of September 30, General Price's Missouri Cavalry galloped through camp on its way to what would be a failed campaign in their home state. Much cheering and rebel yelling marked their departure. Forney's Division received orders to prepare to break camp and be ready to march to Camden the morning of October 2. A muster formation of the division had been called the afternoon of October 1 so the troops could witness the execution of Pvt. William M. Patrick of Barnes' Artillery Battery for desertion.[47] Striking the tents the next afternoon, the men sat in the light rain around campfires or dozed under the supply wagons. During periods of idleness nearly everyone in the regiment smoked or chewed tobacco. It was the only commodity the South produced that seemed inexhaustible. The chilly rain continued to fall. Many would have been reminded of the October two years before when they were freezing on the flooded fields of Prairie County.

The next day, the 13th Texas crossed the Saline River and reached the village of Warren at noon. Here, they were reunited with a number of soldiers who had been in the hospital there. Capt. John T. Stark of Company H noted with evident dissatisfaction that one of his soldiers, Pvt. Friend M. Stewart, "under the patronage of Col. Crawford makes his application for discharge without seeking to account for his absence the 3rd of July last where he was dropped from [the] roll." The record indicates that Stewart had been sick in Newton County in December 1862, absent without leave in January and February, and placed on medical leave for sixty days in March and April 1863. Stark evidently believed he was a slacker or possible deserter, but Dr. Hollis did not hesitate to recommend his disability discharge, diagnosing him with tuberculosis.[48] In the light of his first name, it is possible that the prejudice was due to the fact he was a Quaker.

Blessington described the journey to Camden. "The roads were miserably bad, owing to the incessant rains. Our wagons did not arrive until midnight. The country we traveled through was remarkably fertile, but the most of the farms were lying waste, without fences; while briars, and weeds, and young saplings encumbered the rich soil, in place of the golden grain, and rich harvests of corn. In addition to want, there was deep mourning in every house we passed, for dear ones who had bravely laid down their lives in the cause they believed was just."[49] The roads were virtually deserted, and the fog of early morning dripped from overhanging trees into the tunnel-like roadway below. The sun broke through the dark overcast skies on October 5, one day out of Camden.

Arriving four miles east of Camden on October 6, Forney's Division was assigned the duty of preparing fortifications along the waterfront. The 13th Texas moved to a new camp the next day, crossing the Ouachita River at Lone Pine Ferry and moving to within a half mile of town. On Sunday, October 9, Captain Jones of Company K returned from Tyler County with a few recruits and his two deserters. Pvt. Milton Gaines reported that there was a light frost that night. Wednesday the work details from the 8th (12th) Texas and the 13th Texas began on the fortifications on a bend in the Ouachita River about one half mile from town. A fight between two drummers that ended in a fatal stabbing shocked Col. Thomas R. Bonner's 18th Texas Infantry on Thursday. The evening of Sunday, October 16 the men were mustered to observe the execution by firing squad of Capt. John Guynes, formerly commander of Company F, 22nd Texas Infantry. He had been convicted by a court-martial of encouraging his men to desert when the order was received to cross the Mississippi.[50]

It was in this environment that Aaron and George Fagan returned to their unit after five months in the Woodville jail. Captain Jones got them back to Camden just in time to witness an execution. No records exist of any trial, and it is likely that General Waul or Colonel Crawford allowed them to quietly return to duty. Pvt. Aaron Fagan was later transferred to the pioneer corps for the duration of the war.[51] Pvt. George Fagan returned to duty in Company K. It is probable that the administrators of military justice had made their point with the unfortunate Captain Guynes, and that the command did not feel that further extreme punishments were necessary.

The 13th Texas spent a third winter in Confederate service. The Union threat to Arkansas that had caused it to be recalled to that state for a third time did not materialize. After completing the fortifications on the Ouachita River, the division settled into a routine of drill and a tour of picket duty on the road to Monticello, twelve miles from Camden. Blessington commented, "for what purpose I am unable to say, as there was no enemy nearer than Pine Bluff, some eighty miles distant."[52] In mid-November, as the weather and the condition of the roads began to deteriorate, the division was ordered south to winter in a more strategically central location in northern Louisiana.

In the east, a great final conflict was being acted out near Nashville, Tennessee. Gen. John Bell Hood's Army of Tennessee was destroyed by

Chapter 9

Union attacks on December 15–16, 1864. By early January, Hood had retreated into northern Mississippi and was relieved of command. Many
of Hood's veterans joined Gen. Joseph E. Johnston's army in North
Carolina to oppose Sherman's forces. Maj. Gen. Nathan Bedford Forrest's cavalry corps still defended northern Alabama and Mississippi
and a small army guarded the city of Mobile, Alabama. Lee's army, entrenched at Petersburg, Virginia, was besieged and was later in danger
of being encircled by Grant's forces. In the spring of 1865, the scattered
and often isolated Confederate forces would find an effective defense
against Federal forces impossible.

1. Diary of John T. Stark, September 14, 1864, H. B. Simpson Research Center, Hill
College, Hillsboro, TX.

2. CSR, M323, rolls 75-79. Pvt. Thomas Cliburne died in Woodville, Tyler County,
Texas, May 13, 1924. James A. Birdwell was exchanged Apr. 20, 1864, at Blair's Landing,
Louisiana. Of Privates Edward Tyler of Company C, L. C. Jordan of Company H, and Joe
Fortner and C. S. McGee of Company K there exists no later record.

3. Edwin C. Bearss, *Steele's Retreat from Camden and the Battle of Jenkins' Ferry* (Little
Rock, AR: Arkansas Civil War Centennial Commission, 1967), 1–4. Steele's forces entered
Camden Apr. 15, 1864.

4. Blessington, *Campaigns of Walker's Texas Division*, 241–48.

5. "Minutes of the District Court," MS, Volume D, Criminal Docket No. 597, [1852-
1872], 190; Hewett, *Texas Confederate Soldiers*, 1: 433. Charges against Phillip Williams
were not dropped until November 1865, six months after the end of the war. Aaron and
George Fagan were arrested along with Jacob Rainey. This may have been Pvt. J. G. Raney
of the 16th Texas Cavalry (dismounted) of Scurry's brigade.

6. Lt. Col. Anderson Floyd Crawford to Maj. Gen. John G. Walker, Jan. 18, 1864, CSR,
M323, roll 76, Anderson F. Crawford, personal papers.

7. Ibid.

8. O.R., ser. 1, 34, pt. 1, 819–20; Johnson, *Red River Campaign*, 174; Johansson, *Peculiar
Honor*, 115; Bearss, *Steele's Retreat from Camden*, 36–7, 78–9.

9. Taylor, *Destruction and Reconstruction*, 356; Parrish, *Richard Taylor: Soldier Prince of
Dixie*, 402–4.

10. Diary of Milton P. Gaines, Apr. 20, 1864, Charles Ham Papers, Anderson County.

11. Judy Watson McClure, *Confederate from East Texas: The Civil War Letters of James
Monroe Watson* (Quanah, TX: Nortex Press, 1976), 23.

12. Johansson, *Peculiar Honor*, 114.

13. CSR, M323, roll 75, John H. Burnett, abstract from a register "containing Rosters of

Commissioned Officers, Provisional Army Confederate States."

14. Carson, *Desk of Henry Ralph*, 90.

15. CSR, M323, rolls 75–79, Anderson F. Crawford, Charles R. Beaty, Elias T. Seale, and William F. Seale.

16. Bearss, *Steele's Retreat from Camden*, 9. Woodlawn was fourteen miles southwest of Camden.

17. Diary of John T. Stark, Apr. 27, 1864, H. B. Simpson Research Center, Hill College.

18. R. S. Wilson, "Jenkins' Ferry," *Confederate Veteran* 18 (1910): 486.

19. Diary of Milton P. Gaines, Apr. 27, 1864, Charles Ham Papers, Anderson County.

20. Diary of John T. Stark, Apr. 29, 1864, H. B. Simpson Research Center, Hill College.

21. Bearss, *Steele's Retreat from Camden*, 148-9.

22. It is not clear from primary sources whether the 13th Texas was engaging the main Federal force or attacking the 40th Iowa and 2nd Kansas (Colored) which were on the opposite bank of the creek firing into the Confederate left flank. The latter seems more likely.

23. Diary of John T. Stark, Apr. 30, 1864, H. B. Simpson Research Center, Hill College.

24. Brig. Gen. Thomas N. Waul to Maj. Gen. John G. Walker, May 23, 1864, O.R., ser. 1, 34, pt. 1, 818.

25. Blessington, *Campaigns of Walker's Texas Division*, 260-63.

26. Capt. James B. Rounsaville to his family, ca. May 13, 1864, Papers of James B. Rounsaville, USAMHI.

27. Ibid.

28. Diary of John T. Stark, Apr. 20, 1864, H. B. Simpson Research Center, Hill College.

29. Brooksher, *War Along the Bayous*, 224. The last of the Union invasion force left Simmesport and reached the safety of the Mississippi River on May 21, 1864.

30. Parrish, *Richard Taylor: Soldier Prince of Dixie*, 403.

31. Blessington, *Campaigns of Walker's Texas Division*, 271–72.

32. Diary of Milton P. Gaines, Jun. 16–Jul. 22, 1864, Charles Ham Papers, Anderson County.

33. Johansson, *Peculiar Honor*, 129–30; Capt. James B. Rounsaville to Mattie Bond, Sep. 25, 1864, James B. Rounsaville Papers, USAMHI. Captain Rounsaville states, "The soldiers who left on account or through fears of having to cross the Mississippi River have nearly all returned."

34. Johansson, 129.

35. CSR, M323-80, Truett, Thomas F.

36. Blessington, *Campaigns of Walker's Texas Division*, 272.

37. Diary of Milton P. Gaines, Jul. 22–Aug. 22, 1864, Charles Ham Papers, Anderson County.

38. Blessington, 276.

39. Ibid., 275.

40. Ibid., 276.

41. Ibid., 277; Diary of Milton P. Gaines, Aug. 27–Sep. 7, 1864, Charles Ham Papers, Anderson County.

42. Diary of John T. Stark, Sep. 14, 1864, H. B. Simpson Research Center, Hill College.

43. Ibid., Sep. 17, 1864.

44. James B. Rounsaville to his niece Mattie Bond, Sep. 25, 1864, Papers of James B. Rounsaville, USAMHI.

45. Blessington, *Campaigns of Walker's Texas Division*, 277–78; Diary of John T. Stark, Sep. 26, 1864, H. B. Simpson Research Center, Hill College.

46. Diary of Milton P. Gaines, Sep. 26, 1864, Charles Ham Papers, Anderson County.

47. Ibid., Oct. 1, 1864.

48. Diary of John T. Stark, Oct. 3, 1864, H. B. Simpson Research Center, Hill College; CSR, M323, roll 79, Friend M. Stewart, muster records and personal papers. Captain Stark was not present at the time of Stewart's unexplained absence, having departed for thirty days' leave on Jun. 19, 1864.

49. Blessington, *Campaigns of Walker's Texas Division*, 279.

50. Ibid., 279–80; Diary of Milton P. Gaines, Oct. 9–15, 1864, Charles Ham Papers, Anderson County.

51. CSR, M323, roll 76, Aaron Fagan. The muster of Apr. 1865 indicates Private Fagan had been transferred to the Pioneer Corps on Nov. 1, 1864.

52. Blessington, *Campaigns of Walker's Texas Division*, 280.

Chapter 10

Home With Their Shields

"I would like . . . to see if you have improved much on
Master Jeff's diet or not. As for myself I fatten every day.
If the war lasts much longer I shall apply to Mas' Jeff
for transportation as I am getting almost too corpulent
to march afoot."[1]
—Sgt. Maj. Henry Ralph, 13th Texas Cavalry

Camden's fortifications were completed toward the end of the
week of November 7, 1864. The weather was beginning to turn cool
and wet, and moving to winter quarters was on everyone's mind. After
brigade chapel services on Sunday, November 13, the division began
to pack up. The initial goal was Camp Sumter, near Lewisville, Arkansas. On Monday, they marched south to camp near Mount Holly, as
heavy rains began to turn the usually poor roads to ankle deep mud.
For the next four days, rain and mud slowed the column to a crawl. The
supply wagons fell farther and farther behind. Pvt. Milton Gaines recorded, "We waded in water from shoe mouth to waist deep [until we]
got three miles west of Lewisville." When the division reached Camp
Sumter early Friday afternoon, the weather cleared and the rain was
replaced by a cold north wind. The tents were stranded somewhere
with the quartermaster wagons so the Texans camped in the open and
enjoyed good fires on Saturday and Sunday. The regiment left Lewis-

ville, Arkansas, on November 21 for Minden, Louisiana. Private Gaines wrote, "The ground was frozen wading the little Bodeau Creek [Bayou Bodcau] two hundred and three yards knee deep. . . . Crossed the large Bodeau 1 1/2 miles wide the bottom ground frozen."[2]

For the next seven days the division moved south along the military road to Minden. For much of the time it was overcast with a cold north wind, but there was no more rain. The weather cleared on November 27. Reaching the outskirts of Minden the next day, a temporary camp was set up until a more permanent site could be located in the pinewoods west of town. That night Gaines was detailed to guard "some board piles in the woods 400 yards from camp," probably to prevent their use as a convenient supply of fuel. Pvt. Peyton Raglin of Company K wrote his wife, Martha, in Tyler County on Sunday, December 4, 1864. "They give us leave to cut timber for cabins so we may figure on being here a good spell." Private Gaines described the area as "four miles south of [the] Minden and Shreveport road." The 13th Texas quickly took advantage of this opportunity and built about twenty cabins fourteen by sixteen feet in size. Private Gaines wrote, "built log cabin with chimney in order, in line." Men skilled in building "mudcat" chimneys worked quickly as those less skilled scouted for flat hearth rocks and hauled red clay. Double bunk frames were made from white oak poles and lashed together. Soldiers too weak to chop and haul timber split shingles and stripped poles for the roofs. Blessington reported "many of the troops were careless in building their cabins, owing to the fact that there was no certainty of our remaining any definite period of time; but the cold weather now set in, which left them no alternative but to get into their cabins as soon as possible."[3]

The site was christened "Camp Magruder" after their recent commander in Arkansas. Blessington described it as "situated to the right of the military road leading from Shreveport to Camden, in the midst of a pine ridge. On the south-west was a deserted field, well adapted to the exercise of drilling." It was fortunate that the East Texans were experienced cabin builders, because "on the morning of the eighth, it commenced to sleet; during the night it commenced to freeze, and the next morning the ice was fully two inches thick."[4] Those who did not take the project seriously must have spent an uncomfortable night. Those who did would have felt they were "sittin' in high cotton," as the old Southern phrase went.

On December 12 the units were paid two months' wages in old issue currency, which was soon virtually worthless. The division paymaster, Maj. H. W. Williams, encouraged the men to invest in twenty-year Confederate government bonds paying eight percent interest rather than taking the cash. There is no record of the number of soldiers who expressed this degree of confidence in the Confederate States' longevity. Most of the married men sent their pay home. The others played cards or wagered their money away on practically anything having a dubious outcome. Perhaps to counter the excesses inspired by the government's generosity in distributing extra rations of tobacco, coffee, and devalued currency, Gen. Edmund Kirby Smith ordered that December 16 was "A day set apart to fast and pray."[5]

The routine of camp life was very agreeable to the soldiers of the 13th Texas after the many months of hardship that had preceded it. Some men were granted thirty days' leave and arrived back in East Texas in time for Christmas. A few old books and newspapers made the rounds of the literate. Blessington recalled, "With abundant material for the purpose, they soon manufactured tables, shelves, and benches." The various units competed for recognition for the best and cleanest quarters. The usual work details associated with camp life went on but did not occupy so much time or energy that anyone was inclined to complain about them. Cold evenings were spent around fireplaces filled with the snap of burning pine. Some read aloud and others told the long drowsy stories that belong only to times of unhurried reflection. They were good, peaceful weeks, and could only have been improved by spending them at home with one's own family. Maj. Gen. John Forney, the division commander, broke the camp's sleepy monotony on the afternoon of Saturday, January 7, 1865. He ordered the staging of a "sham battle" with blank cartridges for the benefit of some visiting local ladies and dignitaries. Private Gaines of Company D noted, "The artillery fired one round each [of] forty-two cannons." There was a good turnout, and afterward, the troops were "strongly convinced that it was easier to participate in a hundred 'sham battles' than one sure-enough battle."

Drill remained a prominent part of the training schedule; it was conducted at the division level at a field four miles from the camp. Some units had mascots of sorts during the period. Pvt. Peyton Raglin of Company K wrote to his wife, "[Lieutenant] Perry Nicks . . . has the ugliest cur dog you ever seen it followed us all the way from Camden and has spots." The variety of the soldiers' rations was considerably expanded that month. Private Gaines recalled that on January 11–12, in addition to white flour and bacon, "It was the first time that coffee and tobacco was ever issued to us."[6]

Another occasion to show off the division came on January 17, 1865, when Gen. Kirby Smith, commander of the Trans-Mississippi Department, visited them. Maj. Gen. Simon Bolivar Buckner, described by Blessington as "the hero of Fort Donelson," and commander of the District of Louisiana, accompanied him, along with a large following of civilians. The "grand review" included three hours of drill directed by Generals Buckner and Forney which proved "highly gratifying to the ladies who had come from all parts of the country." Milton Gaines wrote, "Ladies, children, and negroes out to see and hear the drums, fife and brass bands." It was considerably less gratifying to the soldiers, who returned to their quarters late and very tired. Soon the aroma of fresh biscuits, coffee, and bacon from the kitchens dispelled their weariness. Fires lit the half open doors of the cabins, and the card players resumed their places around the rough pine tables outside. Blessington commented, "The utmost contentment and good feeling prevailed among the men, and all seemed determined to enjoy the days of the winter months."[7]

Sooner or later, such idyllic times must end. In the case of the 13th Texas and Forney's Division it proved to be sooner. They left Camp

Magruder on the morning of January 26, 1865, bound for Shreveport. No sooner did they get out of sight of the comfortable cabins than a drenching rain began to fall. It continued the next day, but stopped briefly on the morning of January 27 after they crossed the Red River at Shreveport on a pontoon bridge and moved to a campsite one mile east of the city. The site was not particularly well situated; wood and water had to be hauled by hand from half a mile away. All the work details were completed, and at 4:00 PM, a major cold front began to pass. The initial thunderstorms had high wind and hail. High winds and rain continued through the night. The morning light revealed only two tents still standing out of the entire division. The soldiers sat around the saturated coals of extinguished fires, wrapped in wet blankets. Equipment was scattered everywhere. When it was clear that no breakfast was forthcoming, the soldiers began to organize the wreckage. Drizzle kept falling until late afternoon, when the wind shifted to the north and the cold set in. Men stood around campfires drying clothes and blankets. Many would have questioned the wisdom of leaving Camp Magruder.[8]

The next day, January 30, 1865, an incident occurred that makes it clear why many Texas troops despised General Forney. A division review was ordered at a drill field some five miles from camp. As usual, a number of soldiers were sick or too weak with fevers and other ailments to keep up with the formations. Forney ordered his "body guard," a company of cavalry, to collect all these unfortunates and force them to march in front of their horses. As the healthy part of the division performed the review, the stragglers were compelled to march around the perimeter of the field in a ragged formation pressed by the mounted troops. Blessington complained, "This treatment of the sick was loudly denounced by both officers and men." 1st Lt. Bruno Durst of Leon County, Company A, saw the practice in a totally different light, writing that General Forney, "Has a Squadron [of] Cavalry to follow the Division during drill, whose duty is to pick up the drags and those who step momentarily aside to attend to the calls of nature. These are collected and made to walk a ring while the drill goes on. But the boys take it all in fun."[9]

Milton Gaines of Company D was granted thirty days' leave at the end of January. Lt. Bruno Durst wrote that the timing was unfortunate since, "Floods of rain pour upon us almost continually, while streams are filled to the highest mark. So much so that it is virtually impossible to travel." Gaines borrowed a pony and set out for Anderson County and his wife and home he had not seen in nearly seventeen months. The rain was almost constant and at one point, the horse lost its footing fording Boats Creek and was swept along by the current and emerged swimming on the same eastern bank it had left earlier. Gaines and the pony spent the remainder of the afternoon warming up and getting dried off. Fording the Neches River was equally challenging, and for a second time it was impossible to tell if the horse was in contact with the bottom. After spending a few days at home, Gaines returned the pony to its owner's family and rode back to the regiment on his mule. In an exchange that was probably ongoing, the mule was loaned to another furloughed soldier and sent back to Anderson County with a parcel of letters.[10]

It began raining again on the morning of January 31, and camp was moved to an area with adequate wood and water. The men kept to their tents as much as possible. The rain varied in intensity, but it did not clear until the morning of February 6. The division relocated again the next day to an area nearer a drill field. Guards were posted, drill practice took place each morning, clean up and work details filled the afternoon, and "dress parade" or evening formation took place before supper. Their location near Shreveport led to a very different sort of camp life than that to which they were accustomed. Many ladies visited camp and were duly escorted through the area by regimental and company officers. The division brass band played on various occasions during the day, adding a festive and holiday atmosphere. At evening formation on Tuesday, February 14, it was announced that the ladies of Shreveport, as well as those of Caddo and Bossier Parishes and Harrison County, Texas, would host a grand review and barbecue for Forney's Division on Saturday. Many soldiers trimmed hair and beards and did their best to present a slightly less piratical appearance. Some even delayed departing on leave because of the promised festivities. Regimental Sgt. Maj. Henry Ralph wrote a friend serving at Marshall, Texas, "I have a furlough for sixty days & start home maybe tomorrow & maybe I will remain until after the festival & start next Sunday."[11]

Saturday, February 18, 1865, dawned as clear and pleasant as anyone could have hoped. The division formed two opposing battle lines on the parade field about 10:00 AM. Hundreds of spectators were on hand. The commanders of the two battle lines were to be General Kirby Smith and General Magruder. After reviewing their troops, the generals gave the orders to the brigade commanders for the conduct of the sham battle. The regiments executed their attacks, complete with simulated artillery fire. The smoke, deafening noise, and bloodthirsty yells were too much for some of the onlookers, who wept or fainted, thinking perhaps of loved ones fighting in the east or those already lost. Following the mock battle, the division honored the 130 survivors of the 3rd Louisiana Infantry Regiment, whose heroism and sacrifice had been demonstrated on both sides of the Mississippi. After three cheers and the presentation of arms, each soldier in the division was issued a jigger of whiskey, filed off the field, and stacked arms.

Lt. Bruno Durst wrote that sixteen tables, each seventy feet long, were spread with "all the substantials, necessary to make us relish our grub for instance, 140 hogs, light bread and potatoes to match, mutton, turkeys, chickens, cake, pie, etc. and etc."[12] The good ladies of Shreveport, prepared to urge the soldiers to help themselves following a grace which remained forever unspoken, were likely much in awe at the speed with which vast platters of food were reduced to bones and rinds. Pies neatly cut often proved in practice to be a single portion. If the gentle ladies directed their attention to some other table, sweet potatoes and biscuits stuffed with pork soon disappeared into ammunition pouches and trouser pockets. Following this feast, the troops walked to the area surrounding the speakers' podium. The speeches were a tribute from the people and army of Louisiana to the courage and dedication of their Texas brothers. As evening progressed and the division bands played in the distance, the soldiers returned to their tents in small groups, dazed by the unaccustomed quantity and variety of food.

Later, Lt. Bruno Durst related,

> At night a party was given by Waterhouse's Brigade on board the capacious steamboat *La Fourche*. I went down in company with Captain [Riley J.] Blair and Dr. [Thomas H.] Hollis by invitation from one of the committees. Found, however, when we arrived that it was rather an aristocratic affair given especially to Generals Smith, Forney, MaGruder, Fagan, Boggs and Staffs, and [we] were expected to pay $30 per head in order that we might have the privilege of standing in the corners and look on, while the Chiefs' retinues danced. When we learned this much, we asked to be excused—and they, fool-like I suppose, excused us. So we (smiled) and at once set out for our quarters. There ended the great Fete given in honor to the boys for their bravery displayed at Mansfield and Pleasant Hill.[13]

The division stayed at the Shreveport camp until the morning of February 21. Before leaving Shreveport, the officers of the 13th Texas said goodbye to Capt. John T. Stark of Company H. Stark had been ill since the previous October and was finally compelled to resign his commission on February 25, 1865. Lt. Thomas J. Brack took command and served as the Newton County boys' third and final commander. The march that day was only ten miles to a site that had been selected near Bayou Pierre on the old Mansfield Road. Four Texas Cavalry Regiments were "dismounted" there as the 13th Texas had been, and a fourth brigade was added to the division. Col. Charles DeMorse's 29th Texas Cavalry was added to Waul's Brigade.[14] It was now even more difficult to find corn and fodder for so many horses. The division rested at this camp through Sunday, March 5. Lt. Bruno Durst wrote, "We are living tolerably well at this time—get flour, some bacon, pickled beef, and molasses as well as sugar sometimes."[15]

In an earlier address, General Buckner had warned the troops "against indulging in unreasonable expectations of peace." It was their duty to "prepare for a prolonged struggle to rescue the independence to which we are so clearly entitled." The soldiers of the 13th Texas sensed a change in the air more profound than the signs of spring in the woods of Louisiana. Sgt. Maj. Henry Ralph had written a few weeks earlier, "There is a great deal of talk of peace here among the soldiers. Many think it will be soon, and God grant it may be but I can see no prospect whereas to ground my hopes of it being soon." On February 25, Lt. Bruno Durst added, "The peace prospects, once so flourishing, have again expired. Nothing remains but grim visages of war, with all its grim forebodings."[16]

It was Sunday evening, March 5, 1865, in the regimental officers mess when Col. Anderson Crawford indicated that he wanted to propose a toast. While this was not an unusual event following their frugal meals, the excellent bourbon that passed around the table certainly was. The normal fare would have been a bottle of "old commissary," a distillation whose age was reckoned in weeks rather than years. When the drinks had been poured, Crawford stood and raised his glass. The commanders and staff stood as well. Crawford said he had been advised by General Forney, who had received orders from Gen. Kirby Smith that the division would depart in the morning for Texas. The glasses were barely empty when the cheering and backslapping began. Many a "thank God" would have been spoken. Lt. Col. Charles R. Beaty added that their destination would be Camp Groce, near Hempstead, Texas.

Commanders returned to their company areas and gave the good news to the lieutenants and first sergeants. They quickly spread the word to the soldiers, many of whom had not been home in three years. Excited conversations would have been heard as they prepared to march at first light. After lining up on the road in the morning, they were ordered to face about, and they marched ten miles north toward Shreveport. This confusion was cleared up that evening, and on March 7, they turned southward and traveled eleven miles in a driving rainstorm. When the men reached Mansfield on the eighth, the people turned out to cheer as they passed through. On the eleventh the division camped at Carroll's Mill, where it had rested after the battle of Pleasant Hill. Milton Gaines wrote, "Some of the boys went down to the Pleasant Hill battle ground and got some of the bones of the dead fallen brave soldiers."[17]

As they continued south through the pine forests, the rain ended on the March 13 when a very cold norther blew through. Reaching Keatchie the next day, the regiment was greeted enthusiastically, "every door, window, and house roof was crowded with eager spectators." Blessington recorded fifty-three miles and several days of travel between Mansfield and Keatchie. This was probably due to initial plans to cross the Sabine River farther south, but finding it too high, the Texans were forced to return upriver. Lieutenant Durst of Company A had written a few weeks earlier that rain and high water, "is indeed a poor excuse with our Division Commander."[18]

On Wednesday, March 15, 1865, Forney's Division crossed the state line into Texas in northern Panola County. Reaching Grand Bluff the next day the division found the Sabine River nearly fifty yards wide, running six or seven feet deep. The next day, by pulling the ferry "very rapidly" they were able to cross safely. As the leading element of the division, Waul's Brigade, including the 13th Texas, had quite foolishly crossed the Sabine River at night on March 14.[19] Continuing three more miles, they camped somewhere north of Carthage. Soldiers too ill to stay with the unit were sent on to the hospital in Rusk, where seven were admitted on March 19. Camp was moved two miles to a clear stream lined with cottonwood trees on March 18. The area was very rich in game, and the troops were allowed to hunt. That evening and the next day the menu probably included venison and pork and various game birds. The next few weeks were also times for reunions, as relatives and friends learned that the soldiers had returned. Pvt. Milton Gaines wrote that his wife "Mary came to see me near Cannon's Bridge on the Neches River."[20]

Monday, March 20 found the division passing through a country of clear running streams and old, open forests. Traveling to the southwest, the troops reached Rusk on March 25, and camped two miles from Crockett three days later. Here the 13th Texas had entered Confederate service just over three years before. Private Gaines noted that the actual dismounting of the 29th Texas Cavalry took place at Crockett. There were evidently concerns about mass desertions, and Gaines wrote, "I had been on guard twenty-four hours put on again at night in heavy rain. Thundered and lightening to guard the dismounted cavalry in mud and water."[21]

The regiment stayed there until the morning of April 2. General Forney ordered company drill twice a day. The troops probably considered this inappropriate given their location, and downright silly, given the military situation. The companies dutifully fell in their formations in the surrounding pastures. As commands were given, some wit responded, in cadence with the movements and in a proper parade ground bellow, "Beef, beef, and no drill!" This infectious, if insubordinate, chant spread throughout the division in a matter of minutes. In no time the division headquarters informed the regimental commanders that anyone hollering for beef should be summarily arrested. This ended the chanting but certainly not the attitudes that spawned it.[22]

Beginning their journey again on April 2, the Texans reached the Trinity bottoms that evening, and crossed the river the next day. For the next few days the division moved about twelve to fifteen miles a day through the farmlands of Madison and northern Grimes County. At noon on April 8, 1865, they arrived at the notable resort of Piedmont Springs in north central Grimes County. They made camp near the stream fed by the three sulphur springs that had caused it to become a famous health resort visited by such guests as Sam Houston and General Beauregard. The housing provided for the numerous wealthy

---

patrons of the spot was a turreted one hundred-room hotel with wide verandas, a ballroom, and a fieldstone façade.[23]

Here, the division made arrangements with the proprietor, Mr. Leander Cannon, to leave the soldiers who were too ill to travel. Orderlies were detailed to see to the men's needs. Eleven men were fortunate enough to be checked in to what was probably the Confederacy's most elegant hospital. They were noted on the 13th Texas' final regimental muster of April 31, 1865, as being at Piedmont Springs since April 10.[24] The companies said farewell to the soldiers before they left for Hempstead on April 13. The division arrived at Camp Groce, two and a half miles from Hempstead, on Saturday, April 15, 1865. Blessington recalled that there were many visitors to welcome the soldiers back home. There were also profoundly disturbing reports from the east that Gen. Robert E. Lee and the other major commanders had surrendered. The government at Richmond had been captured, or had fled the country. A hundred conflicting rumors circulated. The soldiers sensibly ignored most of the greater exaggerations and continued to serve and perform their duties in the usual manner. They were a very large undefeated army, and as yet there were no enemy troops in Texas. Because of the absence of many of the senior officers on leave, Col. Anderson Crawford was General Waul's acting brigade commander. Lt. Col. Charles R. Beaty was listed as sick in quarters, leaving the acting command of the 13th Texas to Maj. Elias T. Seale. Cpl. Solomon Wishard of Company I, Orange County, served as the last regimental color bearer.[25]

Generals Magruder, Smith, and Forney addressed the troops over the next few weeks. The courage to defend their homes was all that was needed. Texas would provide the rest. The harvest had been good, the natural resources were inexhaustible, and the defeated troops east of the river would flock to their banner. Unlike the Mississippi, no river in Texas was navigable for the Union gunboats. Magruder said, "The enemy threatens our coast, and will bring his great, undivided resources for a successful invasion of the State. Let him be met with unanimity and Spartan courage, and he will be unsuccessful, as he has been in

Texas." General Forney, the division commander, directed his remarks at those who were wavering. "Should the enemy invade this country in large force, you surely cannot believe that your generals would be guilty of the madness of sacrificing your lives, without a strong probability of success." In a letter from his headquarters at Shreveport, General Smith was perhaps the most openly emotional. "With you rest the hopes of our nation, and upon your action depends the fate of our people. I appeal to you in the name of the cause you have so heroically maintained—in the name of your firesides and families, so dear to you—in the name of your bleeding country, whose fate is in your hands. Show that you are worthy of your position in history. Prove to the world that your hearts have not failed in the hour of disaster, and that, at the last moment, you will sustain the holy cause which has been so gloriously battled for by your brethren east of the Mississippi River."[26]

At a brigade drill on April 24, the announcement was made that President Abraham Lincoln had been killed. Division drill also continued and on April 29, Private Gaines recalled, "Division drill[,] run[ning] through the mud and water half leg deep. Colonel [George Washington] Carter made a speech to fight and a swarm of bees settled near his head."[27] It can be assumed that Carter's comments were brief.

Many of the men were granted leave in late April. At the time the regiment's last adjutant, Lt. Ernest G. Geisendorff, prepared the April 1865 muster, the 13th Texas had only 225 soldiers left on the rolls. Of this number, 179 were listed as on leave, on detached service, sick in hospitals in Camden, Rusk, Keatchie, Shreveport, Piedmont Springs, and Crockett, or absent without leave. Only forty-six soldiers were actually present for duty.[28]

Shortly after May 1, it became clear that Gen. Edmund Kirby Smith was negotiating the surrender of the Trans-Mississippi Department. This caused confusion and divisions in the camp that could not be cured. On May 19, 1865, the remainder of the troops left Hempstead. Each company was allowed one wagon for its baggage and supplies. Milton Gaines wrote his final entry on May 25, "Got home, I was out three years three months and three days in all." The majority of the East Texans would have been home by the end of May. There was still time to clear fields, build fences, and put in a crop. On May 26, 1865, Gen. Kirby Smith's chief of staff signed the terms of surrender. The Confederate Army of the Trans-Mississippi and the 13th Texas Cavalry ceased to exist when Generals Kirby Smith and Magruder signed the formal surrender aboard the Union ship *Fort Jackson* at Galveston on June 2, 1865.

1. Carson, *Desk of Henry Ralph,* 116–17, Sgt. Maj. Henry Ralph to Private G. P. May, February 15, 1865.

2. Diary of Milton P. Gaines, Nov. 18, 21, 22, 1864, Charles Ham Papers, Anderson County; Blessington, *Campaigns of Walker's Texas Division,* 280–81.

3. Blessington, *Campaigns of Walker's Texas Division,* 281; Diary of Milton P. Gaines, Nov. 29, Dec. 2, 1864, Charles Ham Papers, Anderson County; Pvt. Peyton Raglin to Martha Raglin, Dec. 4, 1864, Manie Blewett Pipkin Library, Woodville, Texas.

4. Blessington, *Campaigns of Walker's Texas Division,* 281.

5. Diary of Milton P. Gaines, Dec. 16, 1864.

6. Blessington, *Campaigns of Walker's Texas* Division, 285; Diary of Milton P. Gaines, Jan. 7–12, 1865, Charles Ham Papers, Anderson County; Pvt. Peyton Raglin, Dec. 4, 1864, Manie Blewett Pipkin Library, Woodville, Texas.

7. Blessington, *Campaigns of Walker's Texas Division,* 284; Diary of Milton P. Gaines, Jan. 17, 1865.

8. Blessington, 286–87.

9. Blessington, 287; Bruno Durst, "A Confederate Texas Letter: Bruno Durst to Jet Black," *Southwestern Historical Quarterly* 58 (July 1953): 94–96.

10. Diary of Milton P. Gaines, Jan. 28, Mar. 8, 10, 1864, Charles Ham Papers, Anderson County; Durst, "A Confederate Texas Letter," 95.

11. Sgt. Maj. Henry Ralph to Private G. P. May, Feb. 15, 1865, Carson, *Desk of Henry Ralph,* 116–17.

12. Durst, "A Confederate Texas Letter," 95; Blessington, *Campaigns of Walker's Texas Division,* 289.

13. CSR, M323, roll 79, John Thomas Stark, personal papers; Durst, "A Confederate Texas Letter," 95–96. Capt. Riley J. Blair was the 13th Texas' quartermaster and Dr. Thomas H. Hollis was the regimental surgeon.

14. Blessington, *Campaigns of Walker's Texas Division,* 292–95. The new fourth brigade consisted of Col. George Flournoy's 16th Texas Infantry, Col. Thomas R. Bonner's 18th Texas Infantry, Col. Eli Baxter's 28th Texas Cavalry (dismounted), Col. John H. Caudle's

34th Texas Cavalry (dismounted), and Col. J. W. Wells's Regiment of Texas Cavalry (dismounted).

15. Ibid.

16. Carson, *Desk of Henry Ralph*, 116; Blessington, *Campaigns of Walker's Texas Division*, 291; CSR, M323, roll 79, John Thomas Stark; Durst, "A Confederate Texas Letter," 94.

17. Blessington, *Campaigns of Walker's Texas* Division, 297; Diary of Milton P. Gaines, Mar. 11, 1865, Charles Ham Papers, Anderson County.

18. Lt. Bruno Durst to Capt. J. N. Black, Feb. 25, 1865, *Southwestern Historical Quarterly*: 95.

19. Diary of Milton P. Gaines, Mar. 14, 1865, Charles Ham Papers, Anderson County. Major General Waul was in Texas recovering from the wounds he suffered at Jenkins' Ferry, but as the senior brigade commander, his unit would have had the honor of being the first in the division column.

20. Ibid., Mar. 18, 1865.

21. Ibid., Mar. 26, 1865.

22. Blessington, *Campaigns of Walker's Texas Division*, 301.

23. Tyler, *New Handbook of Texas*, 5: 192–3.

24. CSR, M323, rolls 75–80, Muster of April 1865, Privates Arthur Bearden, Co. H, James T. Cotton, Co. D, Dalphon Garlington, Co. H, W. Goodman, Co. G, N. Hill, Co. F, Robert Mays, Co. H, Henry McKinsey, Co. B, D. Prescott, Co. K, Peyton Raglin, Co. K, Howard Taulbee, Co. H, and Cpl. James Walters, Co. H.

25. CSR, M323, rolls 75-80, Muster of April 31, 1865.

26. Blessington, *Campaigns of Walker's Texas Division*, 303–6.

27. Diary of Milton P. Gaines, Apr. 29, 1865, Charles Ham Papers, Anderson County.

28. CSR, M323, rolls 75-80, Muster of Apr. 31, 1865. This muster is inaccurate in some instances. Both Pvt. Milton P. Gaines and Sgt. Maj. Henry Ralph are known to have been present; neither is listed.

Chapter 11

Epilogue

"I want to be at home where I can get a good water to drink and milk and butter to eat and clean clothes to [wear] and where I can go to church on Sunday."[1]
—Pvt. Lorenzo Dow Fulton, Company D, 13th Texas

Unlike their friends and brothers who served east of the Mississippi, the soldiers of the 13th Texas Cavalry suffered no serious defeat in battle and were never disarmed. Most were paroled only as Union occupation forces moved through their home counties. Some, like Capt. Charles H. Jones of Tyler County, probably delayed their personal surrender until it was discovered that he could not vote or run for office without it.[2] Capt. William D. Wood of Gould's 6th Cavalry Battalion related that rather than returning to the Yankees the famous guns of the "Val Verde" Battery, captured in New Mexico, they were dismounted and buried by Captain Nettles and his men near Fairfield in Freestone County, Texas.[3] The average enlisted soldiers, like Privates Milton P. Gaines or Lorenzo D. Fulton of Anderson County, had little interest in anything beyond their families, homes, and farms. The coming of peace and their return to Texas answered nearly every prayer they had written during the three years of war.[4]

County histories in East Texas are filled with tales of resistance to Reconstruction, both active and passive, often involving veterans of the

13th Texas. In 1866, Lt. Col. George Armstrong Custer and a Union cavalry unit on their way to the western frontier decided to camp on the grounds of the county courthouse in Jasper, Texas. Late that evening, at the height of an intense thunderstorm, the roofs of their tents were riddled by gunfire, leading to a very wet night.[5] West of the Neches River in Tyler County, Federal authorities sent five soldiers to arrest several citizens near Colmesneil who were accused of failing to release their slaves. Local veterans allegedly ambushed the Yankees and hid their bodies deep in the woods, covering the graves with leaves and pine straw. Neither the graves nor the perpetrators were ever discovered. In Tyler County, the incident was known as the "Battle of Billums Creek."[6]

Such anecdotes should be viewed with a high degree of skepticism. Most Confederate veterans in East Texas quietly resumed the same occupations they had pursued before the war. Reconstruction, while galling to many former Confederates, had an only marginal effect on the ability of veterans to be elected to political office. In an interesting example in Houston and Cherokee Counties during the Twelfth Texas Legislature (1870–71), the citizens first elected James R. Burnett, former adjutant of the 13th Texas and brother of Col. John H. Burnett. When Burnett was forced to resign as "an impediment to reconstruction," J. Crockett English, previously the commander of 13th Texas, Company C, replaced him. When Crockett English was forced out, the people of the district elected Frank Rainey, who had served with Randal's 28th Texas, Company G, and reelected him to the Thirteenth Legislature. It is clear that the East Texas veterans had no intention of remaining on the political sidelines.[7]

Col. John H. Burnett (1830–1901) was active in Houston County civic affairs after his resignation in April 1864, publishing *The Crockett Quid Nunc* newspaper with his brother James. He announced his intention to run for lieutenant governor early in 1865, but the election was never held.[8] Burnett remained in Crockett until 1866, when he sold his property and mercantile business and moved his family to Galveston. By 1875, his interests included contracting, building, and cotton brokering. He later had extensive interests in railroad construction and property development. Burnett moved to Houston in 1899 and became president of the Planters and Merchants Bank. At the time of his death on June 24, 1901, he was said to have been the largest owner of real property in southeast Texas.[9]

Col. Anderson F. Crawford (1829–1867) returned to his plantation in Jasper County to find that many of his former slaves had fled. The local economy had depended almost exclusively on large plantations and cotton production, and was particularly hard hit by recession. It is estimated that the population of the county seat was only 360 in 1870. Crawford died of pneumonia on January 10, 1867, at the age of thirty-seven in Keatchie, Louisiana, near the site of his regiment's greatest success. His family returned to Georgia after his death.[10]

Maj. Elias Thompson Seale (1829–1880), returned to Jasper County at the conclusion of the war but soon found the area no longer viable due to the destruction of the plantation economy. He became established in Beaumont, where he was an investor or promoter in an environment rich in timber and railroad speculation. Later, supposedly as the result of financial reverses, he took his own life on November 2, 1880.[11]

Capt. John Thomas Stark (1831–1893), the second commander of Company H, lost his wife Martha to illness in late 1863. Following the war, he returned to Newton County and married the widow of Capt. William Blewett, Nancy Adams, and moved to Orange County where they raised a large family. He was widowed a second time and later married Donna Smith. Stark remained proud of his service and at his request, was buried with the "Dreadnaughts" flag under which the Newton County company had fought.

Capt. John Thomas Bean (1817–1885) of Company K returned to his farm in Tyler County after his resignation in June 1863. His son Floyd recalled that after the war, the troops, "Returned to find the carpetbaggers and Northern troops under Major Saenger, in charge of Woodville and the territory. [At] once he began organizing a force of his fellow woodsmen to 'go and get Saenger,' but only [agreed] after much argument, that that would be the wrong course to follow." He remained active in civic affairs, but his health had been impaired to such an extent that he was unable to resume the leadership role in county business that he held before the war. Bean died at his home January 18, 1885, and was buried in Egypt Cemetery.[12]

Capt. Jerome N. "Jet" Black (1829–1898) of Company A was disabled by fever following the action at Lake Providence and returned to Leona in Leon County in the summer of 1863. After he regained his health, local history recorded that he was commissioned a second time, but no official record exists. After the war, he was reelected sheriff. Black died in Leon County in 1898 after a long illness.[13]

In May 1865 Capt. James Brown Rounsaville (1836–1897) of Company E returned to Crockett where his mother and sisters kept a boarding house. He was married to Caroline Elizabeth "Cally" Adair on July 19, 1865. Cally was the daughter of Dr. William W. Adair and Candia Lockette. The Rounsavilles farmed in Henderson County and raised eleven children. James died at the age of sixty in Chandler, Texas, and was buried in Tyler in the Concord Cemetery.[14]

Capt. Charles H. Jones (1833–1880), the second commander of Company K, returned to his general mercantile business in Woodville, Tyler County. In 1866, he was elected to the Eleventh Legislature to represent Tyler and Hardin Counties. By 1870, his business was flourishing and his household included his wife, four children, two African-American and one white domestic servant, a clerk, and a partner, O. P. Gilder. Jones was active in the local Masonic Lodge. Suffering from poor health, Jones sold his business and retired with his family to his farm about 1878. He died at the age of forty-six on August 23, 1880, and was buried in Magnolia Cemetery in Woodville.[15]

Capt. James Steele Hanks (1809–1898), the first commander of Company D, returned to Anderson County in the spring of 1863. Hanks had lost his son James, who had served in Company B of the 5th Texas Infantry, in the battle of Richmond, Virginia. His younger son died of disease the year he returned. In December 1863 Hanks sold a large leather tanning facility in Mound Prairie and later invested part of the proceeds in buying nearly 14,000 acres of forfeited land at county tax auctions. In 1866 he was elected to represent Anderson County in the Eleventh Legislature. Hanks remained a well-respected member of the community until his death in 1898, and was always referred to as "Colonel" Hanks.[16]

Lieutenants Bruno and Horatio Durst of Company A, Leon County were among a very small number of native Texans who served in the 13th Texas. Their father, John Durst, had settled in the area near Leona prior to Texas Independence. Bruno was elected to serve as representative of Leon and Madison Counties in the Eleventh Legislature. It was later written, "After the war was over, they returned to their homes, and like Cincinnatus of old, took hold of the plow they had left in the furrow, and contented they pursue the noblest and most independent occupation of them all—the cultivation of the earth."[17]

Lt. Ernest Godwin Geisendorff (1838–1897), the last adjutant of the 13th Texas, was elected Tyler County Clerk almost immediately following his return in June 1865. He married Aplice Foster a brief time later, and began what later became a large family. Geisendorff was a partner in a substantial dry goods business, Stewart and Geisendorff, in Woodville, brokering hides, lumber, and cotton in addition to the retail trade. In 1876 he was listed as an officer in the local Masonic Lodge. He served as Tyler County Judge just prior to his death. Geisendorff died of influenza at the age of fifty-eight on April 30, 1897. He was buried in Magnolia Cemetery in Woodville.[18]

Lt. John J. Burroughs, M.D. (1833–1901), after his capture at Lake Providence, Louisiana, was moved through a number of Federal prisons, spending the last year of the war at Fort Delaware, where he was paroled on June 6, 1865. As evidence of the great respect felt by the soldiers of Company K for Dr. Burroughs, he was elected 1st Lieutenant in August 1863 in spite of his status as a prisoner of war. Burroughs moved his family from Woodville to Houston, Texas, in the late 1860s. He established a successful surgical practice there, with offices at 86 Main Street. Feeling close ties to Tyler County, he continued to advertise in the *Woodville Eureka* during the 1880s. Dr. Burroughs died in 1901, and was buried in Glenwood Cemetery in Houston.[19]

Lt. William Perry Nicks (1831–1915) returned to Woodville and resumed his career as an attorney in partnership with Sam A. Willson, a veteran of the "Woodville Rifles," Company F, 1st Texas Infantry, of Hood's Brigade. In December 1867, he married Mary Jane Kavanaugh, daughter of a pioneer Methodist minister. Nicks' early law partners included Edwin Hobby, the father of Texas Governor William P. Hobby, and Samuel Bronson Cooper, later a six-term congressman from East Texas. He moved his practice to Crockett in the late 1870s, but returned to Woodville a few years later. With Cooper, he mentored the aspiring attorney John Henry Kirby, who went on to found Kirby Lumber Company and the Houston Oil Company. W. P. Nicks was elected to three terms as District Attorney, served as Tyler County Judge, and as the Judge of the First Judicial District in 1903–1905. He died at the age of eighty-four on June 15, 1915, and was buried in Magnolia Cemetery, Woodville, Texas.[20]

Pvt. Milton Pinkney "Pink" Gaines (1842–1917) returned to Anderson County on May 25, 1865. He and his wife, Mary Catherine King, had nine children. After the war he became a successful truck farmer and stock raiser. Increasing the size of his farm by buying land from time to time, he eventually owned a large plantation of 2,400 acres. He was remembered affectionately as the person who often used the phrase "bless my time," in conversation. A charter member of the Concord Baptist Church, Gaines donated the first church organ. After the death of his first wife, he married Cammie Conaway on May 30, 1902, in Palestine, Texas. They had six children. He died suddenly on the night of Nov. 29, 1917. Milton Gaines was buried in the Gaines Cemetery, near Montalba, in Anderson County. His daughter Eva transcribed his diary used in this work.[21]

The final mention found of Burnett's 13th Texas Regiment is in an article in *The Crockett Weekly Courier* of July 24, 1891. Under the heading "The Reunion of Burnett's Regiment," it was reported that both Col. John H. Burnett and his son Oscar would attend. "Quite a number of the survivors of Burnett's Regiment met in the courthouse this morning and indulged in handshaking and speechmaking." Texas Adjutant General Wilburn King and W. B. Wall joined Capt. James S. Hanks of Anderson County speaking to the veterans.[22] Regarding a reunion of Gould's Battalion there in Crockett on July 22–23, 1891, the reporter commented, "[They] suffered untold hardships, living in swamps winter and summer. Their number[s] were greatly depleted by sickness and diseases incident to camp life. At their reunion there will be perhaps not more than one hundred of the original members present." These remarks were equally applicable to Burnett's Regiment, whose average age was about sixty. Despite intentions that "a permanent organization will be perfected," there is no later record of regimental reunions. The last known veteran of the 13th Texas in Tyler County, Robert Graham Foster, died on March 17, 1925.[23]

The most perfect epitaph for the 13th Texas is probably contained in the welcome to its only reunion, written by the editor of the *Crockett Weekly Courier*. "There is nothing in the gift of the people or the government too sacred or exalted for these defenders of a once-dear cause. Pensions they have not and can not get. But they have more in the loving, grateful devotion of those for whom they fought. It is theirs and will ever be till patriotism ceases to be a virtue and love of country becomes a fiction."[24]

The motivation of the soldiers of Burnett's regiment was the same fundamental patriotism that drove their grandfathers to serve during the American Revolutionary War. They were convinced that the actions of the Republican administration of President Abraham Lincoln amounted to efforts to establish a federal tyranny in direct opposition to the rights of the states and to the provisions of the Constitution. Lincoln's actions and policies during the conflict did nothing but reinforce their belief. While the threat to the institution of slavery had dominated the minds of many of the secessionists, the majority of the regiment's soldiers had no personal investment in slaves. They probably would have agreed with their former commander, Gen. Richard Taylor, that the "extinction of slavery was expected by all and regretted by none."[25] The veterans of the 13th Texas could look back on their service to the struggling Confederacy in terms of the fulfillment of duty and a deep sense of personal honor not dependent on the military outcome of the war. Regardless of later conclusions concerning the strategic value of the conflict in the Trans-Mississippi, the driving purpose of the soldiers of this regiment was the protection of their homes and families from invasion and occupation. Judged by that standard, they were successful.

1. L. D. Fulton to Susan Fulton, undated [ca. Oct. 1863], Carol Fulton Ahmad Papers, San Antonio, Texas.

2. CSR, M323, roll 77, Charles H. Jones, "Parole of Honor," Aug. 24, 1865; *Members of the Texas Legislature*, 54. Jones was elected as the representative of Tyler and Hardin Counties to the Eleventh Legislature, Aug.–Nov. 1866.

3. Wood, *Officers and Men Raised in Leon County*, 49.

4. L. D. Fulton to Susan Fulton, undated [ca. Oct. 1863], Carol Fulton Ahmad Papers, San Antonio, Texas.

5. James M. McReynolds, "A History of Jasper County, Texas, Prior to 1874," thesis, Lamar State College of Technology, 1968, 102.

6. Moseley, *Pioneer Days of Tyler County*, 88–89.

7. *Members of the Texas Legislature*, 57–76; Hewett, *Texas Confederate Soldiers*, 1: 70, 158, 432.

8. *Crockett Quid Nunc*, Feb. 14, 1865.

9. Tyler, *New Handbook of Texas*, 1: 835.

10. Ibid., 2: 171; Laura V. Nielson, Apr. 10, 2000, personal correspondence; *Galveston Daily News*, Jan. 10, 1867; Bruce Allerdice, personal communication, Sept. 21, 2003.

11. William Seale, Apr. 25 and Nov. 21, 2001, personal correspondence.

12. Wheat, *Sketches of Tyler County History*, 186; Dean Tevis, "Capt. Jack Bean," *Beaumont Enterprise*, Apr. 14, 1935.

13. Wood, *Officers and Men Raised in Leon County*, 29–30.

14. Brian E. Rounsavill, Nov. 7, 2001, personal correspondence; *Texas Weekly Quid Nunc*, Jul. 25, 1865.

15. *Members of the Texas Legislature*, 54; "Ninth Census of the United States, Population

Schedule," Tyler County, TX, Microfilm M593-1606, household 5; "Tenth Census of the United States, Population Schedule," Tyler County, Tex., Microfilms T-9-1329 and T-9-1330, household 222.

16. Ule, *Pioneer Stock*, 18–19.

17. Wood, *Officers and Men Raised in Leon County*, 30–31.

18. Sandra Geisendorff Keyes, Geisendorff Family Papers, Sugar Land, TX; *Woodville Eureka*, Jan. 6, 1883, 2; "Register of Elected and Appointed State and County Officials," Texas State Library, Microfilm roll EL-14.

19. CSR, M323, roll 75, John J. Burroughs; *Woodville Eureka*, Jan. 6, 1883, Sep. 20, 1884.

20. "Minutes of the District Court, Tyler County," Vol. D [1852-1872]; "Tenth Census of the United States, Population Schedule," Houston County, 232; *The Beaumont Daily Journal*, Jun. 15, 1915, 2; "Register of Elected and Appointed State and County Officials," Microfilm rolls EL 12-16.

21. Charles H. Ham, Mar. 12, 2001, personal correspondence.

22. Hewett, *Texas Confederate Soldiers*, 1: 553. William B. Wall, formerly Lieutenant, Company I, 1st Texas Infantry, Hood's Brigade.

23. Gravestone, "13th Texas Cavalry, C.S.A.," Ebenezer Cemetery, Tyler County, Texas. Foster had been one of the youngest in the regiment, joining in 1862 at the age of 17.

24. *The Crockett Weekly Courier*, Jul. 24, 1891.

25. Taylor, *Destruction and Reconstruction*, 288.

Appendix A

13th Texas Cavalry Regiment (dismounted) Roster of soldiers who died on active duty March 1862–May 1865

NAME	LOCATION	DATE	CAUSE	UNIT
Addison, B. M.	Near Pine Bluff, Ark.	2.24.63	Disease	G
Alford, Noah S.	Camp Burnett, Tex.	4.10.62	Disease	H
Baker, Richard	Camp Nelson, Ark.	11.11.62	Disease	I
Bearden, Seaborn	Camp Nelson, Ark.	10.24.62	Disease	H
Berry, Martin W.	Arkansas	9.8.62	Disease	D
Bishop, M. B.	Shreveport, La.	3.26.63	Disease	G
Blackwell, Jerimiah	Little Rock, Ark.	1.14.63	Disease	D
Blewett, William	Little Rock, Ark.	9.19.62	Disease	H
Blount, Calvin C.	Jasper, Tex.	9.3.63	Disease	G
Bowen, Whitfield	Camp English, Ark.	7.20.62	Disease	G
Bowen, William S.	Camp English, Ark.	7.25.62	Disease	D
Brack, Burrell	Little Rock, Ark.	12.25.62	Disease	H
Brasher, James L.	Camp English, Ark.	7.16.62	Disease	C
Brown, William H.	Camp Rogers, La.	1.3.64	Unknown	A
Burk, Andrew J.	8 mi from Des Arc, Ark.	10.16.62	Disease	E
Burk, John D.	Little Rock, Ark.	2.6.63	Disease	E
Butler, Thomas D.	Little Rock, Ark.	12.26.62	Disease	E
Caldwell, Cyrus W.	Camp English, Ark.	7-8.62	Disease	B
Carleton, James B.	Pleasant Hill, La.	4.9.64	KIA	H
Clark, James	Camp Beaty, Ark.	8.4.62	Disease	E
Clark, Jesse W.	Camp Nelson, Ark.	11.9.62	Disease	A
Clark, Oliver P.	Camp Burnett, Tex.	5.21.62	Unknown	A
Clark, William W.	Pleasant Hill, La.	4.9.64	KIA	C
Cochran, Calvin J.	Pleasant Hill, La.	4.9.64	KIA	F
Cole, Clark	Camp English, Ark.	8.1.62	Disease	I

NAME	LOCATION	DATE	CAUSE	UNIT
Coleman, Wm. F.	Camp Nelson, Ark.	10.8.62	Disease	D
Collins, Andrew W.	Camp Nelson, Ark.	11.29.62	Pneumonia	H
Collins, Creed M.	Searcy Valley, Ark.	11.2.62	Pneumonia	H
Cox, Melville B.	Little Rock, Ark.	12.21.62	Camp Fever	H
Crawford, B. C.	Pleasant Hill, La.	4.9.64	KIA	G
Davis, George W.	Camp Nelson, Ark.	11.13.62	Disease	H
Dehart, Wynant	Walnut Hill, Ark.	8.7.62	Disease	H
Delaney, James	Camp Nelson, Ark.	1.12.63	Disease	G
Delaney, Jefferson B.	Camp Nelson, Ark.	1.7.63	Disease	G
Denman, Albert H.	Camp Nelson, Ark.	11.17.62	Disease	F
Denman, Prentice S.	Camp Nelson, Ark.	11.13.62	Disease	F
Denton, Catha M.	Camp Nelson, Ark.	11.30.62	Disease	B
Dickerson, Van G.	Camp Nelson, Ark.	12.2.62	Disease	B
Dubose, Abner B.	Arkansas	2.3.63	Disease	G
Dubose, Peter P.	Camp Nelson, Ark.	10.14.62	Typhoid F.	H
Durdin, Wm. Jas.	Princeton, Ark.	6.11.64	DOW	K
Eason, Francis M.	Little Rock, Ark.	1.20.63	Disease	F
Ellis, O. L.	Pleasant Hill, La.	4.9.64	KIA	B
Ethridge, James	Bayou Meto, Ark.	12.1.62	Disease	K
Evans, William G.	Walnut Hill, Ark.	8.3.62	Disease	D
Fairchild, J. B.	Camp Nelson, Ark.	11.10.62	Disease	I
Ford, Ira	Arkansas	8.29.62	Disease	D
Furr, Benjamin C.	Pine Bluff, Ark.	2.1.63	Disease	B
Gaston, George A.	Pine Bluff, Ark.	1.20.63	Disease	D
Gillespie, James W.	Camp Blair, Ark.	7.16.62	Disease	I
Gillespie, Joseph	Des Arc, Ark.	10.29.62	Disease	A
Gilliland, Samuel B.	Camp Blair, Ark.	7.6.62	Disease	F
Glover, William Y.	Marksville, La.	1.22.64	Drowned	A
Goldman, William	Shreveport, La.	3.18.65	Disease	C
Grainger, Frank F.	Near Little Rock, Ark.	12.4.62	Disease	I
Green, John	On the March, Ark.	8.11.62	Disease	K
Haden, Geo. A.	Camp Nelson, Ark.	1.23.63	Disease	B
Hanson, George W.	Enroute Devall's Bluff	10.6.62	Disease	H
Henson, Timothy W.	Bayou Meto, Ark.	11.26.62	Disease	C
Hall, Samuel H.	Camp Nelson, Ark.	11.20.62	Disease	B
Hallmarke, Geo. G.	Camp Nelson, Ark.	11.1.62	Disease	B
Herring, J. L.	Camp English, Ark.	7.21.62	Disease	I
Herrington, Giles	Camp Nelson, Ark.	11.18.62	Disease	K
Hodges, Chapman R.	Camp English, Ark.	7.22.62	Disease	C
Holdbert, Joseph M.	Pine Bluff, Ark.	2.24.63	Disease	F
Jones, Archibald	Camp English, Ark.	7.24.62	Disease	G
Jones, G. R.	Camp Magruder, La.	1.12.64	Disease	G
Keen, Asa M.	On the March, Ark.	8.23.62	Disease	K

NAME	LOCATION	DATE	CAUSE	UNIT
Kennedy, James J.	Camp Bayou Meto	12.10.62	Disease	G
Lambert, John	Pine Bluff, Ark.	2.20.63	Disease	E
Linsey, Thomas H.	Pine Bluff, Ark.	2.26.63	Disease	D
Long, Levi G.	Little Rock, Ark.	1.4.63	Disease	A
Mahaffy, William	Walnut Hill. Ark.	8.24.62	Disease	I
Mann, David G.	Camp Nelson, Ark.	11.19.62	Disease	K
Mann, James M.	Camp Nelson, Ark.	10.27.62	Disease	K
Manning, Francis S.	Camp Burnett, Tex.	5.18.62	Disease	A
Marshall, Alson	Little Rock, Ark.	1.1.63	Disease	I
Martin, James M.	Little Rock, Ark.	1.10.63	Disease	F
Martin, William	Pleasant Hill, La.	4.9.64	KIA	F
Mayes, Andrew G.	Little Rock, Ark.	10.19.62	Disease	F
McBride, Lewis A.	Camp Beaty, Ark.	8.6.62	Disease	E
McCarty, William H.	Camp Nelson, Ark.	11.22.62	Disease	E
McClung, Carlile	Lake Providence, La.	6.9.63	KIA	F
McDougal, W. F.	Pleasant Hill, La.	4.9.64	KIA	C
McWilliams, Patrick	Walnut Hill, Ark.	7.30.62	Disease	H
McWilliams, Wm. H.	Camp Nelson, Ark.	11.9.62	Disease	H
Miller, James T.	Camp Nelson, Ark.	11.12.62	Disease	E
Mills, Isaac N.	Camp Nelson, Ark.	12.14.62	Disease	F
Mitchell, A. J.	Camp Nelson, Ark.	11.28.62	Disease	E
Mitchell, John W.	(PW) New Orleans, La.	5.24.64	Disease	E
Mitchell, Joseph	Near Pine Bluff, Ark.	1.16.63	Disease	K
Mitchell, Thomas J.	Newton, Tex.	7.25.64	DOW	H
Moffatt, James C.	Crockett, Tex.	3.8.62	Murdered	C
Moore, Allen J.	(PW) St. Louis, Mo.	2.22.63	Disease	-
Moore, John F.	Near Pine Bluff, Ark.	1.15.63	Disease	A
Morgan, E. A.	Camp Nelson, Ark.	11.11.62	Disease	I
Newman, Archibald	Walnut Hill, Ark.	7.22.62	Disease	H
Nobles, James L.	Camp Nelson, Ark.	1.11.63	Disease	G
Norwood, James E.	Walnut Hill, Ark.	8.8.62	Disease	G
Parker, Micajah	(PW), Alton, Ill.	10.9.64	Disease	A
Parsons, W. T. J.	Little Rock, Ark.	12.12.62	Disease	K
Perryman, Matthew	Camp English, Ark.	7.20.62	Disease	K
Price, Weyman A.	Pleasant Hill, La.	4.9.64	KIA	D
Potter, Charles L.	Walnut Hill, Ark.	8.6.62	Disease	H
Pruitt, John B.	Colombia County, Ark.	8.26.62	Disease	K
Pullen, Dewitt W.C.	Camp Nelson, Ark.	12.2.62	Disease	K
Ratcliff, James A.	Little Rock, Ark.	12.21.62	Disease	K
Rawls, H. Jackson	Camp Blair, Ark.	7.29.62	Disease	K
Reed, Charles A.	Camp Nelson, Ark.	12.19.62	Disease	A
Reed, Thomas M.	Camp Nelson, Ark.	11.13.62	Disease	A
Reynolds, James	Near Pine Bluff, Ark.	2.18.63	Disease	B

NAME	LOCATION	DATE	CAUSE	UNIT
Rice, Francis M.	Princeton, Ark.	9.8.62	Disease	B
Richards, Robert W.	Camp Nelson, Ark.	10.31.62	Disease	B
Richardson, James	Camp Nelson, Ark.	11.12.62	Disease	A
Richardson Wm. F.	Pleasant Hill, La.	4.9.64	KIA	C
Rounsaville, Thos. J.	Keatchie, La.	5.1864	DOW	C
Rutledge, John B.	Little Rock, Ark.	1.23.63	Disease	H
Scarborough, James	Camp Nelson, Ark.	11.17.62	Disease	D
Sheffield, Augustus	Little Rock, Ark.	2.15.63	Disease	K
Simmons, DeKalb	Camp Nelson, Ark.	12.5.62	Disease	E
Simmons, Elias	Near Pine Bluff, Ark.	2.27.63	Disease	E
Simms, A. Hubbard	Little Rock, Ark.	2.21.63	Disease	K
Smith, James W. A.	Camp Blair, Ark.	7.28.62	Disease	K
Stafford, H. P.	Little Rock, Ark.	1.17.63	Disease	D
Stark, Samuel H.	Little Rock, Ark.	3.12.63	Disease	H
Stewart, Thomas	Pleasant Hill, La.	4.9.64	KIA	D
Stillwell, Napoleon	Little Rock, Ark.	1.3.63	Disease	A
Stokes, K. K.	Lafayette County, Ark.	7.14.62	Disease	I
Stubblefield, Julius	Little Rock, Ark.	12.16.62	Disease	C
Stubblefield, Wilson	Pine Bluff, Ark.	2.2.62	Disease	B
Thomas, Isaac G.	Camp Nelson, Ark.	12.5.62	Disease	E
Thomas, P. N.	Little Rock, Ark.	10.2.62	Disease	D
Thompson, Wm. H.	Camp Nelson, Ark.	11.26.62	Pneumonia	H
Tucker, Henry H.	Camp Blair, Ark.	7.11.62	Disease	D
Welch, Francis M.	(PW) Ft. Delaware, Del.	6.18.65	Scurvy	F
West, William	Walnut Hill, Ark.	7.24.62	Disease	H
Williams, O. R.	Camp Nelson, Ark.	11.11.62	Disease	I
Williams, Richard	Camp McCulloch, Tex.	6.22.62	Disease	G
Williams, R. D.	Little Rock, Ark.	1.9.63	Disease	E
Williams, T. C. Jr.	Henderson Co., Tex.	4.6.65	Disease	E
Williford, Thomas	Camp McCulloch, Tex.	6.11.62	Disease	A
Wright, Charles W.	Camp Blair, Ark.	7.28.62	Disease	K
York, George W.	Camp Nelson, Ark.	12.7.62	Disease	E
Young, J. W.	Camp Nelson, Ark.	10.25.62	Disease	D
Zeagler, William	Camp Nelson, Ark.	11.10.62	Disease	B

Fatalities: 146. Total Names in Compiled Service Records: 1389. Percentage: 10.4%

Appendix B

Organization of Walker's Division, April 1864

Brig. Gen. Thomas N. Waul's brigade

8th Texas Infantry (also known as the 12th Texas Infantry)

18th Texas Infantry

22nd Texas Infantry

13th Texas Cavalry (dismounted)

Capt. Horace Haldeman's 4th Texas Artillery battery*

Col. Horace Randal's brigade

11th Texas Infantry

14th Texas Infantry

Gould's 6th Texas Cavalry Battalion (dismounted)

28th Texas Cavalry (dismounted)

Capt. James M. Daniel's 9th Texas Artillery battery*

Brig. Gen. William R. Scurry's brigade

3rd Texas Infantry

16th Texas Infantry

17th Texas Infantry

19th Texas Infantry

16th Texas Cavalry (dismounted)

Capt. William Edgar's 1st Texas Artillery battery*

* Although nominally assigned to the brigades, artillery batteries were, in practice, tasked and managed at echelons above the division level.

Appendix C

Commissioned Officers of the Thirteenth Texas Cavalry Regiment (dismounted)

Regimental Field, Staff, & Band

Commander

Colonel John H. Burnett, March 1, 1862–November 15, 1863 (Cheneyville, LA).

Transferred to post duty at Crockett, Texas, Nov. 15, 1863, resigned Apr. 22, 1864.

Colonel Anderson Floyd Crawford, April 23, 1864–June 2, 1865.

Aide-de-Camp

Lieutenant James Russell Burnett, March 1, 1862–July 27, 1862 (Camp English, AR).

Deputy Commander / Executive Officer

Lieutenant Colonel A. F. Crawford, March 1, 1862–April 22, 1864.

Lieutenant Colonel Charles Roambrose Beaty, April 23, 1864–November 1864.

Major Elias T. Seale (from Company G) ca. November 1864–June 2, 1865.

Sergeant Major

Riley J. Blair (Co C) May 24, 1862–Feb. 7, 1863.

James B. Rounsaville (Co C) Feb. 8, 1863–Dec. 2, 1863 (?)

B. C. Crawford (Co G) Feb. 12, 1864–April 9, 1864 (Killed in Action at Pleasant Hill).

Henry Ralph (Co G) Apr. (?) 1864–May 20, 1865.

Chaplain

Chaplain John B. Renfro, March 1, 1862–October 21, 1862 (Camp Nelson, AR).

Chaplain Richard F. Fancher, January 10, 1864–August 26, 1864 (Black River, LA).

Surgeon

Captain William F. Corley (Declined at the time of reorganization, Camp Burnett). March 1, 1862–May 23, 1862.

Captain John M. Hilliard, May 24, 1862–July 28, 1862 (Camp English, AR).

Captain Edward Currie, July 29, 1862–November 15, 1862 (Camp Nelson, AR).

2nd Lieutenant John J. Burroughs, October 29, 1862–June 9, 1863 (Acting Surgeon at Camp Nelson and Little Rock, AR).

Captain Thomas H. Hollis, August 21, 1863–June 2, 1865. (Formerly Staff Surgeon at Camp Terry Convalescent Camp, Little Rock, Arkansas.)

Adjutant

Captain John M. Hilliard, March 1, 1862–May 23, 1862 (Camp Burnett, Tex.). (Captain Hilliard change of duty to Surgeon, May 24, 1862.)

Captain James C. Wooters, May 24 1862–July 27, 1862 (Camp English, AR).

Lieutenant James R. Burnett, July 28, 1862–November 20, 1862 (Camp Nelson, AR).

Captain J. Pat Henry (from Company I), November 21, 1862–January 10, 1865 (Camp near Shreveport, LA).

2nd Lieutenant Ernest G. Geisendorff (from Company K), January 11, 1865–June 2, 1865. (Recommended for promotion to 1st Lieutenant, he had served as acting adjutant May 10, 1864–January 10, 1865.)

Quartermaster (AQM)

Captain Armstead Thompson Monroe, March 1, 1862–December 10, 1862 (Camp Bayou Meto, AR).

1st Lieutenant Charles H. Jones (from Company K) Acting Asst. QM, November–December 1862.

Captain Riley J. Blair, December 11, 1862–June 2, 1865.

ACS (Asst. Commissary Service)

Lieutenant Wilson E. Hail, A.C.S., March 1, 1862–Nov. 20, 1862.

Lieutenant James H. Finch, A.C.S., Nov. 20, 1862–No record after 1863.

Commissary Sergeant

Calvin C. Blount (Co G) March 1, 1862–Sep. 3, 1863 (died).

Joe B. Blount (Co G) Sep. 4, 1863–No record after Feb. 1864.

Assistant Surgeon

Lieutenant J. C. Brubaker, A. S.

Lieutenant John L. Cornish, A.S., Nov. 3, 1863–December 2, 1864 (Camp near Minden, LA).

Lieutenant W. P. Means, A.S.

Lieutenant Shadrach J. Collins (Company C), A. S.

Color Bearer / Color Corporal

Pvt. George A. Hadon (Co B) May 24, 1862–Jan. 23, 1863.

Pvt. Ransom P. Horde (Co G) appointed Dec. 10, 1863.

Pvt. Edman F. Bridges (Co C) appointed Aug. 23, 1864.

Cpl. Soloman Wishard (Co I) as of the Apr. 1865 muster.

Chief Musician

H. D. Watson (Co I) Mar. 2, 1862–No record after Feb. 1864.

Appendix C

Company Commanders

Company A (Co E to May 23, 1862) (Leon, Polk & Trinity Counties)
Organized at Leona, Texas. Initial Muster at Crockett, Texas
Captain Jerome N. Black, February 21, 1862–June 9, 1862, (Camp Burnett, TX).
Captain Granderson M. Nash, June 10, 1862–June 2, 1865.

Company B (Co I to May 23, 1862) (Houston County)
Initial Muster at Crockett, Texas
Captain John T. Smith, February 22, 1862–August 10, 1863 (Pineville, LA).
Captain Joshua B. Young, August 11, 1863–June 2, 1865.

Company C (Co B to May 23, 1862) (Houston County)
Initial Muster at Crockett, Texas
Captain George English, February 22, 1862–August 27, 1863 (Cheneyville, LA).
Captain Crockett J. English, August 28, 1863–June 2, 1865.

Company D (Co A to May 23, 1862) (Anderson County)
Organized at Mound Prairie, Texas. Initial Muster at Crockett, Texas
Captain James S. Hanks, February 22, 1862–June 9, 1863 (Resignation tendered near Pine
    Bluff at Camp Bee, AR, April 1863).
Captain John C. Oldham, June 10, 1863–June 2, 1865.

Company E (Co D to May 23, 1862) (Henderson County)
Organized at Athens, Texas. Initial Muster at Camp Shiloh, Texas
Captain William K. Payne, February 22, 1862–August 31, 1862 (Camp English, AR).
Captain James Eastland, September 1, 1862–December 2, 1863 (Near Simmesport, LA).
Captain James B. Rounsaville, December 3, 1863–June 2, 1865.

Company F (Co C to May 23, 1862) (Angelina County)
Organized at Homer, Texas. Initial Muster at Crockett, Texas
Captain Hiram Brown, March 1, 1862–August 27, 1863 (Cheneyville, LA).
Captain Samuel B. Thomas, August 28, 1863–June 2, 1865.

Company G (Co F to May 23, 1862) (Jasper County) "Crawford's Rebels"
Initial Muster at Jasper, Texas
Captain Elias T. Seale, March 1, 1862–November 15, 1863.
Captain Thomas F. Truett, November 16, 1863–August 12, 1864 (Near Harrisonburg, LA).
Captain Elias T. Seale, August 13, 1864–November 1864.
Captain William F. Seale, November 1864–June 2, 1865.

Company H (Co G to May 23, 1862) (Newton County) "Dreadnaughts"
Organized at Newton, Texas. Initial Muster at Jasper, Texas
Captain William Blewett, March 1, 1862–died September 19, 1862, (Little Rock, AR).
Captain John Thomas Stark, September 20, 1862–February 25, 1865 (Shreveport, LA).
Captain Thomas J. Brack, February 26, 1865 – June 2, 1865.

Company I (Co K to May 23, 1862) (Orange County) "Orange Grays"

    Reorganized from State Militia, Orange, Texas. Initial Muster at Crockett, Texas

Captain Samuel A. Fairchild, March 1, 1862 – (?)

Captain Hiram G. Cline, (?) – June 2, 1865.

Company K (Co H to May 23, 1862) (Tyler County) "Jack Bean's Cavalry"

    Organized at Woodville, Texas. Initial Muster at Camp Lookout, Polk County, Texas

Captain John Thomas Bean, March 1, 1862 – October 2, 1863, (Cheneyville, LA).

Captain Charles H. Jones, October 3, 1863 – June 2, 1865.

Commissioned Officers

Company A

Parker, James P. 1st Lt. resigned May 24, 1862

McLendon, Jesse S. 2nd Lt. resigned November 14, 1862

Nobles, James H. 1st Lt.

Yarborough, Wade H. 2nd Lt., reduced to the ranks.

Durst, Bruno 1st Lt.

Durst, Horatio 2nd Lt.

Company B

Wingfield, William E. 1st Lt. dropped May 24, 1862

Wortham, William 1st Lt. resigned November 26, 1862

Long, John. 2nd Lt. (Muster of May 28, 1862, no later record)

Burton, David L. 2nd Lt. resigned August 1863

Broxson, Enoch 1st Lt.

Beckham, Franklin A. 2nd Lt.

Company C

Williams, Wilford W. 1st Lt.

Owen, Robert B. S. 1st Lt.

English, John C. 2nd Lt.

Craddock, Erasmus D. 1st Lt.

Rounsaville, Thomas J. 2nd Lt. died of wounds, May 1864.

Creasey, William H. 2nd Lt.

Payne, Thomas B. 2nd Lt.

Henniss, Sidney O. P. 2nd Lt.

Company D

Oldham, James R. 1st Lt. transferred to 20th Texas Cavalry, Co A.

Gaston, George A. 1st Lt., died January 20, 1863

Akin, David A. 1st Lt., resigned March 24, 1864

Hassel, Nathaniel, 2nd Lt., resigned July 20, 1862

Hudson, George W. 1st Lt.

Tucker, William J. 2nd Lt.

Company E

Teah, Bernard 1st Lt. resigned December 29, 1863

Allen, Claiborne W. dropped May 24, 1862

Cargile, James L. 2nd Lt.

Jennings, Elbert E. 1st Lt.

Etheridge, Lewis 2nd Lt., reduced to the ranks Jan. 30, 1864

Company F

McMullen, 1st Lt. dropped May 24, 1862

Anderson, William R. 2nd Lt. deserted April 11, 1862

Denman, Washington L. 1st Lt. resigned July 23, 1862

Reynolds, Oliver P. 1st Lt. resigned February 18, 1863

Wright, James B. 1st Lt.

Reynolds, Michael J. 2nd Lt.

Mills, Martin V. 2nd Lt. resigned November 4, 1864

Company G

Smyth, Andrew F. 1st Lt. dropped May 24, 1862

Rodgers, Jesse B. 2nd Lt. dropped May 24, 1862

Lee, Moses 2nd Lt. dropped May 24, 1862

Bower, John P. 2nd Lt.

Crawford, William H. 2nd Lt.

McAlister, Mathew 1st Lt.

Glenn, Horace A. 2nd Lt.

Company H

Snell, John J. 1st Lt. dropped May 24, 1862

Roberts, William T. 2nd Lt. dropped May 24, 1862

Dubose, Amos 2nd Lt. dropped May 24, 1862

Hanson, George W. 2nd Lt. died October 6, 1862

Collins, Creed M. 2nd Lt. died November 2, 1862

Williams, John D. 1st Lt.

Hancock, Charles A. 2nd Lt.

Hare, William T. 2nd Lt.

Jones, Francis E. 2nd Lt.

Company I

Bland, Peyton 1st Lt. dropped May 24, 1862

Saxon, Charles H. 2nd Lt. dropped May 24, 1862

Stephenson, Elijah 2nd Lt. dropped May 24, 1862

Haynes, George W. 1st Lt. resigned February 27, 1865

Arrington, David T. 2nd Lt. resigned July 24, 1862

Bland, Oliver 2nd Lt. resigned August 20, 1862

Granger, Frank F. 2nd Lt. died December 4, 1862

Davis, Francis A. 2nd Lt. resigned August 1, 1864

Cotter, Robert 2nd Lt.

Company K

Kelley, M. J. 1st Lt. dropped May 23, 1862

Kirkwood, George W. 2nd Lt. dropped May 23, 1862

Scott, Thomas G. 2nd Lt. dropped May 23, 1862

Burroughs, John J. 1st Lt. taken prisoner of war June 9, 1863

McAlister, Mathew L. 2nd Lt. resigned December 13, 1862

Nicks, William Perry 2nd Lt. (promoted from First Sergeant Nov. 1863)

Geisendorff, Ernest G. 2nd Lt. (appointed as Adjutant Jan. 1865)

Appendix D

Roster of Soldiers by Company

Roster of Company A, Leon County,
first commanded by Captain Jerome N. Black

Autry. William C.

Ayres. Joseph F.

Bain, W.H.

Baldwin. Hart M.

Baldwin, James A.

Barnes, William P.

Bennick, Jacob J., Sgt.

Black, Jerome N. Capt.

Black, William F., Cpl.

Blackledge, Alexander C.

Blassingame, George W.

Better, Andrew Winston

Brown, John, Cpl.

Brown, John P.

Brown, William H.

Brubaker, J. Curry, Asst. Surg.

Bryan,Thomas L.

Cessna, John D., Cpl.

Clark, Jesse W.

Clark, Oliver P.

Coleman, William Wallace, 1st Sgt.

Davis, George W.

Davis, James I.

Davis, John

Davis, Nathan L.

Dickey, John R.

Dickey, William

Driscol, David A.

Driscol, Ephraim C.

Driskett, David A.

Durst, Bruno, 2nd Lt.

Durst, Horatio W., Jr. 2nd Lt.

Durst, William E., Sgt.

Evans, Isaac G.

Fosket, William H.

Frost, Chafin

Gilchrist, Zedrick

Gillespie, Joseph

Glover, William Y., Sgt.

Greene, James G.

Hall, James

Herring, Thomas W.

Inman, Rufus

Jettund, William, 1st Sgt.

Johnson, Lovet B.

Kidd, Albert A.

Kidd, James E.

Long, James

Long, Levi G.

Long, William

Lummis, Alexander

Lummis, James

Manning, Francis S., Sgt.
McElvin, John
Meadow, W.
Moffitt, Alexander
Monroe, James M.
Moore, John F.
Moore, Moses A.J.
Nash, Granderson M., Capt.
Netherland, James
Netherland, Pleasant M.
Nettles, Jesse S.
Newton, Elihu M.
Newton, Robert M., Cpl.
Noble, James H., 1st Lt.
Orenbum, James
Parker, Curren D.
Parker, James B., 1st Lt.
Parker, Micajah C.
Pate, Jesse
Pate, Martin
Perry, Claiborn G.
Polk, Alfred, Cpl.
Proctor, John Thomas, Sgt.
Proctor, William H., Cpl.
Radford, Obediah A.
Rayborn, Leroy
Reed, Charles A.
Reed, George T., Sgt.
Reed, Thomas M.
Revis, William T.
Revis, Wilson 0.
Rhoades, Andrew Jackson

Richardson, James
Roden, Clement C.
Seachrist, Andrew
Shaw, Henry J.
Sherrod, Benjamin F.
Simms, Sidney, Cpl.
Sinclair, James L.
Sinclair, James W.
Sterrett Ewing C.
Stillwell, Charles H.
Stillwell, John A.
Stillwell, Napoleon B.
Stinson, John
Taylor, James H.
Thompson, John W.
Trawick, John
Tubb, Benjamin
Tubb, James M.
Tubb, Jesse E.
Vance, Richard
Vann, Joseph, Cpl.
Vaughan, John
Vaughn, John
Vaughn, William F.
Vest, John W.
Walton, James W.
Warren, J.W.
Whatley, Edmond M.
Williford, Thomas, Cpl.
Willingham, Berry
Willingham, John

Roster of Company B, Houston County, first commanded by Captain John T. Smith

Abney, Madison
Alfred, Aaron J.
Allison, Jacob H.
Allison, Samuel H.
Allison, Thomas J.
Atkinson, Daniel
Atkinson, John
Atkinson, Lewis

Atkinson, William
Baker, Murdock M., Sgt.
Bartee. James W., Cpl.
Beavers, Joseph
Beckham, Franklin A., 2nd Lt.
Bitner, W. D.
Brent, Peter E., Sgt.
Brown, G. W.

Broxson, Enoch, 1st Lt.
Bunn, Eli M.
Burnett, John H., Col.
Burton, David L., 3rd Lt.
Bynum, Jasper L.
Byrd, J. F.
Caldwell, Cyrus W.
Campbell, Alex C., Cpl.
Casteel, Asberry H., Sgt.Maj.
Chears, Andrew J.
Clinton, John T.
Coghill, William W.
Corley, William F., Surg.
Craddock, James W.
Craddock, William W.
Crowson, Obed. L., Sgt.
Cummins, James H.
Day, William W.
Denton, Cathy M.
Dickerson, Darius A.
Dickerson, Van G.
Downs, James E.
Dunnagan, Alfred J.
Dyers, Milton S., Cpl.
Ellis, Benjamin S.
Ellis, James B.
Ellis, Obed L., Cpl.
Furr, Benjamin C.
Furr, Joseph H.
Gibson, John I., 1st Sgt.
Goodman, Benjamin L.
Goodrum, Robert B.
Gossett, F. A.
Gossett Kelsey L.
Gossett, Preston, Cpl.
Haddox, James H.
Haden, George A.
Hail, Edley E.
Hail, Wilson Edwin, Commissary
Hall, Frank
Hall, Samuel H.
Hallmarke, George G., Sgt.
Hallmarke, Thomas L.
Harkins, John B.

Harrell, John J. J. A.
Hartfield, Joseph A.
Hearn, T. L.
Herron, William J.
Hester, Samuel G., Cpl.
Hester, Thomas R.
Hill, E. M.
Hogue, William
Jones, Seborn G. K.
Jordan, James M.
Kaddock, J. W.
King, H. M.
King, John B.
Klingelhefer, August W.
Lacy, John B.
Leaverton, Charles A.
Leaverton, George W.
Legory, Augustus
Long, James S.
Long, John, 1st Lt.
Martin, Henry F.
Mayes, William E.
McKinzie, Daniel
McKinzie, Henry L., Sgt.
McManners, Dawson
Monday, Columbus M.
Moore, James H.
Moore, William H.
Murchison, Morgan R.
Murchison, William M.
Murphy, Samuel C.
Musgrove, Edward F.
Nelson, Charles C. O.
Nelson, Ralph H.
Nite, James M.
Porterfield, John A.
Ragan, David C.
Reynolds, George W.
Reynolds, James
Rhodes, Joseph W.
Rhone, George W.
Rice, Francis M.
Richards, Robert W. R.
Ritchey, John R.

Sanders, J. K.
Sanders, S. A.
Saxon, Robert H.
Scarbrough, L. L.
Shiflett, King D. D.
Skidmore, Clayton D.
Smith, John T., Capt.
Smith, Robert J.
Stepp, Newton L.
Stevens, Thomas
Stewart, Frank
Stewart, James J.
Stone, Robert
Stribling, John C.
Stubblefield, Wilson M., Sgt.
Toney, William T.
Turner, Absalom D.

Turner, William P.
Varnadore, John C.
Wall, John C.
White, Calvin H., Sgt.
White, Stephen H.
Williams, George R.
Wills, Robert W.
Wilson, John M.
Wingfield, Lewis H.
Wingfield, William E., 1st Lt.
Witherspoon, Alexander M.
Wooters, James C., Adjutant
Wortham, William, 1st Lt.
Wright Joseph A.
Young, Joshua B., Capt.
Young, Peter

Roster of Company C, Houston County,
First commanded by Captain George English

Allen, Ethan T.
Allen, John
Armstrong, Wilson W.
Arnold, Elisha
Ashmore, Ebenezer A.
Ashmore, Joseph H.
Ashmore, Licurgus
Ashmore, William J.
Ballard, A.H., Cpl.
Bass, Holley
Bass, John H.
Belott, Andrew J., Sgt.
Blair, Riley J., AQM
Bowman, Edward
Brasher, James L.
Brasher, Thomas E., Sgt.
Bray, Peter J.
Brazier, James L.
Brazier, John A., Cpl.
Bridges, Edmon F.
Bridges, Jackson R., Sgt.
Bridges, James W.
Bryant, J. W.

Burton, Dempsey J.
Cadenhead, Franklin M.
Calhoun, James M.
Calhoun, Theodore A.
Carlton, John S.
Chapman, I. J.
Chapman, John H., Sgt.
Childers, David, Cpl.
Christian, James L.
Clark, Alfred J. S.
Clark, J. 0.
Clark, Thomas T.
Clark, William W.
Collins, Shadrach J., Asst. Surg.
Conner, Andrew J.
Conner, John C.
Covin, Joseph E.
Craddock, Erasmus D.
Craig, John R.
Creasy, William J., 2nd Lt.
Currie, Edward, Surg.
Davis, Howell P.
Dickerson, George N.

Dunkin, David H.
Duren, Philip D.
Duren, William H.
English, Crockett J, Capt.
English, George, Capt.
English, James
English, Richard B.
English, Stephen, Cpl.
English, Thomas
English, William R.
Ezell, Harrison
Foster, Charles W.
Foster, William L.
Freeman, John
Goldman, William
Goodwin, John, Cpl.
Goodwin, Joseph T.
Gregory, A. W.
Grigg, Silas
Grounds, George W.
Grounds, John W.
Grounds, William J.
Hale, Robert C.
Hallmark, John
Handcock, Benjamin
Hennis, Sidney O.P., 3rd Lt.
Henson, Timothy W.
Hicks, Thomas C.
Hodges, Able
Hodges, Chapman R.
Holcomb, Augustus A.
Holley, Washington
Johnson, Davis V.
Jones, William H.
Kerr, Bird F.
Kersey, David 0.
Kevier, J. E.
Killgore, John F.
Kyle, George A.
Kyle, John
Loving, N. C.
Marsh, William Y.
McDougal, W. F.
Meacham, W. J.

Mills, Lazarus Clinton
Moffatt, James C.
Moffatt, Solomon D.
Monroe, Armisted T., AQM
Moore, Benjamin
Morie, Roman
Nelms, William A.
Owen, Robert B. S., 1st Lt.
Patton, George W.
Payne, H. W.
Payne, Jeremiah E.
Payne, Thomas B., 2nd Lt.
Payne, W. F.
Perkins, James W.
Power, Richard
Quaid, Hugh E., Cpl.
Quaid, W. R.
Randal, Lewis H.
Raybome, A.
Renfro, John H., Sgt.
Rice, John R.
Rice, William J.
Richardson, William F., Cpl.
Rodgers, Joseph N.
Roper, T. R.
Rounsaville, James B., Capt.
Rounsaville, Thomas J., 2nd Lt.
Sage, George, Sgt.
Sandlin, William H.
Shaw, Thomas H.
Smith, John M.
Smitherman, James
Speer, John D.
Stephens, Lawrence C.
Stone, James J.
Stow, Alfred T.
Stow, William
Stubblefield, James A.
Stubblefield, Julius Mc.
Stubblefield, Samuel
Sulivan, Charles B.
Sullivan, Samuel D., Cpl.
Thomas, Nelson S.
Trent, John

Turner, Sanford D.
Tyler, Edward
Tyre, Charles P.
Tyre, John T.
Vaughn, Mathew B., Cpl.
Vaughn, Stephen G., 1st Sgt.
Vaughn, Word H., Cpl.
Waddell, William M.
Wagner, J.

Watson, Franklin B.
Weldon, William D.
Wicks, J. S.
Williams, John D., 1st Lt.
Williams, Wilford W.
Wilson, Thomas L.
Wood, E. W.
Wood, Joseph

Soldiers of Company D, Anderson County, first commanded by Captain James Steele Hanks

Akin, David A., 1st Lt.
Allen, Albert J.
Allen, Elisha Poe
Anderson, John C.
Atkins, Richard
Barber, George W.
Barker, E.B.
Beddingfield, J.D.
Bell, George W.
Berry, John E., Sgt.
Berry, Martin W.
Black, Josiah M.
Black, William
Blackwell, Jeremiah
Blancit, Calvin
Bowen, William S.
Boze, John, Sgt.
Brock, Benjamin C.
Brown, Samuel D.
Brown, Thomas
Brown, William S.
Burbanks, L.F.
Butler, Daniel M.
Campbell, James
Campbell, John, Cpl.
Cantrell, John W., Sgt.
Cantrell, Shade
Cantrell, William J.
Cherrytree, Thomas C.
Cinclair, Christopher P.
Coleman, William F.

Cone, Edward
Cone, John
Cotton, James T.
Cotton, P.C.
Cox, James
Craft, George W.
Cuthbertson, S.J.
Dagg, Edward
Elliott, James M.
Evans, David B., Cpl.
Evans, Henry
Evans, John D.
Evans, W.B.
Evans, William G.
Farries, James H., Sgt.
Fitzgerald, James E., Cpl.
Fitzgerald, McA.
Ford, Ira
Fulton, L.D.
Gage, John L., Cpl.
Gaines, Milton P.
Gaston, George A., 1st Lt.
Gilbert, James
Giles, John
Goad, James 0.
Graves, Charles W.
Graves, Harris B.
Grayham, Anderson
Green, Albert G., Hosp.Stew.
Griffin, John M.
Hallum, R.G.

Hanks, James S., Capt.
Hanks, Joshua B.
Harper, Henry C.
Harris, William R.
Hassell, Nathaniel, 2nd Lt.
Hassell, William J.
Haynes, William N., Cpl.
Henderson, Richard C.
Henry, John R., Sgt.
Herrington, William B.
Hickman, B.F, Cpl.
Hickman, Jabez H.
Hickman, William P., Cpl.
Hooker, T.C.
Hopper, Joshua T.
Huddleston, Daniel C.
Huddleston, James
Huddleston, J.A.
Hudson, George W., 1st Lt.
Hudson, Sampson, Bugler
Hudson, William H.
Janes, Isom S.
Johnson, J.A.
Johnson, J. H.
Killan, Elijah J.
Killion, Levi
Lane, John H.
Lee, Olston 0.
Lewis, Spencer P.
Linsey, Thomas H.
Lunn, Andrew
Magee, C.S.
Masters, Romulus J., 1st Sgt.
McKinny, Michael B.
McKinzie, Francis M.
Miller, Reuben C., Cpl.
Miller, Stephen R.
Milling, David Y.
Murphy, Ephraim M.
Nix, William H.
Oldham, Franklin H.
Oldham, James R., 1st Lt.
Oldham, John C., Capt,

Palmer, James H.
Payne,S.H.
Petty, John W.
Price, Josiah
Price, Samuel T.
Price, Weyman A.
Renfro, John B., Chap.
Rogers, M.L.
Save, James M.
Scarborough, James, Sgt.
Simpson, Beauford B.
Sinclair, C.P.
Smith, R.N.
Snowden, J.H.
Stafford, Hartwell P.
Stafford, Uriah M.
Stewart,Thomas
Thomas, Eli W.
Thomas, James M.
Thomas, P.N.
Todd, Andrew K.
Tucker, Henrey. H.
Tucker, William J., 2nd Lt.
Underwood, Reuben H.
Vannoy, John H.
Walker, J.B.
Walsh, Richard
Ward, William C.
Watts, B.F.
Webb, James M.
Wigington, David F.
Wigingion, J.H.
Williams, Ben J.
Wilson, R.H.
Wilson, Washington M.T.
Wilson, William M.
Wolf, Charles S.
Womack, Rufus B.
Woolvenon, John L.
Woolverton, William R., Sgt.
Woosley, David S.
Wright, Raus
Young, Joseph W.

Roster of Company E, Henderson County,
first commanded by Captain William K. Payne

Allen, Claborn W., 2nd Lt.
Aly, John, Far.
Avant, William W.
Ballard, William, Cpl.
Ballow, John W., 1st Sgt.
Barber, Robert V.
Bell, George A.
Boyd, Larkin M.
Bradford, Powell L.
Buie, John A.
Burk, Andrew J.
Burk, John D.
Butler, Elijah M.
Butler, Joseph A.
Butler, Thomas D.
Butler, William A.
Cargile, James L., 2nd Lt.
Carpenter, W.H.
Clanahan, William R.
Clark, James
Conner, Andrew J.
Crawford, John A.
Crawford, William B.
Dill, John W.
Easterwood, Silas D.
Eastland, James, Capt.
Elston, David E.
Etheredge, Lewis, Sgt.
Evans, F.P.
Evans, James J.
Flinn, Powhattan T.
Gardner, Othneil
Gardner, William
Gililland, William B., Music.
Goodnight, Henry
Goodnight, Thomas, Cpl.
Gosnell, Elisha
Gray, Thomas G.
Green, Andrew J.
Green, Samuel S.
Guthrie, James T.

Guthrie, John C.
Guthrie, Samuel H.
Hall, Edward A.
Hanson, Joseph N.
Harkins, Robert T.
Harkins, William P.
Harper, Andrew J., Teamster
Head, Geo. W.
Holloway, James L.
Jennings, Elbert E., 1st Lt.
Jones, Crawford F., Sgt.
Lambert, John
Matthews, John H.
Matthews, Thomas P.
McBride, James, Cpl.
McBride, Lewis A., 1st Sgt.
McBride, Littleton B.
McCarty, John D.
McCarty, William H.
McCollum, William
McDougaid, Duncan J., Cpl.
McMorris, George W.H., Sgt.
McMorris, John T., Sgt.
Meatis, E.M.
Meeks, Elijah, 1st Sgt.
Miller, Andrew W.J.
Miller, James T.
Miller, John B.
Mitchell, Andrew J.
Mitchell, John W.
Mitchell, Samuel H.
Mitchell, Wilson J.J.
Morehead, James
Neill, G.C., Jr., 2nd Lt.
Netherland, Lewis
Norfleet, Newton W.
Payne, Andrew J.
Payne, William K., Capt.
Piearcy, John W.
Reid, James S., Teamster
Reynolds, Charles

Rounsaville, James B., Capt.
Rushing, Felix
Rushing, William R., Sgt.
Sanders, William K.
Shelton, J.
Simmons, DeKalb
Simmons, Elias
Simmons, Lafayette
Teah, Bernard,1st Lt.
Thomas, Isaac G.

Tison, William T.
Webb, William E.
Weldon, William D.
Westbrook, John W.
Williams, Robert D., 1st Sgt.
Williams, Thomas C., Sgt.
Williams, Thomas C., Jr., Cpl.
Williams, William
Witherspoon, Abel N.
York, George W.

Roster of Company F, Angelina County, First commanded by Captain Hiram Brown

Allen, Asa T.
Anderson, William R., 2nd Lt.
Arnold, Gilford
Babb, George W.
Baird, Albert G., Cpl.
Banks, William F.
Berry, Andrew J.
Berry, Hugh A. P.
Berry, John L.
Berry, Samuel L.
Brashears, Jesse W.
Brazile, John M.
Brazile, William
Brewer, William R.
Brissauw, Alexander
Broadaway, John
Brookshire, Jesse W.
Brown, Hiram, Capt.
Brown, Richard O.
Brown, William H.
Bruer, William K.
Burke, Matt W.
Burks, William F.
Byler, William L.
Byrd, Lundy C.
Chesnut, J. C.
Clover, John
Cochran, Calvin J.
Cochrane, Abraham B., Sgt.
Collins, Thomas F.

Cramer, Aaron
Crutchfield, Jasper J.
Cupp, Andrew J.
Dearby, J.A.
Denman, Albert H.
Denman, Prentice S.
Denman, Washington L., 1st Lt.
Denman, William
Denning, J.H.
Eason, Francis M.
Ellis, Richard, Cpl.
Ewing, James L.
Fairchild, Elijah, 1st Sgt.
Fairchild, George W.
Forrest, William
Gann, Samuel
Gann, William B.
Gilbert, William
Gilliland, James L., Sgt.
Gilliland, Samuel B.
Graham, Dempsey E.
Graham, Isaac N.
Graham, John L.
Gray, T.S.
Hambry, T. J.
Harrison, Edward J.
Head, Geo. W.
Herrington, James
Higinbotham, Francis M.
Hill, N.

Holdbert, John D.

Hope, Thomas

Ivy, Cyrus, Sgt.

Ivy, James S.

Johnson, George W.

Jones, Calway F.

Jones, John F.

Jones, Martin M.

Jones, William M.

Keer, Joseph

Kerby, James A.

Kilgore, William R.

Kirkly, I. C.

Landtroop, William S.

Larue, James

Lindsey, Alfred M.

Mankins, Lindsey

Mann, John

Mantooth, Calvin

Mantooth, Daniel

Mantooth, Samuel

Martin, James M.

Martin, William

Massingill, George W.

Massingill, William

Massingill, William J.

Mathews, S.

Mayes, Andrew G.

McClendon, Eli W.

McClung, Carlisle, Sgt.

McKinney, James

McMullen, Robert A.

McMullen, William R., 1st Lt.

Miller, Alexander J.

Mills, Isaac N.

Mills, Martin V., 3rd Lt.

Mills, Rufus J., Sgt.

Nesbert, James

Olivan, Lucas

Oquin, Baldwin

Owen, J.L.

Page, James L.

Parker, Hardy, Cpl.

Pearson, John T.

Quin, B. O.

Reynolds, Michael J., 2nd Lt.

Reynolds, Oliver P., 1st Lt.

Rhote, J. C.

Roberts, W. C.

Shirey, Arthur W., Sgt.

Smith, Benjamin E.

Smith, Gilford M., Sgt.

Spivey, Moses W.

Spivey, Sherwood F.

Spivey, William C.

Steame, Charles A.

Stegall, Henry L.

Stevens, Thomas

Stevens, William, Music.

Stripling, Elijah R.

Suttles, John, Cpl.

Suttles, Thomas D.

Swagerty, James C.

Taylor, William M., Cpl.

Thomas, John, Sgt.

Thomas, R. W.

Thomas, Robert

Thomas, Samuel B., Capt.

Thompson, Thomas S.

Thomton, J.

Trawick, Stephen T.

Treadwell, James, Sgt.

Tubbs, Thomas D.

Walker, Phillip A.

Walker, Thomas R.

Ward, William C.

Warren, Noah

Welch, Benjamin W.

Welch, Francis M., Cpl.

White, Benjamin F.

White, Thomas G.

White, William M.

Wilkerson, James P.

Wilson, Pleasant R.

Woods, Henry M.

Woods, William

Wright, James B., 1st Lt.

York, Harrison

York, Thomas T.

Appendix D

Roster of Company G, Jasper County,
first commanded by Captain Elias T. Seale

Adams, Jerry
Addison, B.M.
Addison, William L.
Armstrong, James T.
Barnett, John L.M.
Barrett, Willis T.
Beaty, Charles R., Lt. Col.
Beaty, Thomas B.
Biscamp, Augustus F.
Bishop, A.T.
Bishop, M.B.
Bishop, Milton C.
Bishop, Tillman D.
Blewett, William, Captain
Blount, Calvin C., Comsy. Sgt.
Blount, Francis M.
Blount, Joe B.
Boone, James F.
Bostick, William K.
Bowen, Whitfield
Bower, John P.
Bower, Thomas W.
Boyctt, Noah
Byerly, Micajah
Byerly, W.F.
Byrd, John D.
Calhoun, John A.
Chapman, Jesse
Childers, J.P.
Claud, Benjamin F.
Crawford, Anderson F., Lt. Col.
Crawford, B.C., Sgt. Maj.
Crawford, William H., 2nd Lt.
Dean, William P.M.
Delaney, James
Delaney, Jefferson B.
Delaney, Martin P.
Delano, Oliver J.
Dubose, Abner B.
Dubose, Button J.
Erwin, James F., Sgt.

Ferguson, Alfred J.
Ferguson, John W.
Glenn, Horace A., 3rd Lt.
Goodman, Charles G., 1st Sgt.
Goodman, George W.
Goodman, W.
Gray, Horatio N., Ord. Sgt.
Green, John
Grimes, William
Harron, J.M.
Hart, Nathan M., Sgt.
Hilliard, John M., Surg.
Hoarde, David L., Cpl.
Hoarde, Ransom P.
Holton, John D.
Horn, Chesly A., Sgt
Horn, Weston C.
Jones, Archibald Jones, G.R.
Jones, Joseph H., Sgt.
Jones, Thomas C., Cpl.
Jordan, Andrew C.
Jordan, Thomas A.
Kennedy, James J.
Knighton, William F.
Kyser, H.W., Capt.
Lee, Moses, 3rd Lt.
Leamy, Miles
Lettany, Ulysses
Lewis, John W.
Magee, George W.
Magee, Green F., Cpl.
Magee, William L.
Mashaw, James A.
McAlister, Mathew, 1st Lt.
McFarland, Richard J., Sgt.
McMahon, James D.
McRae, John H.
McRae, Robert C.
Merrill, William
Monk, William W.
Morgan, Reuben

Morgan, William
Morris, Jonathan T.
Morris, L.D.
Murry, Allen J.
Musick, Austin
Nobles, James L.
Norwood, James E.
Owens, M.
Owens, Stephen H., Sgt.
Pace, Eli
Pace, James B.
Peacock, Claiborne, Sgt.
Peacock, William J.
Powell, John A.
Powell, Joseph B., Sgt.
Ralph, Henry
Rawls, William J.
Rees, James M.
Rees, Orlando C.
Rees, Orlando U.
Rogers, Elly B., Sgt.
Rogers, Jesse B., 2nd Lt.
Rogers, Shadrach J.
Ross, William
Scruggs, William A.
Seale, Elias T., Maj.
Seale, J.J.
Seale, T.R.

Seale, William F., Capt.
Sellers, Simeon M.
Short, Jackson J.
Smith, Green B.
Smith, John G., Cpl.
Smith, Uriah A.
Smyth, Andrew F., 1st Lt.
Taylor, Amos K., Cpl.
Trotti, James H., Cpl.
Trotti, Joshua F.
Truett, Thomas F., Capt.
Truett, W.H.
Walker, James M.
Ward, James W.
Ward, Joseph A.
White, Edwin
Wigley, John
Wigley, Paschal A.
Williams, B.W.
Williams, E.N.
Williams, George W., Cpl.
Williams, Joseph G.
Williams, Richard
Williams, William W.
Wilson, William
Wood, Singleterry T.
Zeagler, John
Zeagler, William

Roster of Company H, Newton County, first commanded by Captain William Blewett

Alford, Noah S.
Bearden, Arthur
Bearden, John
Bearden, Sebom
Birdwell, James A.
Blewett, William, Capt.
Booker, Thomas J.
Brack, Burrel
Brack, Henderson F., Ord.Sgt.
Brack, Thomas J., Capt.
Brister, George W.
Byerley, George W.

Cade, Drury B.
Cade, Robert
Cade, Thomas
Carleton, James B., Cpl.
Carleton, Joel H.
Clark, Harrison
Cobb, Ezekiel, Cpl.
Cochran, William A.
Collins, Andrew W.
Collins, Creed M., 2nd Lt.
Collins, James D.
Collins, Lewis J.

215

Colville, John P.
Cooper, Wyley C.
Cottingghame, J.M.C.
Cox, Melville B.
Cox, William
Davis, George W.
Deggs, Dixon M.
DeHart, Winant, Cpl.
Dickey, Patrick J.
Dougharty, Francis B., Cpl.
Dougharty, J.M., Sgt.
Dougharty, Marshall J.
Downs, William W., Sgt.
Dubose, Amos, 3rd Lt.
Dubose, John, Music.
Dubose, Peter P.
Duke, Rufus
Ehrstien, Benard
Fancher, James
Fuller, Elijah
Fuller, Henry C.
Fuller, John M.
Fuller, Samuel L.
Fuller, William L.
Garlington, Dalphon R.
Garlington, Stephen W.
Gilbert, James M.
Gilchrist, William C.
Glover, William J.
Goolsbee, Adison E.
Goolsbee, John N.
Goolsbee, Zabud E.
Griggs, Lerov
Griner, Timothy M.
Hall, William M.
Hancock, Charles A., Ord.Sgt.
Hanson, George W., 2nd Lt.
Hare, Alfred D.
Hare, William T., 2nd Lt.
Harville, William L.
Herrin, Andrew J.
Hext, Robert P.
Hogue, Aureluis H.
Horger, John M.

Jenkins, James J.
Jones, Francis E., 3rd Lt.
Jones, John H.
Jones, Samuel F.
Jones, Sarshall R., Bugler
Jordan, Abraham M.
Jordan, Daniel
Jordan, Lemuel C.
Joyner, Robert
Kimmey, John F.
Kimmey, Seabom C.
Layton, George W.
Litle, William T., Sgt.
Love, Andrew J.
Love, James J.
Marshall, Alexander
Marshall, William R.
Martin, William L.
Mattox, Joshua H., Sgt.
Mayes, William S.
Mays, Robert
McMahon, Friend R.
McMahon, Joel D., Cpl.
McNoughton, Allen
McWilliams, Patrick H.
McWilliams, William H., Jr.
McWilliams, William H., Sr.
McWilliams, Wright H.
Newman, Archibald
Parrott, William I.
Peacock, Claiborne, Sgt.
Peacock, William
Porter, Timothy D., Cpl.
Potter, Charles L., Cpl.
Powell, John H.
Ramsey, Benjamin
Ramsey, Doctor F.
Rhodes, Arnold
Roberson, George W.
Roberts, Francis R.
Roberts, Samuel D.
Roberts, William T., Lt.
Rutledge, John B.
Rutledge, William

Simmons, James F.

Simmons, Pleasant R., Sgt.

Simmons, Stephen J.

Simmons, William W.

Smith, Jonathan L.

Smith, Levi, Sgt.

Smith, V.S.

Smith, William

Snell, Adam H.

Snell, John J., 1st Lt.

Snell, William D.

Stark, John T., Capt.

Stark, Samuel H.

Stewart, Friend M.

Stfinger, Cornelius

Taulbee, Howard M., Black.

Thompson, Thomas P.

Thompson, William H.

Trottie, John L.

Walters, James A., Cpl.

Walton, Leander J.

West, Richard, Cpl.

West, William

Westbrook, Joshua H.

Williams, John D., 1st Lt.

Willson, David H.

Wilson, David H., Sgt.

Woods, Allen

Woods, Calaway

Woods, Hiram

Woods, Raford C.

Woods, Ransom D.

Woods, Walton, Music.

Woods, William H.

Roster of Company I, Orange County, first Commanded by Captain Samuel Fairchild

Adams, James K.

Arrington, David T., 2nd Lt.

Atkinson, John W.

Baker, G.B.

Baker, Green

Baker, Joseph

Baker, Richard

Ballard, John J.

Beard, William

Bell, M.J.

Black, Ezekiel, Sgt.

Bland, Oliver, 3rd Lt.

Bland, Payton, 1st Lt.

Braly, J.D.

Brewer, John D., Sgt.

Burton, Owen, Cpl.

Burton, T.

Cane, N.E.

Chisem, H.P.

Clark, Oliver

Clark, Robert F.

Cline, Hiram G., Capt.

Cole, Absalom B.

Cole, Clark

Cole, James

Cooper, Jonathan

Cooper, Uriah

Cooper, William

Cotier, Robert, 2nd Lt.

Crabtree, J.M.

Davis, Francis A. Jr., 2nd Lt.

Day, Henry

Day, R.H.

Day, Thomas, Cpl.

Deer, A. W., Sgt.

Delano, Charles

Fairchild, George W.

Fairchild, Henry J., Cpl.

Fairchild, J.B., Sgt.

Fairchild, J.I.

Fairchild, Samuel A., Capt.

Fairchild, William L., Far.

Finch, James H., Asst. Comsy.

Finch, Philepus, 1st Sgt.

Fredrick, Trezanio
Gill, James B.
Gill, Thomas B.
Gillespi, James W., Cpl.
Gilley, John, Cpl.
Grainger, Frank F., 2nd Lt.
Grayston, R.P., Ord. Sgt.
Green, P.M.
Grongia, Michael
Hannon, William H.
Hardin, Napoleon B.
Hannon, Joshua, Black.
Harrington, D.T.
Harris, Benjamin D., 1st Sgt.
Harris, Pressley A.
Hart, Thomas W., 1st Sgt.
Hawthorn, James I.
Haynes, George W., 1st Lt.
Henry, J. Pat, Adj.
Henry, W.C.
Herring, J.L.
Hill, Stephen
Holden, Samuel H.
Humble, Jacob M., Music.
Humble, James K., Music.
Ingram, Tilman, Sgt.
Jackson, N.H.
Jarroll, Stephen
Jordan, H.
Jordan, Josiah
Lagrange, Milia
Linscomb, Joseph
Linscomb, Napoleon
Long, J.B.
Mahaffy, Amos
Mahaffy, William
Marshall, Alson
McCienan, William, Cpl.
McClusky, James
McLain, Alexander
McLain, James
McLane, Andrew J.
McLane, Ephraim
McMillan, William

Millaman, Ira B.
Minshew, Robert R.
Moore, Henry G., Sgt.
Moore, James
Moore, James A.
Morgan, E.A.
Morgan, J.
Morgan, W.L.B.
O'Donald, Thomas, Sgt.
Parker, A. J.
Parker, Thomas J.
Pattillo, George H.
Pattillo, James H.
Perkins, Lucious Q.
Pevito, Alfred
Pevito, John
Pevito, Samuel
Pinson, Harvey H.
Raley, B.B., Lt.
Richardson, William
Riley, Edward J., Sgt.
Sanders, John
Saxon, Charles H., 2nd Lt.
Shaver, B. F., Music.
Sheshon, Joseph
Singleton, Joseph H.
Smith, Benjamin
Smith, W.J., Sgt.
Steger, William C., Sgt.
Stephenson, Elijah, 2nd Lt.
Stephenson, W.A., Cpl.
Stokes, K.K., Cpl.
Turner, Aaron M.
Walker, J.D.
Walters, T.C.
Watson, D.
White, H.
Whitmire, Sibley D.
Williams, O.R.
Winn, Rufus A.
Wishard, Solomon
Woodred, T.
Young, Joseph

Roster of Company K, Tyler County,
first commanded by Captain John Thomas Bean

Allen, S.W.

Anderson, George W., Cpl.

Anderson, J.K. Polk

Barclay, Robert

Barclay, Walter

Barksdale, Jonathan C.

Bean, John T., Capt.

Bell, John M.

Bivins, James

Black, John R., 1st Sgt.

Brantly, David

Brown, Bryant

Burk, Ahaz J.

Burk, Arch T.

Burk, James M.

Burroughs, John J., 2nd Lt.

Busby, John W., QM Sgt.

Butler, John

Carroway, D.M.H.

Chancy, Randolph

Chancy, Thomas

Chancy, W.

Clark, Loring G.

Clark, Robert W., Sgt.

Clark, Wesley S.

Clark, William

Clibum, Thomas

Collier, Joseph W.

Cruse. Anderson P.

Dauzat, Ludgar

Darden, James R., Sgt.

Darden, William H.

Davis, William W.

Devens, A.N.

Dickens, Richard N.

Dickson, T.

Dilliard, John B.

Dillon, James T.

Dunn, John

Durdan, William J., Sgt.

Durham, H. L. Turner

Durham, James K.

Durham, Solomon S.

Durham, William S.

Enloe, D.C.

Ethridge, James

Fagan, Aaron

Fagan, George

Fortner, Joseph, Cpl.

Foster, Nathaniel J.

Foster, Robert G.

Fowler, George W., Sgt.

Freeman, Ely W.

Futch, Isaac G.

Gause, Luther

Geisendorff, Ernest G., 2nd Lt.

Gilder, Jacob A.

Gilder, Oliver P.

Goode, John H.

Goode, Josiah W.

Grayham, John T.

Green, John

Grimes, Allen

Hall, W. Riley

Halmark, James M.

Harrison, Elbert A., Cpl.

Harrison, William

Hawkins, Benjamin F.

Hawkins, John H.

Hawkins, Stephen

Hawthorn, Joseph H.

Hays, John H.

Hendricks, Theodore T.

Herrington, Giles, Cpl.

Hooker, Robert

Hopson, Shade A.

Jackson, James A.

Johnson, L. Augustus

Jones, Charles H., Capt.

Jones, Daniel

Keen, Asa M.

Kelley, M.J., 1st Lt.

Kincaid, William J.

Kirk, Joseph M.

Kirkwood, George W., 2nd Lt.

Lea, William R., Ord.Sgt.

Long, William T.

Loyed, George

Magee, C.S.

Manley, William

Mann, David G.

Mann, James M.

Mann, John P.

Mapes, McCagher F.

McAlister, Mathew L., 3rd Lt.

McAllister, William J.

McKinney, Calvin, Cpl.

Minyard, John J., Sgt.

Mitchell, Joseph

Moody, A.

Moody, Jacob

Moody, Levi

Mullins, Samuel P.

Murry, Allen J.

Nicks, W. Perry, 2nd Lt.

Nowlin, Martin D., Cpl.

Orr, William

Parr, John A.

Parsons, Joseph J.

Parsons, W.T. Jourdon

Pearson, J. Thomas

Perden, David

Perryman, Mathew T.

Phelps, James A.

Phillips, James M.

Phillips, John L.

Phillips, Marion J.

Phillips, William

Pinson, Patrick H., Sgt.

Pipes, W.

Powers, William B.

Prescot, D.

Pruitt, John B.

Pullen, Dewitt W.C.

Raglin, Peyton

Raley, George W., Sgt.

Ratcliff, Edward T.

Ratcliff, James A.

Ratcliff, R.K.

Rawles, H. Jackson

Register, Harrison

Richardson, G.W.

Rigsby, Benjamin F.

Rigsby, James M.

Sanders, Alfred G., Sgt.

Sanders, J.B.

Sanders, Peter

Sandlin, Alexander K.

Sapp, Addison J.D.

Scott, Thomas G., 3rd Lt.

Scott, Washington M., Sgt.

Shamburger, Augustus, Cpl.

Sheffield, Augustus M.

Simms, A. Hubbard

Slater, Mathew

Smith, Elbert

Smith, James W.A.

Taylor, George 0.

Thornton, Lewis T.

Tompkins, David C., Sgt.

Tompkins, Delaney E.

Tompkins, G.S.

Tullas, Albert

Vaughn, William S.T.

Walters, Henry J.

Walters, Lemuel

Weaver, William J.

Wheeler, John H.

Wiggins, William D.

Bibliography

MANUSCRIPTS

Hill College, H. B. Simpson Research Center, Hillsboro, Texas
13th Texas Cavalry (Dismounted) files (William Blewett, G. B. Layton,
Sherwood F. Spivey, John Thomas Stark, Milton P. Gaines.)
18th Texas Infantry file (John C. Porter)
22nd Texas Infantry file (John Simmons)

Lamar University, Mary and John Gray Library, Beaumont, Texas
National Archives and Service Administration. Compiled Service
Records of Confederate Soldiers Who Served in Organizations
From the State of Texas (microfilm M323, reels 75–80). Abbreviated
CSR.

**Louisiana State University, Shreveport, Louisiana, Noel Memorial
Library, Archives and Special Collections**
John Ardiss Manry Papers, Collection 215

Texas State Archives, Austin
Confederate Pension Application Files (CPAF)
Muster Rolls, companies G, H, and I of the 13th Texas Cavalry
Photo Archives and Information Services Division
Texas State Troops Records, Brigade Correspondence, 1861–1865
Texas Adjutant General's Office, Correspondence, 1862

Tyler County Courthouse, Woodville, Texas
Minutes of the District Court, Volume D. 1852–1872

University of Texas at Austin, E. C. Barker Library, Center for American History
Bluford Alexander Cameron Papers
Robert Simenton Gould Papers
Henry Eustace McCulloch Papers

U.S. Army Military History Institute, Carlisle Barracks, Pennsylvania. Abbreviated USAMHI in notes.
James B. Rounsaville Papers
Myron G. Gwinner Collection

NEWSPAPERS

Crockett (Texas) Weekly Quid Nunc
Galveston (Texas) Tri-Weekly News
Jasper (Texas) Newsboy
Texas Republican (Marshall)
Tyler (Texas) Reporter

PUBLIC DOCUMENTS

Confederate States of America, War Department. *Army Regulations Adopted for the Use of the Army of the Confederate States, also, Articles of War.* Richmond, VA: West & Johnson, Publishers, 1861.

Day, James M., ed. *House Journal of the Ninth Legislature, Regular Session of the State of Texas, November 4, 1861–January 14, 1863.* Austin, TX: Texas State Library, 1964.

------------, ed. *Senate Journal of the Ninth Legislature, First Called Session of the State of Texas, February 2, 1863–March 7, 1863.* Austin, TX: Texas State Library, 1963.

------------, ed. *Senate Journal of the Ninth Legislature of the State of Texas Regular Session, November 4, 1861–January 14, 1862.* Austin, TX: Texas State Library, 1963.

"Eighth Census of the United States Population Schedule," Houston County, Texas, 1860. MS, Microfilm M653, Rolls 1292–1308.

Kennedy, Joseph G. C. *Agriculture of the United States in 1860: Compiled from the Original Returns of the Eighth Census.* Washington, DC: Government Printing Office, 1864.

Members of the Texas Legislature, 1846–1962. Austin, TX: Legislature of the State of Texas, 1962.

Scott, Major-General [Winfield], by Authority of U.S. Army. *Infantry Tactics, or Rules for the Exercise and Maneuvers of the United States Infantry. Volume I, School of the Soldier and Company.* New York: Harper and Brothers Publishers, 1858.

Statistics of the United States, (Including Mortality, Property, &c.,) in 1860: Compiled from the Original Returns and being the Final Exhibit of the Eighth Census, Under Direction of the Secretary of the Interior. Washington, DC: Government Printing Office, 1866.

United States Congress. *Red River Expedition: Report of the Joint Committee on the Conduct of the War.* Originally published in 2 vols. Washington, DC: Government Printing Office, Senate Document Number 142, 1866. Reprint, Millwood, NY: Kraus Reprint Co., 1977.

United States War Department. *War of the Rebellion: A Compilation of the Official Records of the Union and Confederate Armies.* 128 vols. Washington, DC: Government Printing Office, 1880–1901. Abbreviated as O.R.

PRIMARY SOURCES

BOOKS

Bartlett, Napier. *Military Record of Louisiana: Including Biographical and Historical Papers Relating to the Military Organization of the State.* 1875. Reprint, Baton Rouge: Louisiana State University Press, 1964.

Blessington, Joseph P. *The Campaigns of Walker's Texas Division.* 1875. Reprint, Austin, TX: State House Press, 1994.

Brown, Norman D., ed. *Journey to Pleasant Hill: The Civil War Letters of Captain Elijah P. Petty, Walker's Texas Division, C.S.A.* San Antonio, TX: University of Texas Institute of Texan Cultures, 1982.

Carson, Geraldine Primrose. *From the Desk of Henry Ralph.* Austin, TX: Eakin Press, 1990.

The Confederate States Almanac and Repository of Useful Knowledge for 1862. Vicksburg, MS: H. C. Clarke, 1862.

Debray, Xavier Blanchard. *A Sketch of the History of Debray's 26th Regiment of Texas Cavalry.* 1884. Reprint, Waco, TX: Waco Village Press, 1961.

DeRyee, William, and R. E. Moore. *The Texas Album of the Eighth Legislature, 1860.* Austin, TX: Miner, Lambert & Perry, 1860.

Gallaway, B. P. *Texas, The Dark Corner of the Confederacy: Contemporary Accounts of the Lone Star State in the Civil War.* Lincoln, NB: University of Nebraska Press, 1994.

Hardee, W. J. *Rifle and Light Infantry Tactics for the Exercise and Manoeuvres,* Volume 1, School of the Company. 1855. Reprint, N.p.: James R. Gunn, 1991.

———. *Rifle and Light Infantry Tactics; for the Exercise and Manoeuvres of Troops When Acting as Light Infantry or Riflemen.* Vol. 2, School of the Battalion. Philadelphia, PA: J. B. Lippincott & Co., 1861.

Hewett Janet B., ed. *Supplement to the Official Records of the Union and Confederate Armies.* 100 vols. Wilmington, NC: Broadfoot Publishing Company, 1994–2000.

———. *Texas Confederate Soldiers 1861–1865,* 2 vols. Wilmington, NC: Broadfoot Publishing Company, 1997.

Johansson, M. Jane, ed. *Widows by the Thousand: The Civil War Letters of Theophilus and Harriet Perry.* Fayetteville, AR: University of Arkansas Press, 2000.

Lord, Walter, ed. *The Fremantle Diary: Being the Journal of Lieutenant Colonel Arthur James Lyon Fremantle, Coldstream Guards, on his Three Months in the Southern States.* Boston, MA: Little, Brown, and Company, 1954.

McClure, Judy Watson. *Confederate from East Texas, The Civil War Letters of James Monroe Watson.* Quanah, TX: Nortex Press, 1976.

Spurlin, Charles D., comp. *Texas Veterans in the Mexican War: Muster Rolls of Texas Military Units.* Victoria, Texas: Victoria College, 1984.

Taylor, Richard. *Destruction and Reconstruction: Personal Experiences of the Late War.* New York: Longmans, Green & Co., 1955.

Wood, W[illiam] D. *A Partial Roster of the Officers and Men raised in Leon County, Texas, For the Service of the Confederate States in the War Between the States, with Short Biographical Sketches of Some of the Officers, and a Brief History of Maj. Gould's Battalion and other Matters.* San Marcos, TX: Published by the Author, 1899.

ARTICLES

Barr, Alwyn. "Texan Losses in the Red River Campaign, 1864." *Texas Military History* 3 (summer 1963): 103–110.

Bee, Hamilton P. "Battle of Pleasant Hill—An Error Corrected." *Southern Historical Society Papers* 8 (April 1880): 184.

Cutrer, Thomas W., ed. "Bully for Flournoy's Regiment, We are some Punkins, You'll Bet': The Civil War Letters of Virgil Sullivan Rabb, Captain, Company 'I,' Sixteenth Texas Infantry, C.S.A." *Military History of the Southwest* 19 (fall 1989): 161–90; 20 (spring 1990): 61–96.

-----------, ed. "'An Experience in Soldier's Life': The Civil War Letters of Volney Ellis, Adjutant, Twelfth Texas Infantry, Walker's Texas Division, C.S.A." *Military History of the Southwest* 22 (fall 1992): 109–72.

Duncan, J. S., ed. "Alexander Cameron and the Red River Campaign 1863-1865." *Military History of Texas and the Southwest* 12, no. 4: 246–271; 13, no. 1: 37–57.

Durst, Leon, cont. "A Confederate Texas Letter: Bruno Durst to Jet Black." *Southwestern Historical Quarterly* 58, no. 1 (July 1953): 94–96.

Estill, Mary Sexton, ed. "Diary of a Confederate Congressman." *Southwestern Historical Quarterly* 38 (April 1935): 270–301 and 39 (July 1935): 33–65.

Johansson, Jane Harris and David H. Johansson. "Two 'Lost' Battle Reports: Horace Randal's and Joseph L. Brent's Reports of the Battles of Mansfield and Pleasant Hill, 8 and 9 April 1864." *Military History of the West* 23 (fall 1993): 169–80.

Wilson, R. S. "Jenkins' Ferry." *Confederate Veteran* 18 (1910): 486.

SECONDARY SOURCES

BOOKS

Aldrich, Armistead Aldrich. *The History of Houston County Texas: Together with Biographical Sketches of Many Pioneers and Later Citizens of Said County, Who Have Made Notable Contributions to its Development and Progress.* San Antonio, TX: The Naylor Company, 1943.

Ayres, Thomas. *Dark and Bloody Ground: The Battle of Mansfield and the Forgotten Civil War in Louisiana.* Dallas, TX: Taylor Trade Publishing, 2001.

Bearss, Edwin C. *Steele's Retreat from Camden and the Battle of Jenkins' Ferry.* Little Rock, AR: Arkansas Civil War Centennial Commission, 1967.

Bergeron, Arthur W., Jr. *Guide to Louisiana Confederate Military Units 1861–1865.* Baton Rouge, LA: Louisiana State University Press, 1989.

Brooksher, William Riley. *War Along the Bayous: The 1864 Red River Campaign in Louisiana.* Washington DC: Brassey's, 1998.

Cole, Garold L. *Civil War Eyewitnesses: An Annotated Bibliography of Books and Articles, 1986–1996.* Colombia, SC: University of South Carolina Press, 2000.

Confederate Military History, Extended Edition. Vol. 15: *Texas.* Wilmington, NC: Broadfoot, 1989.

Cooper, William J., Jr. *Jefferson Davis, American.* New York: Alfred A. Knopf, 2000.

Crute, Joseph H., Jr. *Units of the Confederate States Army.* Midlothian, VA: Derwent Books, 1987.

Davis, William C., and Julie Hoffman, eds. *The Confederate General.* 6 vols. Washington, DC: National Historical Society, 1991.

Dougan, Michael B. *Confederate Arkansas: The People and Policies of a Frontier State in Wartime.* University, AL: The University of Alabama Press, 1976.

Elsberg, John, ed. *American Military History.* Washington DC: Center of Military History, United States Army, 1989.

Fitzhugh, Lester N. *Texas Batteries, Battalions, Regiments, Commanders and Field Officers, Confederate States Army, 1861–1865.* Midlothian, TX: Mirror Press, 1959.

Fullenkamp, Leonard, et al., eds. *Guide to the Vicksburg Campaign.* Lawrence, KS: University of Kansas Press, 1998.

History of Leon County Texas. Dallas, TX: Curtis Media Corporation, 1986.

Johansson, M. Jane. *A Peculiar Honor: A History of the 28th Texas Cavalry 1862–1865.* Fayetteville, AR: University of Arkansas Press, 1998.

Johnson, Ludwell H. *The Red River Campaign; Politics and Cotton in the Civil War.* Baltimore, MD: Johns Hopkins Press, 1958.

Kerby, Robert L. *Kirby Smith's Confederacy: The Trans-Mississippi South, 1863–1865*. New York: Columbia University Press. 1972. Reprint, Tuscaloosa: University of Alabama Press, 1991.

Kight, L. L. *Their Last Full Measure: Texas Confederate Casualty Lists*. 3 vols., 1861–1865. Arlington, TX: GTT Publishing, 1997.

Lowe, Richard. *Walker's Texas Division, C.S.A.: Greyhounds of the Trans-Mississippi*. Baton Rouge: Louisiana State University Press, 2004.

Mainer, Thomas N. *Houston County in the Civil War*. Dallas, TX: Publishing Development Company of Texas, 1981.

Marshall, Nida A. *The Jasper Journal, Vol. I*. Austin, TX: Nortex Press, 1993.

Moseley, Lou Ella. *Pioneer Days in Tyler County*. Fort Worth, TX: Miran Publishers, 1979.

Parrish, T. Michael. *Richard Taylor: Soldier Prince of Dixie*. Chapel Hill: University of North Carolina Press, 1992.

Peebles, Ruth. *There Never Were Such Men Before*. Livingston, TX: Polk County Historical Association, 1987.

Reid, Thomas. *Captain Jack and the Tyler County Boys: A History of Company K, 13th Texas Cavalry Regiment, C.S.A.* Woodville, TX: Heritage Village Museum, 2000.

Seale, William. *Texas Riverman: The Life and Times of Captain Andrew Smyth*. Austin, TX: University of Texas Press, 1963.

Simpson, Harold B. *Hood's Texas Brigade: Lee's Grenadier Guard*. Fort Worth, TX: Landmark Publishing, Inc., 1999.

Sifakis, Stewart. *Compendium of the Confederate Armies: Texas*. New York: Facts on File, 1995.

Sitton, Thad. *Backwoodsmen: Stockmen and Hunters along a Big Thicket River Valley*. Norman, OK and London: University of Oklahoma Press, 1995.

Sumrall, Alan K. *Battle Flags of Texans in the Confederacy*. Austin, TX: Eakin Press, 1995.

Ule, Michelle. *Pioneer Stock*. Ukiah, CA: Published by the Author, 2000.

Wakelyn, Jon L. *Biographical Dictionary of the Confederacy*. Westport, CT: Greenwood Press, 1977.

Warner, Ezra J. and W. Buck Yearns. *Biographical Register of the Confederate Congress*. Baton Rouge: Louisiana State University Press, 1975.

Wheat, James E. and Josiah Wheat. *Sketches of Tyler County History*. Bevil Oaks, TX: Whitmeyer Printing, 1986.

Winters, John D. *The Civil War in Louisiana.* Baton Rouge: Louisiana State University Press, 1963.

Wright, Marcus J., comp. *Texas in the War, 1861-1865.* Edited by Harold B. Simpson. Hillsboro, TX: Hill Junior College Press, 1965.

Woodhead, Henry, ed. *Echoes of Glory: Arms and Equipment of the Confederacy.* Alexandria, VA: Time-Life Books, 1991.

Wooster, Ralph A. *Civil War Texas.* Austin, TX: Texas State Historical Association, 1999.

---------. *Texas and Texans in the Civil War.* Austin, TX: Eakin Press, 1995.

---------. *Lone Star Generals in Gray.* Austin, TX: Eakin Press, 2000.

---------. *Lone Star Regiments in Gray.* Austin, TX, Eakin Press, 2002.

ARTICLES

Bollett, A. J. "To Care for Him That Has Borne the Battle: A Medical History of the Civil War." *Resident and Staff Physician* 36 (1991): 107.

Hale, Douglas. "Life and Death Among the Lone Star Defenders: Cherokee County Boys in the Civil War." *East Texas Historical Association* 29, no. 2 (1991).

Jones, Allen W. "Military Events in Louisiana During the Civil War, 1861–1865." *Louisiana History* 2 (Winter 1961): 301–15.

Lale, Max S. "For Lack of a Nail." *East Texas Historical Association* 30 (1992): 34–43.

----------. "New Light on the Battle of Mansfield." *East Texas Historical Journal* 25, no. 2 (1987): 34–41.

Oates, Stephen B. "Recruiting Confederate Cavalry in Texas." *Southwestern Historical Quarterly* 64 (April 1961): 463–77.

Roebuck, Field. "The Camp Nelson Confederate Cemetery: A Tribute to Confederate Heroes." *Confederate Veteran* (November–December 1992): 22–27.

Sartin, Jeffrey S. "Infectious Diseases During the Civil War: The Triumph of the 'Third Army'." *Clinical Infectious Diseases* 16 (April 1993): 580–84.

Tevis, Dean. "Captain Jack: Tyler County Pioneer." *Beaumont Enterprise,* March 14, 1935.

Wooster, Ralph A. "Analysis of the Membership of the Texas Secession Convention." *Southwestern Historical Quarterly* 62, no. 3 (January 1959): 322–35.

------------. "Membership in Early Texas Legislatures." *Southwestern Historical Quarterly* 69 (October 1965): 170.

Wooster, Ralph A. and Robert Wooster. "'Rarin' for a Fight': Texans in the Confederate Army." *Southwestern Historical Quarterly* 84 (April 1981): 387–426.

UNPUBLISHED WORKS

Ashcraft, Allan Coleman. "Texas: 1860–1866. The Lone Star State in the Civil War." Doctoral dissertation, Columbia University, 1960.

Hardison, Keith A. "Orange County and the War for Southern Independence." Unpublished manuscript, Heritage House Museum, Orange, Texas, 1985.

McReynolds, James M. "A History of Jasper County, Texas, Prior to 1874." Master's thesis, Lamar State College of Technology, 1968.

Meiners, Fredericka Ann. "The Texas Governorship, 1861–1865: Biography of an Office." Doctoral dissertation, Rice University, 1975.

Stark, Jeremiah M. "In Memory of a Fallen Confederate Soldier— Thomas J. Mitchell, 1837–1864," Unpublished manuscript, 13th Texas Cavalry files, H. B. Simpson History Complex, Hill College, Hillsboro, TX, 1993.

Index